This book is due on the last date stamped below.
Failure to return books on the date due may result
in assessment of overdue fees.

SMITH AND KRAUS PUBLISHERS
Contemporary Playwrights / Collections

Act One Festival '95

EST Marathon '94: The One-Act Plays
EST Marathon '95: The One-Act Plays
EST Marathon '96: The One-Act Plays
EST Marathon '97: The One-Act Plays
EST Marathon '98: The One-Act Plays

Humana Festival: 20 One-Act Plays 1976–1996
Humana Festival '93: The Complete Plays
Humana Festival '94: The Complete Plays
Humana Festival '95: The Complete Plays
Humana Festival '96: The Complete Plays
Humana Festival '97: The Complete Plays
Humana Festival '98: The Complete Plays
Humana Festival '99: The Complete Plays
Humana Festival 2000: The Complete Plays

Women Playwrights: The Best Plays of 1992
Women Playwrights: The Best Plays of 1993
Women Playwrights: The Best Plays of 1994
Women Playwrights: The Best Plays of 1995
Women Playwrights: The Best Plays of 1996
Women Playwrights: The Best Plays of 1997
Women Playwrights: The Best Plays of 1998
Women Playwrights: The Best Plays of 1999

If you require prepublication information about upcoming Smith and Kraus books, you may receive our semiannual catalogue, free of charge, by sending your name and address to *Smith and Kraus Catalogue, 4 Lower Mill Road, North Stratford, NH 03590. Or call us at (800) 895-4331, fax (603) 643-1831. www.SmithKraus.com*

Thirty 10-Minute Plays for 4, 5, and 6 Actors
from Actors Theatre of Louisville's National Ten-Minute Play Contest

Edited by Michael Bigelow Dixon,
Tanya Palmer, and Brendan Healy

Contemporary Playwrights Series

SK
A Smith and Kraus Book

A Smith and Kraus Book
Published by Smith and Kraus, Inc.
177 Lyme Road, Hanover, NH 03755
www.SmithKraus.com

Manufactured in the United States of America

Cover and Text Design by Julia Hill Gignoux, Freedom Hill Design
Layout by Jennifer McMaster
Cover Photograph by Richard Trigg
Cover Photo: The cast of Marcia Dixcy's *Pyramid Effect.*
(l.–r.: Rob Campbell, Adrianne Krstansky, Heidi Swedberg, Al Proia, Kate Fleming, Del Pentecost)

First Edition: September 2001
10 9 8 7 6 5 4 3 2 1

Library of Congress Cataloguing-in-Publication Data
30 ten-minute plays for 4, 5, and 6 actors from Actors Theatre of Louisville's National Ten-Minute Play Contest / edited by Michael Bigelow Dixon, Tanya Palmer, and Brendan Healy.
—1st ed.
p cm. — (Contemporary playwrights series)
ISBN 1-57525-279-1
1. One-act plays, American. I. Title: Thirty-ten-minute plays for 4, 5, and 6 actors from Actors Theatre of Louisville's National Ten-Minute Play Contest. II. Dixon, Michael Bigelow. III. Palmer, Tanya. IV. Healy, Brendan. V. Actors Theatre of Louisville. VI. Series.
PS627. O53 A18 2001
812'.04108054—dc21
2001034485

Contents

Plays for Six Actors

Acknowledgments

Thanks to the following persons for their invaluable assistance in compiling this volume of plays:

Robert Kemnitz

Stephen Moulds

Karen Petruska

Jeffrey Rodgers

Zan Sawyer-Dailey

Alexander Speer

Amy Wegener

Introduction

What can happen in ten minutes? After an informal survey of friends and co-workers, the answer that kept coming up was—just about anything. It just has to happen quickly. And the plays in this volume bear that out. Lives can be altered irrevocably, relationships can end, or begin, or the possibility can be lost forever. Such events and stories are seemingly limitless, as are the ways in which these stories can be told. So what, if anything, distinguishes the ten-minute play from a full-length play, other than the obvious?

Any play, whatever its length, is made up of a series of moments: encounters between characters that provoke in the audience feelings of anger, amusement, fear, and hopefully, recognition. In a play that lasts two hours, actors have the luxury of using many different moments to reveal their characters' motivations and tactics, to color relationships through subtextual meanings and physical actions, and to clarify the ideas of the playwright with keen and compelling interpretations of the text. In a ten-minute play, the number of moments available to accomplish those same ends is extremely limited, but the goal remains the same—to tell the story with intelligence, passion, and craft, and by telling the story well, to capture the attention, and engage the imagination of the audience.

Playwright Richard Dresser, who has two plays in this volume, says that he challenges himself to write a full-length play in the ten-minute form, rather than write a sketch: "When you apply a three-act structure to ten minutes, it forces a tremendous discipline onto the writing and it creates the possibility for an audience to go through a real theatrical experience." So, whether you're writing, directing, or acting, the key to this form is creating full-length complexity in a very short time. And the best way to achieve that is to go deep, down through many layers of motivation and meaning, and then to distill volumes of intention and feeling into a few brief pages of action.

There it is, the essential difference between working on full-length and ten-minute plays is the emphasis on distillation. Without the luxury of time, dramatic necessity becomes paramount. The collaborators must agree on what is essential, and then work to make it powerful—theatrically, emotionally, narratively, and thematically. These are not full-length plays, but each moment should still be fully dimensional for the artists, and for the audience, fully rewarding.

Michael Bigelow Dixon, Tanya Palmer, Brendan Healy

Plays
for
Four Actors

Slop-Culture
by Robb Badlam

CHARACTERS
BRIAN

DYLAN

DANIELLE

CINDY

SETTING
The present. New York.

Slop-Culture

Brian and Dylan, a pair of twenty-somethings wearing their finest bumming-around-the-house clothes, are on the couch, in the midst of a heated discussion.

BRIAN: Oh, come on!

DYLAN: Can't do it.

BRIAN: That's my answer!

DYLAN: Inadmissible.

BRIAN: But it's true!

DYLAN: Our judges have spoken: The Pillsbury Dough Boy cannot be your role model.

BRIAN: Why not? Poke me in the stomach! I'll giggle!

DYLAN: Judges say: "Talk to the hand, girlfriend."

BRIAN: *(Very put out.)* Man! *(Pause.)* What about Fred from *Scooby-Doo*?

DYLAN: That, we'll accept.

BRIAN: Fred and not Pop'n'Fresh?

DYLAN: It's really for your own good.

BRIAN: *(Resigned.)* Man!

> *(A pause. A grin creeps across Brian's face.)*

BRIAN: *(Nodding.)* Dude… Daphne.

DYLAN: *(Complete agreement.)* Aaaww yeah. You know Fred was givin' her the business in the back of the Mystery Machine.

BRIAN: Aaaaaww yeeeaah. *(Beat. Impressed.)* Fred, man. He was one smooth operator. Had his own sense of style.

DYLAN: Not many guys could pull off the white shirt and ascot and still look tough.

BRIAN: True that.

> *(They nod a moment. A pause.)*

BRIAN: You think Shaggy and Velma ever hooked up?

DYLAN: *(With certainty.)* When they were drunk.

> *(Danielle enters. She has a packet of papers in one hand. She is dressed professionally, but she is very jittery and nervous.)*

DANIELLE: Hey guys. Cindy here?

BRIAN: *(Calling over his shoulder.)* Cindy! Your lawyer's here!

DANIELLE: *(Instantly paranoid.)* Shit! Do I really look like a lawyer? Shit! I need to look like a personnel coordinator! Shit! A lawyer? Shit! Really? Shit!

BRIAN: You could be Marcia Clark's twin.

DYLAN: Dude, that's cold.

BRIAN: Oh, sorry. You'd be the younger, less weathered twin.

DYLAN: *(To Danielle.)* So, what's with the new look? Witness Relocation?

DANIELLE: I'm applying for a job.

DYLAN: Whoa! Whoa! Whoa! I object, Your Honor! *(Steps onto a chair.)* Hear now these words I say: Under no circumstances...I say again for emphasis...no *circumstances...are* you to maintain or operate a frozen yogurt dispenser. Learn from my mistakes, Danielle...I have permanent scars. Let this be a lesson...look on my twisted form and learn...

(Dylan starts to undo his pants.)

DANIELLE: Dylan!

DYLAN: My life is nothing if not cautionary example.

DANIELLE: It's an office job!

(Pause.)

DYLAN: No frozen yogurt?

DANIELLE: No!

(Pause.)

DYLAN: Soft serve?

DANIELLE: Dylan! It's an office.

(Pause.)

DYLAN: *(Contemplative.)* I see. *(Pause.)* So...no dessert or snack vending of any kind?

DANIELLE: *(Emphatic.)* It's an OFFICE!

BRIAN: *(Offering.)* I got my hand caught inside the VCR once. *(Beat.)* I got it out.

DANIELLE: *(Frustrated, to Dylan.)* Is...your sister...home!?

DYLAN: Shower.

(He points vaguely down the hallway. Much on her mind, Danielle exits in that direction.)

DYLAN: Okay. One line. Summarize the show. *Dukes of Hazzard.* Go.

BRIAN: "Kew! Kew! Kew! Fuck you, Duke boys!"

DYLAN: Rosco never said fuck.

BRIAN: That was his subtext. You go. *Gilligan's Island.*

DYLAN: "Gilligan! Drop those coconuts!" BONK! "Oow!"

(Pause.)

BRIAN: Whoa. *(Pause.)* Nice. *(Pause.)* I could see the coconuts.

DYLAN: It's a gift.

(Cindy enters, bathrobe, towel, drying her hair. She is late and in a hurry. Danielle, like a small lap dog, is hot on her heels.)

CINDY: Danni, I can't do this now. I'm late as it is. If I'm late one more time, the agency is going to fire me. Do you realize how difficult it is to get fired from a temp agency?

(Cindy brushes her hair in front of a mirror. She continues dressing and preparing throughout.)

DANIELLE: I need your help!

CINDY: *(Resigned.)* Talk.

DANIELLE: They want me to answer this essay question…

CINDY: What's the question?

DANIELLE: …And I don't think my answer is what they're looking for…

CINDY: What's the question?

DANIELLE: …In fact, I'm sure it's not what they're looking for…

CINDY: What's the damn question?!

DANIELLE: Cindy. Did you ever go to church as a kid?

CINDY: That's the question?

DANIELLE: No. I'm asking. Did you ever go to church?

CINDY: Nope. My Sunday afternoons started with Abbot and Costello and ended with Godzilla. God bless Channel 11. Why?

DANIELLE: Just curious.

CINDY: Thinking of finding Jesus?

DYLAN: And the conversation turns to matters of great import.

BRIAN: I met a Jewish guy once. *(They look at him. He continues, deflated.)* I don't really have a story to go with that.

(The conversation swerves back to Danielle.)

CINDY: Why do you ask, Danni?

DANIELLE: Sometimes I… *(Unsure, but pushes ahead.)* …Well…there's this Baptist Church…in my neighborhood…and…sometimes I go and… I just…I sit outside and listen.

CINDY: To what?

DANIELLE: The singing. It's nice.

CINDY: Why don't you go in?

DANIELLE: I couldn't. I don't… I don't belong.

CINDY: *(Stops. Looks at her.)* Are you okay, Danni?

DANIELLE: They've got something. I can't put my finger on it, but… *(Searching for words.)* …It's… I don't know. They've got—

DYLAN: Milk.

BRIAN: The music in them.

DYLAN: The fever for the flavor of a Pringle.

CINDY: *(Threatening them.)* Don't make me turn this car around.

(Pause.)

DANIELLE: They've got a past.

(Pause.)

CINDY: How do you figure?

DANIELLE: A past. A history. They come from somewhere.

CINDY: Did we spontaneously self-generate, Master Yoda?

DANIELLE: It's different. It's something we don't have. It's a sense of… I don't know…community?

CINDY: What was college?

DANIELLE: Yeah, but don't you see? College pulls you out of *one* community, changes you, and forces you into a *new* one. Then, as soon as you get comfortable, that new community gets jerked out from under your feet after four years.

BRIAN: Six years.

DANIELLE: And where does that leave you? You're a different person now. You can't go backwards. You can't go back home. Because home isn't where you left it. It's different. *You're* different. You don't really fit in anymore. You don't have anything to hang onto. It's like you're…I don't know… marooned.

DYLAN: *Gilligan's Island.*

CINDY: *(Scolding.)* Dylan.

DYLAN: *(On to something.)* No, I'm serious. That's the reason the Professor could build a satellite out of coconuts and twine, but he couldn't patch the hole in the boat. They're *spiritual* castaways. They can't go back to the mainland because they don't belong there anymore. The island has changed them fundamentally. They are home. They just won't accept it because they can't see it. Where they most want to go, they already are. It's very Zen. They hate the island, but it's part of them. They can't deny it. You can take the boy away from the coconuts, but you can't take the coconuts away from the boy.

BRIAN: Coconuts. The great social equalizer.

(Pause.)

CINDY: Dylan?

DYLAN: Yes?

CINDY: Never speak again.

DANIELLE: *(Producing paper.)* What's your earliest and fondest childhood memory?

CINDY: What?

DANIELLE: That's the question. "What's your earliest and fondest childhood memory and what impact do you think the experience has had on you as a person?" *(Beat.)* I need yours. Mine sucks.
(Pause.)

CINDY: *(Thinking.)* Hmm. McDonald's cheeseburger. *(Beat.)* Fridays used to be the big night. Mom would take us to McDonald's as a treat. We'd get all dressed up. She'd put those Happy Meals in front of us and we thought we were at the Ritz Carlton having caviar.

DYLAN: Uh-huh. And you used to tell me that Shamrock Shakes were made of Grimace's brain juice. I've never forgiven you for that.

CINDY: I'd have been derelict in my duties as Older Sister if I hadn't terrorized you.

BRIAN: My folks got divorced when I was three. I don't remember it. I always used to wish Fonzie was my real dad. *(Beat.)* Then I'd cry because the Cunninghams made him live in the garage. So I'd leave cookies in *our* garage. Then the raccoons came... *(He stares off, lost in the unpleasant memory.)*

CINDY: So what's your memory, Danni?

DANIELLE: I can't...

CINDY: Come on.

DANIELLE: It's totally wrong!

CINDY: What is it?

DANIELLE: Do you remember in the opening credits for *Tom & Jerry?* When Tom's sticking his tongue out? And the big bulldog pounds him on top of the head and makes him bite his tongue off?

CINDY: Yeah. *(Danielle is quiet.)* That's IT? That's your earliest, fondest memory?

DANIELLE: *(Smiles.)* Tom looks so embarrassed about it!

CINDY: I think that's probably on the big list of things NOT to write on a job application.

DANIELLE: Duh! *(Beat.)* But it's true. *(Pause.)* Cindy, when my mom was my age she was cooking huge Sunday dinners with her entire family...all the aunts and uncles and cousins and grandparents…they all lived right there in the same neighborhood! Like their own little Sicilian embassy in the middle of Brooklyn! The food. The stories. That community. *(Beat.)* But then my mom moved away and got married…and I grew up in the suburbs. *(Beat.)* I was a kid eating Crunch Berries over *Schoolhouse Rock* at the same age when my mom and my great-great-great-grandmother were making… *(Searching.)* … baklava!

CINDY: Isn't baklava Greek?

DANIELLE: See! *(Beat.)* Cindy, I'm half Italian, and I need help ordering spaghetti at the Olive Garden!

BRIAN: If it helps, I've lost touch with my Viking heritage, too.

CINDY: *(To Brian.)* Don't make me come over there.

DANIELLE: So what do I do? I can't write down the truth. They'll think I'm four years old. I mean, I AM! I might as well be! I feel totally out of place going into an office! Like I've snuck in with my mom's blazer and my dad's briefcase. Petrified they're going to find me out! That they're gonna suddenly look up at me and say, "Silly rabbit! Jobs are for grownups!"

CINDY: So you want my advice?

DANIELLE: YES!

CINDY: Lie.

(Cindy moves swiftly off in the direction of the back bedroom.)

DANIELLE: No shit! How? *(Following her halfway.)* I wanted to use yours, but cheeseburgers and…and…Fonzie's brain juice aren't on *Fortune 500*'s big list of "do's" either!

(Cindy re-enters, dressed and ready. Bag in hand, she is out the door.)

CINDY: I really wish I could be more help, sweetie, but if I don't leave right now, I'll be filling out job applications too. Relax. Be creative. Good luck. *(A quick peck on the cheek and Cindy is gone. A pause. Danielle stares at the door. Then, lets out a frustrated scream.)*

DYLAN: Don't deny the island, Danni.

DANIELLE: What?!

DYLAN: Your past. Your history.

BRIAN: Your coconuts.

DYLAN: Where the castaways most want to go, they already are. The island. It's part of them. Like it or not.

BRIAN: Dude, didn't Gilligan get arrested for dope?

DYLAN: That's not helping the metaphor, man.

BRIAN: Sorry.

DYLAN: So what if our cultural heritage is only twenty-five years of bad TV. It's not much, but it's something. Embrace it. It's ours.

BRIAN: *(Serious.)* Gilligan, drop those coconuts.

DYLAN: *(Serious.)* Bonk.

BRIAN: *(Serious.)* Ow.

(Pause.)

DANIELLE: *(With a faint smile.)* Yeah.

DYLAN: Be proud, Danielle. You go right ahead and bite off that cartoon cat's tongue.

BRIAN: Hear! Hear!

DYLAN: *(To Brian.)* I think our work here is done. *(Motions to door.)* Shall we?

BRIAN: Indubitably! *(Brian and Dylan get up and start out.)* Dude, we got nowhere to go.

DYLAN: *(Without breaking stride.)* Doesn't matter.

(They're gone. Danielle, alone, sits thinking. Then takes up her pen and begins to write—with confidence. A smile creeps across her face. For the first time, she is relaxed. A weight's been lifted—more than the application.)

DANIELLE: *(Laughing.)* No way I'm getting this job.

(Danielle keeps writing. Blackout.)

END OF PLAY

Double Take
by K. M. Chopin

CHARACTERS

INNER WOMAN
OUTER WOMAN
INNER MAN
OUTER MAN

Double Take

Set: a large bed; a night table with a clock on it; a stereo; clothes scattered on the floor—a T-shirt at the foot of the bed. Bodies buried under the covers.

One of the lumps under the covers begins to move. A hand emerges from the foot of the bed. Then a head. Outer Woman is reaching for the T-shirt that lies just out of her reach. After a near-miss stretch, Inner Woman emerges, dressed in the same T-shirt, and observes Outer Woman's gymnastics.

INNER WOMAN: I think you've done it. I think this just may be the stupidest moment of your life. You do realize what you're doing, don't you? You do realize that you are upside down in someone else's bed with no clothes on, and that the man you've just spent the night with is going to wake up any second now and see you like this? Well, it is a tough decision…having him see you naked in broad daylight or letting him think you were a cicada in a former life. I mean, it's a little late to be thinking about clothes now, isn't it? What happened to all that casual spontaneity that got you where you are today?

(A body under the covers stirs.)

OUTER WOMAN: Shit.

(She retrieves the T-shirt and buries herself under the covers, where she puts it on.)

INNER WOMAN: Gotta love that free spirit.

INNER MAN: *(Under covers.)* Oh God.

INNER WOMAN: He's waking up. Come on, you've got the T-shirt—now deal with the situation. This is a pretty special guy or you wouldn't be here. So why don't you just start his day by letting him know that.

INNER MAN: *(Rolls out of bed.)* Oh my God. *(He realizes where he is and who he's with.)* Oh my God.

(Outer Man cautiously pokes his eyes above the sheet to look at the clock.)

INNER MAN: Nine. I wonder if she's awake yet.

(Inner Woman has rearranged herself under covers; her head is now visible.)

INNER WOMAN: All right, fine. Let him wake you up. But you're blowing a great moment.

INNER MAN: Maybe I should let her sleep. But she said she had a meeting this morning. She could hate mornings. Oh, what the hell.

(Outer Man turns to look at Outer Woman.)

INNER WOMAN: Don't forget to breathe.

INNER MAN: She looks so peaceful.

INNER WOMAN: He can see your eyelids twitching.

INNER MAN: She really is a great girl. Different. God, I hope I don't mess things up.

INNER WOMAN: He's regretting it. He's sitting there looking at you wishing that you weren't here.

INNER MAN: I feel like I'm in a Lavoris commercial.

INNER WOMAN: Change his mind. Make him glad you're here.

INNER MAN: Here goes…

(Outer Man strokes Outer Woman's cheek.)

INNER WOMAN: This is it…

OUTER MAN: Morning.

OUTER WOMAN: Morning. *(Another kiss.)* You beat a Coast commercial any day.

INNER WOMAN: Cute.

OUTER MAN: How'd you sleep?

OUTER WOMAN: Pretty well.

INNER WOMAN: Now *that* sounds committed.

OUTER WOMAN: I—like the company.

OUTER MAN: Mmm. Makes two of us. *(He stops short, blinking.)*

INNER MAN: Shit. I left my contacts in.

OUTER WOMAN: Adam… Are you O.K.?

OUTER MAN: Uh, yeah, it's just, uh, my contacts—one's kind of rolled back…

OUTER WOMAN: Oh…well, can I… Do you want me to look, or something?

INNER WOMAN: Look? What, you have X-ray vision? Don't hover. You'll embarrass him.

INNER MAN: Only me. Only to me would this happen.

OUTER MAN: I'll just go… I'll be right back.

(Outer Man exits; Inner Man remains.)

OUTER WOMAN: I'll be here.

INNER WOMAN: Someone, somewhere, must really hate you.

INNER MAN: For a while there it was a great start.

INNER WOMAN: Maybe you're just not meant to be happy.

INNER MAN: Goddammit. The bathroom's a pit. Well, we'll just pick up where we left off. Just slow down and take it easy. *(Pause.)* Nine.

OUTER MAN: Did you say something about a meeting this morning?

OUTER WOMAN: Oh.

INNER WOMAN: Guess he can't wait to get rid of you.

OUTER WOMAN: Yeah. I've got to be in by ten.

OUTER MAN: That's what I thought.

INNER MAN: Great, guy. That sounded just great.

INNER WOMAN: Twenty-four hours ago you were reasonably good friends and now he can't wait to get you out of his apartment.

OUTER MAN: Ten.

OUTER WOMAN: Ten.

INNER MAN: Put your foot in one more time and you could make the track team.

INNER WOMAN: If the friendship is ruined, it's going to be ruined, and that'll be it. What have you got to lose?

INNER MAN: I need to let her know I'm glad she's here. She's got to know that.

INNER WOMAN: You know you don't want to lose this one. This one was a— woosh—. You've know that ever since you met him. You actually under-stood each other. How many times does that happen?

OUTER MAN: *(Enters, mouth full of toothpaste.)* It didn't mean anything, you know. I mean it didn't mean anything. I mean I didn't mean it…your meeting—I didn't mean, I didn't want you to— I mean, the fact is, I may not let you go.

OUTER WOMAN: You're getting toothpaste on the floor. *(Outer Man exits.)* Shit.

INNER MAN: She's pissed.

INNER WOMAN: You've got to learn to say the right halves of your thoughts.

INNER MAN: I'm just racking up the points here. I mean, a woman like her deserves more than some goon dribbling toothpaste on himself. Breakfast in bed with a rose, maybe.

OUTER MAN: *(Entering.)* All I've got is Irish Mocha Mint and a couple of bags of lemon zinger.

INNER MAN: Great. That's three for three.

OUTER WOMAN: Good morning and welcome to the wonderful world of the non sequitur. Let's see… I guess we're talking beverages here, am I right?

INNER WOMAN: The wonderful world of insecure wit is more like it.

OUTER MAN: Uh, beverages…right.

INNER WOMAN: Beverages?!

OUTER MAN: I don't have anything else in the kitchen. Except maybe some Nutter Butters.

INNER MAN: Maybe we could just start over…

OUTER WOMAN: Don't worry. It's okay. If you'll just come back over here I'll have all I need.

OUTER MAN: You got it. *(He exits.)*

INNER MAN: What the hell…?

INNER WOMAN: Maybe he's having a different conversation.

(Outer Man returns.)

OUTER MAN: Why am I putting the toothbrush in the toothbrush rack when there's a beautiful woman here waiting for me?

OUTER WOMAN: Don't ask me. I'm biased.

OUTER MAN: Why don't we just start over?

INNER WOMAN/INNER MAN: Yeah, why don't we?

OUTER WOMAN: Morning.

OUTER MAN: Morning.

INNER MAN: Now this is more like it.

OUTER MAN: You want to know something?

INNER WOMAN: Here it comes. "You're a nice girl, but…"

OUTER MAN: It's nice to have you here.

OUTER WOMAN: Nice.

INNER MAN: Great choice of words, guy.

OUTER MAN: No, that's nothing special. You're not nice I don't mean, I mean, well, you know—I mean, you *know* how I feel about you—

INNER WOMAN: Yeah, right.

OUTER MAN: —it's what I've always said. You're, I don't know—just—different.

INNER MAN: Oh my God.

OUTER WOMAN: Yeah, well around here being different is getting a Cheddar Melt at McDonald's.

INNER WOMAN: Period. End of chapter.

INNER MAN: I think we can guess how she feels about this.

INNER WOMAN: You're going to protect yourself right out of this one.

INNER MAN: Time to cover your losses, buddy.

OUTER MAN: Hey, listen, Di. You know I have a lot of respect for you—

INNER WOMAN: Here we go.

OUTER MAN: I care about you—

INNER WOMAN: Give up now and it's a slow fade to oblivion.

INNER MAN: Do I really want to give up?

INNER WOMAN: If you don't talk now you'll never get another chance. One—woosh—right down the toilet.

OUTER WOMAN: Adam—just hold me for a second, will you? *(They embrace.)*

INNER MAN: Maybe she's not running away. Maybe I couldn't feel this way if she didn't feel something. Maybe I'm just jumping to conclusions.

INNER WOMAN: If you don't tell him, he'll never know it.

OUTER WOMAN: *(Abruptly pulling away.)* I'm just going to the bathroom. I'll be right back.

(She quickly grabs her clothes.)

INNER MAN: On the other hand, maybe I'm not.

INNER WOMAN: Don't do this. You're running away. You've been honest with him before—why should that change? Why should *anything* change? Just tell him. *(To Outer Man.)* Adam, I don't know why I'm doing this. I guess I'm scared—I don't know why. Or maybe I do. Maybe it's because you're more different than a Cheddar Melt. It's just that if I let myself go, I'll be gone. I want to trust you. And that scares me.

INNER MAN: It happens every time. I scare them away. Maybe I was a serial killer in another life and that's how I got the world's largest chunk of bad karma. A chunk of karma. What a concept.

INNER WOMAN: Would that be so hard? It couldn't be harder than knowing you'll never say it.

(Outer Man moves to put tape in tape deck. Inner Man and Inner Woman move to one another.)

INNER MAN: Man, why can't I get this one right? She sees through me, she sees into me. Or she did. And I could use that for a change. I could use someone who really deals with me, and she does. Did. I know I want her. Why won't I let myself try to get her?

(Inner Man and Inner Woman embrace.)

OUTER WOMAN: *(Entering.)* Well. Here we are.

OUTER MAN: *(Starts tape.)* Yeah, here we are.

OUTER WOMAN: Eat your heart out Dorothy Parker.

OUTER MAN: Huh?

OUTER WOMAN: Never mind. It's getting pretty late.

INNER WOMAN: Don't do this.

OUTER MAN: Yeah.

INNER MAN: You're going to let her go.

OUTER WOMAN: I've got to get to that meeting.

OUTER WOMAN/OUTER MAN: Listen—

OUTER MAN: Look, Di. We're friends, remember.

INNER MAN: Stupid. So dumb.

OUTER WOMAN: Yeah. Friends.

INNER WOMAN: Every one you let go by gets in the way of the next one.

OUTER MAN: Maybe we can have coffee tomorrow or something.

OUTER WOMAN: Yeah, I'd like that.

OUTER MAN: You're okay, right?

OUTER WOMAN: Yeah, I'm fine. We understand each other, right?

OUTER MAN: Right.

(Inner Man and Inner Woman embrace a last time, then slowly pull apart.)

OUTER WOMAN: Well, see you round the old homestead.

OUTER MAN: Yeah. Ciao, Baby.

OUTER WOMAN: Ciao.

(She exits. Outer Man pauses, breaks, then turns up the stereo and heads for the bathroom. Lights fade on Inner Woman and Inner Man staring at one another from opposite ends of the stage.)

END OF PLAY

The Road to Ruin
by Richard Dresser

CHARACTERS

CLIFF: A man in his thirties.

CONNIE: His wife.

FRED: A middle-aged auto mechanic.

JIMBO: The proprietor of a Jersey City garage.

SETTING

The middle of a rainy night at Jimbo's Garage. It's in a particularly menacing neighborhood in Jersey City just off the highway. We can see the office of the garage and a small part of the parking lot.

The Road to Ruin

At rise: Darkness. The sound of rain, then two car doors open, a dog barks, and the car doors slam shut. We hear Cliff and Connie's voices in the lot outside the garage.

CONNIE: I will never ride in that car again.

CLIFF: Then how do you plan to get home?

CONNIE: That's a very good question. Since nobody seems to be here.

CLIFF: Maybe I'll take a quick look at it myself.

CONNIE: You can't even get the hood up, I've seen you try!

CLIFF: That was one time, before they showed me where the little catch is.

CONNIE: We've had the car for two years and you can't get the hood up.

CLIFF: Well if I got just a little bit of support from you it might be different. Come on.

(Cliff opens the door to the office of Jimbo's garage. It's illuminated by a fluorescent clock on the wall, a Coke machine, and a neon sign. Connie follows Cliff in out of the rain. They stand in the ghostly light of the office. It contains a desk with a telephone, a wall phone, and horrible clutter. Besides the doorway leading outside, there's a closed door leading into the garage.)

CONNIE: This place better be open.

CLIFF: *(Calling out.)* Hello? Anybody here? *(Connie sits down. She gets out a small mirror and checks herself out. The door to the garage opens, revealing a blinding white light. Fred enters. He is covered with grease. He closes the door, switches on the lights in the office, sits down at the desk, opens the desk drawer, and takes out a sandwich. He eats the sandwich, paying no attention to them. Connie looks at Cliff, challenging him to take charge of the situation. Cliff tentatively approaches the desk.)* Excuse me, sir. We've got a little problem with our car. We were hoping that you could perhaps take a look at it.

FRED: Can't you see I'm on my break?

CLIFF: Oh, right. Sorry. *(Cliff crosses to where Connie is impatiently sitting. A low voice.)* He's on his break.

CONNIE: *(Pained.)* For how long?

CLIFF: *(Clearing his throat.)* Uh, how long would the break be?
(They both watch Fred, but there's no response.)

CONNIE: Maybe he could give us the key to the ladies room.

CLIFF: Yes, uh, sir? Is there a ladies room key? For my wife?
(Without turning to them, Fred points toward the corner. They follow where he is pointing. Connie goes to the corner and gets a cinder block with a ladies room key on it.)

CONNIE: Is this it? *(Fred suddenly puts the sandwich back in the drawer and slams it shut.)*

FRED: People steal, okay? *(Connie picks up the cinder block and starts outside where Fred is pointing.)*

CONNIE: *(To Cliff.)* Would you call Triple A? We haven't got all night and he obviously won't help us. *(Connie struggles out with the cinder block. Cliff takes a quarter from his pocket and goes to the wall phone.)*

CLIFF: Mind if I… *(Fred is intently reading a magazine. Cliff checks the yellow pages, and dials. As he does this, Fred slowly swivels around in his chair and takes Cliff's wallet from his back pocket. Then he swivels back into his previous position as Cliff finishes dialing. Cliff moves toward the doorway, trying to have some privacy from Fred. The phone on Fred's desk rings. Fred answers it. On phone.)* Yes, is this the Automobile Club?

FRED: *(On phone.)* Uh-huh.

CLIFF: I wonder if you can help me. I'm at a station in Jersey City called Jimbo's, and my car is broken down. No one here will help us, and I need to get my car towed. It's very important that I get back to the city because my wife has a job interview tomorrow.

FRED: *(On phone.)* What seems to be the problem?

CLIFF: *(On phone.)* It was going and then it stopped… *(He turns around and sees Fred on the phone. Cliff hangs up the phone. Fred hangs up the phone.)* Why are you talking to me?

FRED: You called. I answered.

CLIFF: Why did it ring here?

FRED: This is the only phone you can call from there. Dial any number and it will ring here. Wanna try again?

CLIFF: Will you fix my car?

FRED: What's wrong with it?

CLIFF: It was running fine and then it started making this sound, like…somewhere between a rattle and…a…moan…and then it stopped, and we were lucky enough to coast down the ramp and right in here.

FRED: Damn lucky.

CLIFF: We thought you could, what is it—give it a jump start or something.

FRED: It was moaning?

CLIFF: Could you at least look at it?

FRED: Not till Jimbo gets here.

CLIFF: You couldn't look at it without him? *(Fred opens another desk drawer and gets out a cup of coffee. He stares at Cliff. Then he gets out a contract from the desk drawer.)*

FRED: Work order. Sign on the X.

(Cliff signs. Fred immediately takes a stamp and loudly bangs it down on the contract in several places. Then he tears out the bottom sheet and files it in a file cabinet, puts another in an envelope, stamps the envelope and sends it down a mail slot. He gives another to Cliff, who puts it in his pocket without looking at it. Connie enters from the garage carrying the cinder block, which she drops in the corner.)

CLIFF: Was it okay? *(No response.)* I mean the bathroom, sometimes in a place like this...but of course maybe they do keep it clean. You never know.

CONNIE: Did he look at the car?

CLIFF: He hasn't actually looked at it, no, but we discussed it.

CONNIE: And?

CLIFF: He can't look at it until the boss shows up.

CONNIE: Why not?

CLIFF: You know union or insurance or something. There must be a good reason.

CONNIE: I want to get my dog and my luggage and go home. *(Beat.)* When is the boss showing up? *(Louder.)* When is he showing up?

FRED: *(Swiveling in the chair to face her.)* You won't be talking so loud. You'll keep your voice down when he shows up.

CLIFF: My wife is a broadcast journalist. She is one of three candidates to be the weekend weather girl on channel 7. So you had better show a little goddam respect when addressing her, my man. *(Headlights outside. Fred immediately puts the coffee cup back in the drawer and hides the magazine he was reading.)*

CLIFF: Good. Maybe now we can get a little service here.

(Jimbo enters. He's soaking wet.)

FRED: *(Very politely.)* How is it out there? *(Jimbo glares at Fred, then turns his attention to Cliff and Connie.)*

JIMBO: Whose car is blocking my driveway?

CLIFF: That's our car. It stalled out and we just coasted in here. We thought maybe we could get help, but no one has lifted a finger. *(Jimbo goes menacingly over to Fred, who cowers.)*

JIMBO: Any telephone calls? *(Jimbo and Fred burst into hysterical laughter.)*

CLIFF: Could it be the spark plugs? I hear that if they get wet it can stall a car.

FRED: *(To Jimbo.)* Don't listen to him. He don't know much. *(Confidentially.)* She was moaning before she stopped.

CLIFF: Moaning is not what I meant!

JIMBO: *(Turning on Cliff.)* I know what's wrong with your car.

CLIFF: Really? *(Beat.)* What?

JIMBO: Your car is depressed.

CLIFF: That's not possible.

JIMBO: No? *(To Fred.)* He says it's not possible. *(Jimbo opens the door to the garage and exits into the white light.)*

CONNIE: Did you call the auto club?

CLIFF: I tried.

CONNIE: Good lord. I'm going to call a cab. I have to start putting on my makeup in…two hours. *(Connie goes to the phone.)*

CLIFF: Don't bother. All the calls go through the desk and he stops them. *(Connie dials and the phone rings on the desk. Connie hangs up the wall phone and the phone on the desk stops. Fred smiles at her.)*

CONNIE: We never should have come to New Jersey.

FRED: You people think a car can't get depressed? Take a peek out back. The whole lot is full of 'em. Just sittin' there. They gave up.

CLIFF: *(Staring out the window.)* What do you do with them?

FRED: Talk to 'em. Try to build up their self-esteem. *(Jimbo comes back in. Fred spins around in his chair and studies the papers on his desk.)*

JIMBO: That was a helluva place to leave your car.

CONNIE: We didn't mean to leave it there—

CLIFF: That's where it happened to stop. Believe me, there was absolutely no planning on our part.

JIMBO: *(To Fred.)* Move it.

FRED: We got no room—

JIMBO: Make room! *(Fred jumps up and goes outside.)*

CLIFF: I signed a work order and I'm going to insist that you live up to it.

JIMBO: He got you to sign?

CLIFF: It's right here. I'm a man who respects a contract. *(Beat.)* How soon can you look at my car?

JIMBO: Depends.

CLIFF: On what?

JIMBO: On how bad it is.

CLIFF: How can you tell how bad it is if you don't look?

JIMBO: You're a wise guy, aren't you? I could put your nose in a lug wrench. Give it a couple of turns and then we'd see how wise you are.

CLIFF: My wife has to put on her cosmetics. If you can't look at the car tonight, then we'll have to leave it here.

JIMBO: I'm all backed up. No way will your car stay here tonight.

CONNIE: Maybe you'd like to buy it.

CLIFF: Connie!

CONNIE: *(Urgent whisper.)* It's a perfect chance to get rid of it!

JIMBO: I don't buy 'em anymore. Too much trouble.

CLIFF: Then what will it cost for you to look at it right now? Fifty bucks?

JIMBO: Put 'er on the table. *(Cliff reaches for his wallet, which is gone.)*

CLIFF: My God, Connie. My wallet—

CONNIE: What?

CLIFF: It's gone—

CONNIE: And I didn't bring my purse—

CLIFF: *(To Jimbo.)* Listen, we seem to have misplaced our money. But we've got every credit card you can name. We have a mortgage, bank cards, securities, mutual funds, IRAs, you name it. We're good for the money.

JIMBO: People like you I see by the hundreds. They never pay up.

CLIFF: Don't judge me by the others! I'll give you my watch!
    (Cliff puts his watch on the desk.)

CONNIE: Cliff, we can't even take the train if we don't have money.

JIMBO: Let me tell you a story. One of 'em came in here, he could have been your twin. Tried to give me a *personal check*. (Pause. Cliff and Connie aren't sure if the story is over.)

CLIFF: What happened?

JIMBO: He turned out to be a bad credit risk. *(Jimbo presses a buzzer on the desk and makes a violent motion out the window. There is a loud, grating sound.)*

CLIFF: Your jewelry, Connie—

CONNIE: Cliff! *(Connie starts taking off her jewelry and putting it on the desk.)*

CLIFF: All of it, Connie! *(Connie moans and takes off more. Jimbo slides it into the desk drawer, which he closes.)*

CLIFF: And if that isn't enough, then we'll give him Ramon—

CONNIE: Not Ramon!

CLIFF: *(To Jimbo.)* She's got a dog in the car that's worth six grand. He just won every prize at the show, for Chrissakes this dog could do your taxes if you want. He's yours. You can barbecue the sucker for all I care. I just want you to know that we are people who are as good as our word—

CONNIE: We are not going to give this man Ramon!

CLIFF: Listen to reason, Connie. We are going to give him whatever he wants. We have no car and no money—

(Fred comes in pushing a little hand truck with a cube of compressed metal on it.)

JIMBO: I've changed my mind. You can leave your car here now because we have the room.

FRED: Where do you want it, boss?

CONNIE: *(A small stricken voice.)* That's our car, isn't it?

CLIFF: What have you done?

CONNIE: My God. Ramon! Where is Ramon? *(To Fred.)* Was there a dog in there?

FRED: *(To the metal block.)* Here boy! Here boy! *(To Connie.)* He don't come when you call.

JIMBO: Put 'er way in back. They're last in line and they got no money.

CLIFF: I loved that car! *(Turning on Jimbo.)* How could you do that?

JIMBO: *(Turning to Fred.)* You can get cleaned up, Fred. *(Fred wheels the hand truck into the garage.)*

JIMBO: *(To Cliff.)* See? Take away your money and you're just like everyone else.

CONNIE: Come on, Cliff. We'll walk.

JIMBO: I give you two blocks, maybe three. Then they'll get you.

CONNIE: Nobody's going to "get us."

JIMBO: A healthy pair like you? You get picked up and bought and sold and bought and sold and pretty soon you're on the other side of the world bent over in the hot sun harvesting cocoa plants. *(Beat.)* The only way to leave this place is in a car. And you ain't got one.

CLIFF: Okay. We'll wait here—

JIMBO: You wait here you gotta work. That way you'll be able to get another car.

CLIFF: Okay, we'll work tonight. I don't mind.

JIMBO: What can you do? Can you fix things? *(Beat.)* Course not. Professionals. Can't do a damn thing and I got three acres of cars turning into scrap iron.

CLIFF: I could talk to the cars…try to cheer 'em up.

CONNIE: God, Cliff.

JIMBO: Fair enough. And maybe some day one of 'em will be yours. *(Beat.)* Course I gotta charge you rent.

CLIFF: Fine. Take it out of my pay. *(Beat.)* How much do I get?

JIMBO: It's all in the contract you signed.

CLIFF: What contract? *(Cliff looks blank. Then he hurriedly gets out the paper he signed.)* My God. I thought it was a work order. I'll never get away... Connie...

JIMBO: It's already gone to the central office. Try to break a contract with them...

(Fred enters, wearing Bermuda shorts, sunglasses, and sandals with high black socks. He's carrying a work shirt, which he tosses on the chair. He stops at the desk and puts on Cliff's watch. Fred takes out his wallet—which is Cliff's wallet—and carefully counts out some bills, which he gives to Jimbo.)

FRED: That's the last of it. I'd say we're square, boss.

JIMBO: *(Looks at his watch.)* Your shift is done, Fred. *(Beat.)* Seven years to the day. Now you got your choice of cars. *(Fred goes to the wall where a number of keys are hanging. He selects one.)*

FRED: *(To Cliff.)* The pay's okay, but the rent's worse.

(Fred starts for the door.)

CLIFF: You're leaving?

FRED: I done my time.

CONNIE: Could you give us a ride? Oh, please, just get us across the bridge—

JIMBO: Not this one. He works here now.

CONNIE: Then take me, please, Manhattan's right over there—

CLIFF: Connie!

FRED: I guess I could do that.

CLIFF: What about me?

JIMBO: You signed up to have your car fixed—

CLIFF: How can you fix it now?

JIMBO: It'll take time. Gotta send out for parts. And there's a whole slew of people in front of you. You'll meet 'em, living in their cars, wandering through the lot out back. Nice folks who ran into some car trouble. You gotta wait your turn, just like everyone else.

CONNIE: I'll come back for you, Cliff. As soon as I get the job—

FRED: That's what they all say. *(Beat.)* I was coming through here with the wife and kids. A week's holiday at the shore, you know? We get off the highway to look for a place to eat. The car stalls, right out front. We thought we were lucky, a garage right handy. Jimbo put the car out back with the others. We kept waiting for it to get better, but it never did. Months go by, I'm pumping gas, we're living in the car wash. This wasn't much of a place for the kids to grow up, so one morning the wife says she's gonna take the kids and make a break for it, try to get out and get help. That was six and a half years ago. Some vacation.

CONNIE: Cliff, you know I'd stay if it weren't for the job.

CLIFF: I know, darling. *(Beat.)* Maybe I'll see you on TV.

CONNIE: I sure hope so, Cliff. *(They embrace. Then Connie and Fred leave. Cliff watches them.)*

JIMBO: The sooner you start the sooner you can leave. That's just common sense.

(Cliff takes off his shirt and puts on the work shirt that Fred brought out. It fits perfectly, and has Cliff's name over the pocket. Cliff opens the door to the garage and steps into the white light. Blackout.)

END OF PLAY

The Morpheus Quartet
by John Glore

CHARACTERS

1ST VIOLIN: Female.
2ND VIOLIN: Male.
CELLO: Male.
VIOLA: Female.

The Morpheus Quartet

In black.

1ST VIOLIN:	2ND VIOLIN:	CELLO:	VIOLA:
Warm bath red	Oh, brother,	Night machine	Twenty-one,
wine Mozart	where are you	one thousand	twenty-two,
plays a	Kreisler come	pistons fire	twenty-three,
breeze over	and get its	up a bullet	twenty-four,
the water	dinner time	flashing	twenty-five

(Light bumps up.)

VIOLA: It's 3:42 AM.

CELLO: I'm in my car. My black car. My vintage, black, metallic-black Mustang LX 5.0 with blackout trim and silvered moonroof.

1ST VIOLIN: Silver moon in a black, black sky.

CELLO: My cello's in the co-pilot's seat and we're cruising aimlessly, sailing down an empty freeway—

1ST VIOLIN: Empty and free.

CELLO: —when suddenly I realize that I'm late for a concert. And I can't remember which concert hall we're playing, and *I don't know where I am—

2ND VIOLIN: *(*Simultaneous.)* I don't know where he is.

CELLO: *(Continued.)* —and it dawns on me that I've never even looked at the music we're supposed to play tonight.

1ST VIOLIN: Music plays.

CELLO: *And—*

VIOLA: I'm...

CELLO: I'm in my underwear. *In* the driver's seat—

VIOLA: In a fever—

1ST VIOLIN: In the background.

CELLO: —*in* my under *wear.

2ND VIOLIN: *(*Simultaneous.)* Where is he?

VIOLA: In the middle of the night, my fever-baked brain refuses to let me sleep. Not physical fever, although that maybe too. Emotional fever. Craving. Desirous. Overcome with...

1ST VIOLIN: Beautiful music.

VIOLA: —fever. I try counting the measures in Shubert's *D minor Quartet*, the "Death and the Maiden" quartet. I make it well into the second movement but my eyelids still feel spring-loaded. So I decide to focus my mind, which has been *sailing aimlessly

1ST VIOLIN: *(*Simultaneous.)* Sailing.

VIOLA: *(Continued.)* in steamy tropical seas for well over three hours now, to focus it on one thing.

CELLO: My pants.

VIOLA: His *cello.

1ST VIOLIN: *(*Simultaneous.)* Cello and piano.

VIOLA: I abandon myself to thoughts of his cello, the shape of it nestled between his strong legs, its curves emerging seamlessly out of the curves of his thighs.

1ST VIOLIN: Tracing elegant curves of sound in the still night air.

VIOLA: The color of it, like sunlight filtered through Coca-Cola, rich and warm as it picks up the highlights in his hair, then darker near the edges, until it bleeds into the perfect blackness of his tuxedo trousers.

CELLO: *Where are my goddamn pants?

2ND VIOLIN: *(*Simultaneous.)* Where is that damn...

CELLO: I'm driving trouserless down the freeway. I reach behind me and frantically sort through a pile of laundry on the back seat, which seems to be all shirts, every single one of them with a large, yellow stain on the front of it. But no pants. Well.

1ST VIOLIN: Well.

2ND VIOLIN: He's missing.

VIOLA: Well.

CELLO: I'll just have to hope no one notices.

VIOLA: *(Sing-song.)* Soooo.

1ST VIOLIN: So the black sky and the silver moon and this music, which is unlike any I've ever heard or played before. Indescribable. Sweet and pungent and breezy and still and brilliant and—

2ND VIOLIN: Great.

1ST VIOLIN: Indescribable. And I find that I'm in a state of—

VIOLA: —perfect—

1ST VIOLIN: —silken—

VIOLA: —trousers.

1ST VIOLIN: —ecstasy.

VIOLA: I smell the cherry smell of wood, the aged varnish, and I *imagine that

1ST VIOLIN: (*Simultaneous.) Imagine that.

VIOLA: (Continued.) if I run my tongue along the surface of the cello it will taste like wheat soaked in sweet ale. And I put my cheek up close to the strings, and I can feel their vibrations move the surrounding air into a tiny, pulsing breeze.

2ND VIOLIN: I can't find him anywhere.

VIOLA: And now, with the breeze from his strings kissing my cheek, I become aware that his knees are on either side of me, nearly touching my arms, and *a shudder goes through me,

1ST VIOLIN: (*Simultaneous.) I shudder.

VIOLA: (Continued.) from my shoulders down into my womb. And for a moment—

CELLO: The darkness is getting thicker somehow,

VIOLA: I become the cello...

CELLO: but my halogen headlamps cut through it, and the broken white line flashes underneath me—

VIOLA: —his fingers racing up and down my fingerboard—

CELLO: —like tracer bullets in a World War II movie.

VIOLA: —the caress of his thighs, the heat from his cheek next to my pegbox, the smell of cinnamon on his breath.* But then he stops playing and makes a face and tries to tune my strings, only he can't, *I* can't get it—

(*1st Violin moans with pleasure.)

2ND VIOLIN: I can't find him.

VIOLA: —I can't please him. And then I'm separate again, looking back at the cello between his legs. And I'm crying.

CELLO: Okay.

VIOLA: Why am I crying?

CELLO: Everything's under control.

2ND VIOLIN: My cat, Kreisler, is missing.

CELLO: Then a cat appears out of the black jelly to my right, a white Jaguar XJS with opaque windows and twin silver tailpipes. It zips in front of me nearly clipping my front fender and I'm instantly furious. SHIT!!!

2ND VIOLIN: Damn it.

VIOLA: God damn it to hell.

CELLO: He could have killed me, he could have messed up my car!

VIOLA: To stop the tears, I peer steadily into the blackness of the cello's sound hole—

1ST VIOLIN: And as I lie here listening to this indescribable music…

VIOLA: —the right sound hole, the one closest to his hand, *his

CELLO: (*Simultaneous.) That

VIOLA: (Continued.) bow-wielding,

CELLO: scum-sucking *snake.

VIOLA: (*Simultaneous.) snake-charming hand.

1ST VIOLIN: …I become aware of the room I'm in. A small, intimate, safe little room, yet it seems to go on forever, and through the ceiling I can see the heavens, the black, black sky and a silver moon and stars that flicker like a thousand candle flames.

CELLO: I'll smoke him.

VIOLA: I feel myself become smoke and drift sleepily through the cello's curving sound hole and into the body of the instrument.

2ND VIOLIN: I can feel Kreisler's absence in the house, which is not my house, but the house of my parents, the one I used to live in as a boy.

VIOLA: The smell inside the cello is musty, like a summer house in winter, and the music*,

1ST VIOLIN: (*Echo.) And the music…

VIOLA: (Continued w/o holding.) which I expected to be deafening, is only a faint, persistent stir in the background. I walk through the door *immediately ahead of me—

2ND VIOLIN: (*Simultaneous.) I move from room to room.

VIOLA: (Continued.) —and into a dark, empty space.

1ST VIOLIN: And a feeling begins to seep into my bones, a feeling of—

2ND VIOLIN: Searching.

1ST VIOLIN: —of—

VIOLA: Such loneliness.

1ST VIOLIN: —of wholeness unlike any I've ever experienced. It's so complete that I begin to think I must have reached my moment of *death.

VIOLA: (*Simultaneous.) *Death.

CELLO: Die, you asshole.

2ND VIOLIN: Searching for him, for Kreisler, but he's *nowhere to be found.

VIOLA: (*Simultaneous.) Nowhere.

2ND VIOLIN: *(Continued.)* What if he's dead?

CELLO: So I stand on my accelerator

2ND VIOLIN: I go out into the yard.

CELLO: *(Continued.)* and careen ahead into the *blackness—

VIOLA: *(*Simultaneous.)* Darkness.

2ND VIOLIN: It's black outside, not dark, but black.

CELLO: —until I'm four inches, no three, from the back bumper of that Jaguar son-of-a-bitch.

2ND VIOLIN: So I walk into the woods to look for the cat.

CELLO: But—of course—with me riding his bumper, he hits the brakes. The red eyes in the tail of the Jag fry my eyeballs, my foot is through the floor, my spleen is in my *throat and he disappears

1ST VIOLIN: *(*Simultaneous.)* It's like I've disappeared…

CELLO: *(Continued.)* into the blackness in front of me.

2ND VIOLIN: And now I'm on a flagstone path in the middle of the woods, which appear to go on *forever,

1ST VIOLIN: *(*Simultaneous.)* —forever…

2ND VIOLIN: *(Continued.)* and it seems as though I can see behind me and in front of me at the same time, but still, *nowhere do I see Kreisler.

VIOLA: *(*Simultaneous.)* Nowhere.

1ST VIOLIN: *(*Simultaneous.)* —into nowhere.

2ND VIOLIN: *(Continued.)* I try to call his name—

CELLO: Christ!

2ND VIOLIN: —but I seem to have lost my voice, or at any rate no sound*

VIOLA: *(*Echo.)* No sound.

2ND VIOLIN: *(Continued w/o holding.)* comes out and it flashes through my mind, if a foot falls in the forest and there's no one* there to hear it…

VIOLA: *(*Echo.)* No one.

2ND VIOLIN: *(Continued.)* … And this makes me suddenly very sad. I'm lost,*

VIOLA: *(*Echo.)* I'm lost.

2ND VIOLIN: *(Continued w/o holding.)* and Kreisler is gone and I'm in a black, black forest and there's no one to hear. And I begin to cry, to wail, in fact, deep, soulful wailing.

VIOLA: Where am I? What am I doing here?

2ND VIOLIN: But then a voice behind me calls my name. Without turning I know it's Jimmy's voice, Jimmy, whom I haven't seen since the day he died, and there he is, Jimmy, my brother, standing in front of me, my cat Kreisler wound in his arms as though they were one creature. And Jimmy's voice seems to come from Kreisler's mouth as he says,

1ST VIOLIN: But I'm not dead.

VIOLA: Am I dead?

CELLO: I'm not dead yet. If that's how he wants to play it, okay. So I floor the Mustang, squinting to see those red dragon eyes up ahead, and then I *find him.

2ND VIOLIN: (*Simultaneous.) I found him.

CELLO: (Continued.) He's there and I'm catching up. Or he's slowing down to let me catch up.

(In the following speech, [words in brackets] should also be spoken by 1st Violin; {words in italic brackets} should also be spoken by Viola; /words between slashes/ should also be spoken by Cello.)

2ND VIOLIN: Jimmy, {I'm lost}, I say, and /he smiles/ and sits down beside me on the ground. [No one knows] who I am. You don't know [who I am], I tell him. You {never} did know. And I {never} knew who you were, and /he nods/ and hands me an old toy car. It's the replica of James Bond's /steel-gray/ Aston Martin, with the /bullet-proof/ shield and the ejector seat, {the one} Jimmy and I used to fight over when we were kids. And Jimmy and I are /in that car/ now, driving down a [silver] ribbon of highway, with Kreisler still [sleeping] in his arms, the wind [blowing] through our hair and we laugh, a laugh as [deep] and [soulful] as the [{wailing}] only a moment ago.

CELLO: I ease up behind him, laughing tightly in the direction of my cello, as I ride the Jag's back bumper, and then I

CELLO:	2ND VIOLIN:
SLAM the gas pedal to the floor	And Kreisler stretches into a taut curve.

CELLO:
and I

CELLO:	VIOLA:	2ND VIOLIN:
throw the wheel right then back again left and before he knows what's hit him he's eating road grit in my rearview mirror.	lie down with my face against the wall of the dark room my body assuming the curve of the dry wooden wall.	And Jimmy and I laugh again,* a full rumbling laugh *(*1st Violin laughs.)*

CELLO: AaaaaaaaaHA!

    (Beat.)

1ST, 2ND and VIOLA: And after a while—

2ND VIOLIN: our laughter subsides.

VIOLA: I finally fall asleep.

1ST VIOLIN: an epiphany breaks my horizon.

2ND VIOLIN: And I look at Jimmy—

CELLO: Then I get a look at his face for the first time—

2ND VIOLIN: —at my brother's face—

CELLO: —no, at *her* face.

1ST VIOLIN: Like an aurora.

CELLO: Into the beautiful eyes

2ND VIOLIN: —and I see my reflection in his eyes,

CELLO: of the *woman* driving the Jag,

2ND VIOLIN: which becomes the rippling image of my nine-year-old face

CELLO: her hair piled casually atop her head—

2ND VIOLIN: reflected in the crystal water of that mountain pool,

1ST VIOLIN: And I hear myself telling myself in a crystalline voice—

2ND VIOLIN: on that perfect summer day

CELLO: —careless wisps caressing her long summer neck and I realize—

1ST VIOLIN: "Life is more."

2ND VIOLIN: when Jimmy drowned.

CELLO: —I know this woman.

1ST VIOLIN: "Our experience of life is like the sound of a single violin, beautiful in its way

2ND VIOLIN: Playing in the water,

1ST VIOLIN: —but wire-thin

2ND VIOLIN:	CELLO:
without a care,	And now
	the game
	has changed
1ST VIOLIN:	and the
and without largeness.	two of us
	are side
2ND VIOLIN:	by side
our twin lives…	

1ST VIOLIN: *(In the clear.)* The full music of life is so much more.

2ND VIOLIN:
…one minute there…

CELLO:
dancing a dance of
machines and flesh at 90
miles an hour down a
ribbon of tracers in a
black-jelly night and
she's looking at me and
I'm looking at her and
it's electric and
it's music and
it's sex and
it's—

1ST VIOLIN:
It's the music of all instruments
playing at once.

2ND VIOLIN:
…the next minute gone.

1ST VIOLIN:
In an eternal dance.

2ND VIOLIN:
Like a dream.

VIOLA:
A dream flows through me.

1ST VIOLIN:
Each single note
of that music
has no beginning
and no end.

CELLO:
—a concrete bridge
abutment.

2ND VIOLIN:
And now here we are.

VIOLA:
In the dream I follow
the curving wall into a
new room

1ST VIOLIN:
Your momentary experience
of it is only the
point at which it
intersects with
your mole-blind
consciousness,
but that note,

2ND VIOLIN:
*My brother and I.

CELLO:
*(*Simultaneous.)*
My cello and I are
hurtling toward a
bridge abutment

1ST VIOLIN: *(Continued.)*
all the notes,
of all the
instruments
have always
ever will sound.

VIOLA:
lit only by candles,

2ND VIOLIN:
As though we had never
woken up

CELLO:
at a *hundred MPH
with nowhere to turn

VIOLA:
*(*Simultaneous.)*
hundreds of them
of all shapes and sizes

VIOLA:
and I *sigh.

CELLO:
   *(*Simultaneous.)*
   and I *scream

2ND VIOLIN:
   *(*Simultaneous.)*
   and I laugh a quiet laugh.

1ST VIOLIN: And for an instant—I hear the music of it all. For an instant I can hear it all forever.

2ND VIOLIN: But now what do I do, Jimmy?

VIOLA: A beckoning chair…

1ST VIOLIN: This is only a dream, *of course.

CELLO: *(*Simultaneous.)* We fly through the blackness and land gently *in the center of a dark empty space.

VIOLA: *(*Simultaneous.)* …in the center of the room.

2ND VIOLIN: And Jimmy says, "You should play your music."

VIOLA: *And waiting to be breathed…

1ST VIOLIN: *(*Simultaneous.)* And when I wake up I won't remember my epiphany,

CELLO: I'm alive.

1ST VIOLIN: I'll have only the dry residue of the dream.

VIOLA: …with the air in the room…

1ST VIOLIN: But it doesn't matter.

CELLO: And I see I'm on the stage where we're supposed to *play and I'm

2ND VIOLIN: *(*Simultaneous.)* "Play your music."

CELLO: here just in time—

VIOLA: —is the music.

CELLO: —for the music.

1ST VIOLIN: I've heard that music.

2ND VIOLIN: "I am your music."

1ST VIOLIN: And maybe some day I'll be able to play it for someone else.

VIOLA: And the others *are here now

1ST AND 2ND: *(*Simultaneous.)* And the others

CELLO: are *here

VIOLA: *(*Simultaneous.)* he and

1ST VIOLIN: you *and

2ND VIOLIN: *(*Simultaneous.)* and you and

CELLO: *she.*

ALL FOUR: We're all in the room

VIOLA: of candles

2ND VIOLIN: with Jimmy

ALL FOUR: and we play

2ND VIOLIN: deep soulful

1ST VIOLIN: indescribable

VIOLA: music

2ND VIOLIN: as deep as

VIOLA: the color of his hair

CELLO: the moment of her eyes

1ST VIOLIN: the unsoundable chord

2ND VIOLIN: a crystal pool.
   (Breath.)

1ST VIOLIN: And for a brief, everlasting moment…

VIOLA: 3:56 AM.

1ST VIOLIN: It's perfect.
   (Lights fade.)

END OF PLAY

A Private Moment
by Stephen Gregg

CHARACTERS

CHANG and ENG BUNKER: Chinese-born twins joined by an eight-inch band of flesh that connects their abdomens. They stand side by side facing each other slightly. Most often each rests his inside arm on the other's shoulder.

SALLY YATES: Mid-twenties, the daughter of a plantation owner.

ADELAIDE: Early twenties, Sally's sister.

TIME AND PLACE

A study in a house in North Carolina in the mid-nineteenth century.

A Private Moment

Lights come up on a study. Chang and Eng enter with Sally. From another room, we hear conversation and maybe a piano.

SALLY: I think it's a library. No, it's just another room with chairs in it. I've never seen so many chairs in one house.

CHANG: I'm glad to be away from the others.

SALLY: What would people do with this many chairs? It's as if all they do all day is sit down in different places.

CHANG: You're nervous.

SALLY: There must be fifty chairs in here.

CHANG: Are you uncomfortable with being alone with me?

SALLY: No, I just—I do think it's strange, so many chairs. I don't think you could fit fifty people in here standing. If you wanted all the chairs filled, you'd have to have them come in in batches of five.

CHANG: Why are you nervous?

SALLY: Ten batches. I'm not.

CHANG: Should we go back?

SALLY: No, I'm comfortable. We should sit.

(She sits. Chang and Eng remain standing.)

CHANG: Thank you for exploring with me. I was restless.

SALLY: You must be tired of being the center of attention.

CHANG: It makes it difficult to have a private conversation.

SALLY: *(Pause.)* I don't think if I owned fifty chairs I'd have them all be the same style.

CHANG: And I want to have a private conversation with you. How are you?

SALLY: I'm all right. Not perfect. I've had a headache since 1842.

CHANG: I'm sorry to hear that.

SALLY: Sometimes people laugh. But it's true.

CHANG: It must be very uncomfortable.

SALLY: It's always there. Sometimes it's better and sometimes it's worse. But it never goes away.

CHANG: How is it now?

SALLY: It hurts. A little worse than usual.

CHANG: I'm sorry. Does it hurt too much to talk privately?

SALLY: No. *(Beat.)* Almost privately.

CHANG: Completely private. My brother is not here.

SALLY: You're making fun of me.

CHANG: No. It's a talent of mine. Long ago my brother and I discovered that there are times when it is convenient for one or the other not to be here. So one leaves. The other takes control.

SALLY: I find that difficult to believe.

CHANG: He can't hear you. Ask him something.

SALLY: That won't prove anything. I was talking to him three minutes ago.

CHANG: Yes. But when I came in here he surrendered control.

SALLY: Why would he do that?

CHANG: Because he knew I wanted to talk with you alone. This is the eighth time I've spoken to you.

SALLY: Thank you for keeping track.

CHANG: Most girls do not speak to me more than once. But you and your sister are always friendly. You don't seem scared the way some others do.

SALLY: Adelaide says it's because of Mama.

CHANG: She taught you to be brave.

SALLY: No. She weighs six hundred pounds.

CHANG: Really?

SALLY: We think so. Nobody actually knows how to measure. She's the largest woman in North Carolina, maybe in the whole country. So we're used to odd-shaped people. Your brother smiled.

CHANG: He can't hear us.

SALLY: *(To Eng.)* You smiled.

CHANG: He's not here. We can talk about anything we like. We could talk about him if we wanted to. It's perfectly safe. I'll tell you a secret of his.

SALLY: I don't think you'd better.

CHANG: A secret which he would certainly object to my telling. Are you ready? Eng is very fond of your sister. You see? No reaction.

SALLY: They've barely spoken.

CHANG: Eng is shy. Does your sister care for him? *(Beat.)* He's not here.

SALLY: No, she doesn't.

CHANG: I see. Thank you for telling me. I will keep it in confidence. *(Beat.)* I could tell you a secret of mine as well.

SALLY: All right.

CHANG: I enjoy speaking with you.

SALLY: I enjoy speaking with you.

CHANG: I enjoy it very much.

SALLY: Thank you. We should maybe get back.

CHANG: First I need to ask you…

SALLY: What?

CHANG: You will not offend me if you say no. I would like to continue to speak to you privately sometimes.

SALLY: That would be fine.

CHANG: But I need to know, why am I speaking to you?

SALLY: Because I'm charming.

CHANG: And if I were speaking to you a year from now, why would I be speaking to you?

SALLY: The same reason.

CHANG: I see. This is difficult.

SALLY: I know.

CHANG: I'm going to tell you a story. You may have already heard it. It was in the newspapers. When I visited Philadelphia, I lost a watch, a gift from my mother, and I was distraught. Dozens of people came to my aid. They asked me questions: "When did I last have it on?" And I had no idea. So I said, because it might be true, that I think I last had it on a trolley. But as I said it, I realized that no, I had no idea when I last wore it. I couldn't remember seeing it for the last week. But it was too late. People were already organizing trolley search parties. It was in the newspaper. Siamese Brother Loses Precious Keepsake. The mayor had the trolley company give us a schedule. People divided up into groups and each searched a different trolley line. All of this activity set into motion because I was too dishonest to say I don't remember. Now whenever I think of Philadelphia, I get an uneasy feeling in my chest. I could have saved them so much trouble. *(Pause.)* Do you understand?

SALLY: I think so.

CHANG: How's your head?

SALLY: It hurts.

CHANG: I need to know. Should I have any hope at all?

SALLY: Yes.

CHANG: Thank you. May I hold your hand?

SALLY: No.

CHANG: Have you ever held a man's hand before?

SALLY: Yes.

CHANG: Why won't you hold my hand?

SALLY: I'm embarrassed.

CHANG: We're alone.

SALLY: No we're not.

CHANG: We're as alone as we ever will be. One more time. Should I have hope?

SALLY: I think so.

CHANG: Then hold my hand.

SALLY: It's too early.

CHANG: What doesn't your sister like about my brother?

SALLY: I'm not sure.

CHANG: Is it this? *(He indicates the band.)*

SALLY: No.

CHANG: What then?

SALLY: I don't like to talk about a person when he's not here. But it's not that. Why would it be? It's so small. It's barely there. May I touch it?

CHANG: You won't hold my hand, but you want to touch my belly button?

SALLY: I'm sorry is that...? It is. I never noticed. I don't look, to be polite.

CHANG: Go ahead.

SALLY: No that's all right.

CHANG: Please.

SALLY: I'd better not.

CHANG: I won't be able to feel it.

SALLY: *(Touches the band.)* Not at all?

CHANG: Pressure only.

SALLY: Can he?

CHANG: He's not here.

SALLY: But if he were?

CHANG: No.

SALLY: It's harder than I thought. It does feel strong.

CHANG: Once, Eng fell out of bed and hung there sleeping until I woke up and pulled him back.

SALLY: What's it made of?

CHANG: I don't know.

SALLY: Is there any chance you might be separated?

CHANG: It might be possible, yes.

SALLY: Would you want to be?

CHANG: Yes. Very much so. Now please hold my hand. *(She takes his hand.)* Thank you.

SALLY: You're trembling.

CHANG: I'm nervous. Stay like this for a moment.

SALLY: Thank you for asking to hold my hand. I don't think your brother would have done that. That's why Adelaide doesn't like him. He's not passionate enough. She's never even seen him laugh or smile or... You're really shaking.

CHANG: It's difficult. But I am enjoying this.

SALLY: I am too. I didn't expect this. I didn't expect it at all. Your hand feels nice.

CHANG: Yours is warm.

ENG: Someone's coming.

(Chang and Sally move apart.)

SALLY: I thought you weren't here.

ENG: I wasn't. In my head I was standing in the doorway. I thought I should mention that somebody was approaching.

(Pause.)

SALLY: But there is no one approaching.

ENG: I heard footsteps. Go back to whatever you were talking about.

(Long pause.)

CHANG: May we try again?

SALLY: I think we should get back.

(Adelaide enters.)

ADELAIDE: There you are.

ENG: Hello, Adelaide.

ADELAIDE: We've been missing you. You stole our celebrities. Sally!

SALLY: What?

ADELAIDE: Look at all these chairs.

SALLY: I know.

ADELAIDE: Am I interrupting something?

SALLY: Of course not.

ADELAIDE: I told Daddy I'd find you. Don't be long.

SALLY: We won't.

ENG: Good to see you, Adelaide.

ADELAIDE: Good to see you.

(Eng gives her a large smile. She looks from him to Sally and exits.)

SALLY: We should get back.

CHANG: First, may I give you a kiss?

SALLY: No.

CHANG: On the hand.

SALLY: All right.

CHANG: Or the cheek.

SALLY: I don't think so.

CHANG: As a promise.

SALLY: A promise of what?

CHANG: That there might be future meetings like this. In private, sometimes.

(After a moment. She turns her cheek to the side for him to kiss. He does so.)

CHANG: Thank you. Very much.

(They begin to exit, her arm resting on his.)

CHANG: How do you feel?

SALLY: I'm in remarkable pain.

(Lights fade as they exit.)

END OF PLAY

Loyalties
by Murphy Guyer

CHARACTERS
RUDY

KATRIN

MONIKA

JACOB

SETTING
A dining room.

Loyalties

Scene: A round table with four chairs. Solid oak. A white linen tablecloth. In the center of the table sits a half-consumed chocolate cake. Also, two bottles of champagne. One empty, the other half full. There are four settings at the table. Each with a glass of champagne and a plate stained with the remains of chocolate cake. Four crumpled linen napkins. Upstage left is a large wooden door.

At rise: We see Monika, Jacob, Katrin, and Rudy seated at the table. Monika and Katrin are both wearing dresses of simple cut and style. They evoke no particular period of fashion. Jacob is wearing a plain black suit, worn and bohemian. He wears a white shirt. No tie. Rudy wears the brown pants of a military uniform, with a matching brown T-shirt. Brown socks and no boots.

RUDY: He's done a remarkable job, no doubt about it. Thanks to him this country is back on its feet again…Where's the cake knife?

MONIKA: Here, hon.

RUDY: People are starting to act like citizens again. They're starting to care about more than just making it through the next day.

KATRIN: That was because of inflation.

RUDY: Sure it was. Hell, I'm not blaming them. They had no choice. Anybody else for more cake? *(To Monika.)* Birthday girl?

MONIKA: Well, maybe just a little. Not too much though… No Rudy, smaller. Smaller! Rudy! I can't eat all that! What are you doing? Take some of that back. You'll ruin my waistline.

RUDY: To hell with your waistline. You're getting too skinny anyway. I got nothing to hold on to anymore.

MONIKA: Rudy! Not in front of the guests.

RUDY: What guests? It's your sister.

MONIKA: *(Giggling.)* He's got a one-track mind, I swear.

RUDY: *(Offering cake.)* Katrin?

KATRIN: No more for me, thanks.

RUDY: Jake? Cake? Cake, Jake?

JACOB: No thanks.

RUDY: How's that for poetry? What do you think? Think I've got a future?

JACOB: It's Jacob.

RUDY: No good. Can't use it. Doesn't rhyme with cake. Can't be poetry if it doesn't rhyme.

JACOB: Think of it as blank verse.

RUDY: Ha ha. Good one, good one... What did I do with my fork?

MONIKA: You dropped it on the floor. I'll get you another one.

RUDY: Forget it. I'll use Jake's. *(He wipes Jacob's fork off with his napkin.)* Where was I? Oh yeah—no, no, I'm not blaming them. They were scared to death. And why wouldn't they be? Their life savings were being wiped out right in front of their eyes. Millions of people out of work? No, it was a desperate situation, no doubt about it. But what made it really bad was that there wasn't anybody in charge. There wasn't any confidence in the future because there wasn't anybody to inspire it. I mean let's face it, since we lost that goddam war, this country has been in a daze. People suddenly just lost faith in all the traditional values. I mean forget discipline. Forget self-sacrifice. It was just me, me, me. Either something had to change or this country wasn't going to make it.

MONIKA: But it has changed.

RUDY: That's what I'm saying. That's my point. The whole situation has turned around. Inflation is down, crime is down, the military is strong again, and the communists are running scared. Hell, no wonder the election was such a landslide. For the first time in twenty years, people can finally feel proud of their country again.

MONIKA: Tell them about that woman at the newsstand.

RUDY: I'm getting to that. Will you let me finish?... You're not going to eat your cake?

MONIKA: I can't. It's too much I told you.

RUDY: Jesus Christ. Give it to me... Here's a perfect example of what I'm talking about. The other day I went into this newsstand to buy a paper. And there was this old lady there. Must have been around sixty, sixty-five. Didn't look like she had much money. Anyway, from the moment I walked in, all that woman did was stare at me. And I thought to myself, "Oh no, here we go again. She's going to throw a fit."

MONIKA: That happened a couple of weeks ago. This woman saw Rudy at the train station and started screaming at him. He didn't even do anything. She started screaming. What was it that she called you?

RUDY: I don't know. She was crazy.

MONIKA: It was really filthy.

RUDY: She was nuts. She was like one of those mad dogs that go into convulsions every time a uniform walks by.

JACOB: Did you shoot her?

RUDY: Ha, ha, ha. I should have.

KATRIN: Jacob.

JACOB: Just asking.

KATRIN: Don't start.

RUDY: Oh come on Katrin, he's just joking.

KATRIN: I mean it, Jacob.

MONIKA: What's wrong? What's going on?

KATRIN: Jacob's had too much to drink.

RUDY: Oh hell, Katrin, let the guy enjoy himself. Pay no attention to her, Jake. Eat, drink, and be merry.

JACOB: Thanks, Rude.

RUDY: Ha, ha. Good one, good one.

MONIKA: Come on Rudy, finish your story.

RUDY: Right, right. So anyway I pay for the newspaper and I'm just about to walk out the door when this old lady grabs me by the arm. And I thought to myself, "Here it comes." And you know what she does? She pulls me down and whispers, "It makes me proud to see young men in uniform again. God bless you. We could use more like you."

MONIKA: Isn't that sweet?

RUDY: How about *that?* Now that kind of thing just wasn't happening a few years ago.

MONIKA: And it's true. It does make you feel proud.

RUDY: The woman actually had tears in her eyes.

MONIKA: I love that story.

JACOB: How do you know she wasn't crazy?

KATRIN: Jacob.

RUDY: What?

MONIKA: No, no, that was the other one.

KATRIN: That's enough.

RUDY: Wait a minute, wait a minute. I want to hear what he has to say.

KATRIN: He's drunk. He's just being contrary.

RUDY: What did you mean by that?

JACOB: I just think it's interesting that's all.

MONIKA: What's interesting?

JACOB: That you assume that the woman who berated you was insane while the one who flattered you was perfectly normal.

MONIKA: She was berating him in a public place.

JACOB: He was flattered in a public place.

MONIKA: But she was screaming.

JACOB: The insane never whisper?

RUDY: You're not saying that it's crazy to be patriotic, I hope.

JACOB: I wouldn't call it absolute proof of sanity.

MONIKA: What's wrong with patriotism?

RUDY: Nothing. It's perfectly natural.

JACOB: So is death and disease.

RUDY: And what is that supposed to mean?

JACOB: Just because a thing is natural doesn't make it desirable.

RUDY: If patriotism is anything, it's a cure.

JACOB: It seems to me more like a symptom.

MONIKA: Of what?

JACOB: Of personal weakness.

MONIKA: What's weak about feeling patriotic?

JACOB: To feel patriotic is to feel superior. To celebrate one country is to implicitly denigrate all others. And the feeling of superiority that comes with patriotism is a coward's superiority. It risks nothing. The man who proclaims the greatness of his country is a man who doesn't have the courage to proclaim his own individual greatness.

RUDY: Are you saying that patriots are cowards?

MONIKA: But what about all the men who have died for their country?

JACOB: They did not "die for their country."

RUDY: The hell they didn't!

JACOB: They were killed while trying to kill for their country.

RUDY: Well, however you want to put it, the fact is that they sacrificed their lives for the good of their country!

JACOB: Soldiers do not go into battle with the intention of sacrificing anything. Least of all their lives. And how you *put it,* as you say, means everything. The expression "He died for his country" did not originate with the dying soldier. It was invented by a political eulogist for political purposes. He needed to reassure the grieving parents and to recruit more young heroes to take the dead soldier's place. It's rhetoric. The manipulation of words for emotional effect to achieve a political purpose.

RUDY: You're the one who's manipulating words for effect.

JACOB: What effect?

RUDY: To win people over to your sick point of view.

JACOB: I don't care whether you agree with my point of view or not. I'm a poet, not a politician. I say what I say because I believe it's true.

MONIKA: But what about the Olympics? Didn't you feel proud when this country won all those medals?

JACOB: Individual athletes won those medals. And their pride is the honest pride of individual effort. The people who appropriate that pride in the name of patriotism are nothing more than chauvinistic cannibals. Their own achievements have so little value they have to confiscate the achievements of their so-called country.

RUDY: The achievements of a country *are* the achievements of its people!

JACOB: The achievements of Mozart are not the achievements of Austria.

RUDY: Mozart is a product of Austria.

JACOB: You make him sound like an industrial export.

RUDY: He was born and raised in Austria.

JACOB: So were millions of others, whose only talent was for giving birth to millions more.

MONIKA: But without Austria there would have been no Mozart.

JACOB: Austria is a political invention, like all countries. It was not created for the purpose of cultivating Mozarts, and so it has no right to claim his genius for its own.

RUDY: So you feel no loyalty to your own country.

JACOB: No.

RUDY: After all this country has given you.

JACOB: I don't see that this country has given me any more than Austria gave to Mozart.

MONIKA: But what about the language? You couldn't write poetry without that.

JACOB: Not everyone who speaks the language is a poet. And not every poet speaks this language.

RUDY: What *do* you feel loyalty towards?

JACOB: My work, my friends.

RUDY: And what about the rest of the world? What about belief in a cause?

JACOB: The world can take care of itself. My only cause is my own mind.

RUDY: It would be a hell of a world if everyone felt the way you did.

JACOB: Almost no one does. They never have and probably never will. And it's still a hell of a world in spite of that.

RUDY: And if your country were suddenly attacked you wouldn't defend it?

JACOB: I'm not a soldier. I'm a poet. I have no interest in fighting. My only interest is to understand the truth as best I can.

RUDY: Yeah, some poet! You've never even been published.

MONIKA: Rudy!

RUDY: Well it's true, isn't it?

KATRIN: Thanks, Monika.

MONIKA: We were talking. It just came up. You didn't say it was supposed to be a secret.

RUDY: I mean if we're only supposed to say things because they're true...

MONIKA: Stop it, Rudy. Don't be spiteful.

RUDY: Who's being spiteful? I just always thought that you had to be published before you could call yourself a poet.

KATRIN: Jacob happens to be a very fine poet.

RUDY: Yeah, well, you seem to be the only one who thinks so.

KATRIN: Everyone will think so someday.

RUDY: And since when did you become such an expert on poetry?

MONIKA: Alright, Rudy, stop it.

RUDY: You probably never even *read* a poem until you met him.

MONIKA: Rudy, stop it. Leave my sister alone.

RUDY: No, no, come on, we're supposed to be telling the truth here, right?

MONIKA: Katrin has been reading books ever since she was a little girl. She's read more than you and me put together.

RUDY: How do you know how many books I've read?!

KATRIN: Look, let's just stop this, alright?

RUDY: I mean, how the hell can somebody just *decide* that he's a poet. If that's all it takes, maybe I'll just decide that I'm a doctor. He doesn't need to publish, and I don't need to take a medical exam! How's that?

MONIKA: Oh be quiet. You're being ignorant.

RUDY: Don't call me that! Don't you ever call me that!

MONIKA: Well, stop picking on everybody.

RUDY: You're supposed to be my wife!

MONIKA: But Katrin's my sister.

RUDY: Well it's time you decided whose side you're on.

MONIKA: But you're not being fair. If Jacob wants to call himself a poet, why can't he? Who cares if he's been published or not? Do you have to kill somebody before you can call yourself a soldier?

RUDY: Hey, I don't care what the hell he calls himself! But I'll be damned if I'm going to sit here and listen to him call patriots cowards.

KATRIN: He never said that.

RUDY: Because let me tell you something, *Jake!* I'm patriotic. And so is everybody else in my squad. Now are you going to tell me that those men don't have courage?

JACOB: I can't see that it takes much courage to mindlessly march to your own death on someone's command.

RUDY: Are you saying that soldiers are mindless?!

(The following exchange accelerates and overlaps.)

JACOB: You fight when you are ordered to fight. I call that not having a mind of your own.

RUDY: You sonofabitch.

MONIKA: Rudy!

RUDY: I'm defending freedom, you bastard!

MONIKA: Rudy, stop it!

JACOB: Right …

KATRIN: Jacob.

JACOB: …as long as I don't exercise it by disagreeing with you.

KATRIN: Jacob! That's enough!

RUDY: You know what you are?

MONIKA: Come on, Rudy!

RUDY: You're a selfish fucking egotist!

MONIKA: You're ruining the party!

JACOB: And you're an interchangeable part.

(In one rapid movement, Rudy lunges at Jacob, pulls him from the chair, and punches him hard in the belly. Jacob crumples to the floor. The following exchange coincides.)

MONIKA: Rudy! For godsake!

KATRIN: STOP IT!

MONIKA: Leave him alone! *(Katrin rushes to Jacob.)*

RUDY: If you hate this country so much, why don't you just leave it?

KATRIN: You stay away from him.

MONIKA: Come on Rudy, stop it, that's enough.

JACOB: I intend to.

RUDY: Yeah, well do us a favor and make it soon.

KATRIN: Monika! Get him out of here.

JACOB: Will next week be soon enough?

MONIKA: Come on Rudy, you have to get ready. You'll be late.

RUDY: *(As he exits off right.)* Goddam little fucking traitor.

KATRIN: Bastard!

MONIKA: It's not all his fault!

KATRIN: Who attacked who, Monika?

MONIKA: Well tell Jacob to keep his mouth shut.

KATRIN: Why? He's right.

MONIKA: Rudy is not a coward!

KATRIN: You call what he just did an act of courage?

MONIKA: He was provoked!

KATRIN: Yes. By the truth.

MONIKA: Get out! Get out of our house, both of you! Get out and stay out! I don't care if you are my sister! I won't let you come in here and call my husband a coward! Rudy happens to be one of the bravest men I ever met! *(She exits.)*

KATRIN: Are you alright?

JACOB: Leave me alone.

KATRIN: Well that was childish.

JACOB: It was true.

KATRIN: So what? Did you have to say it?

JACOB: I meant about leaving next week.

KATRIN: What?

JACOB: I *am* leaving next week.

KATRIN: ...For where?

JACOB: Paris.

KATRIN: ...For how long?

JACOB: I'm not planning on coming back.

KATRIN: ...And what about me?

JACOB: I have nothing to offer you, Katrin. I have no money and I don't see how I could expect to get any anytime soon.

KATRIN: Well, maybe I have my own money. Did you ever think of that?

JACOB: Do you?

KATRIN: ...No.

JACOB: I can't support you, Katrin. I can't take that responsibility. It would interfere with my work.

KATRIN: So you have to leave because of your work.

JACOB: Yes.

KATRIN: Well I don't see why. You've been working just fine right here.

JACOB: I haven't been working just fine here. That's why I'm leaving.

KATRIN: And you think you'll be able to work any better in Paris?

JACOB: I can't stay in this country. It's spiritually bankrupt.

KATRIN: And what about me? Am I spiritually bankrupt too?

JACOB: I didn't say that.

KATRIN: No, I'm just an albatross, right?... Right?!

JACOB: I'm sorry.

KATRIN: Fine. Well, I hope you and your work will be very happy together. *(She crosses to the door.)* Rudy was right. You're a selfish sonofabitch.
(She exits. Jacob remains on the floor. After a moment, Rudy re-enters from stage right. He is now in full uniform. It is a Nazi uniform. He carries his boots. He sees Jacob and stops. They stare at each other for a long moment. Jacob rises and exits out the door. Rudy sits and drops his boots. Monika enters and goes to clear the table. After a pause, Rudy bursts out emotionally.)

RUDY: Is it me?! Am I crazy? Am I wrong? Is it wrong to love your country? Is it wrong to be willing to fight for it? I love this country, goddammit! I love it! I know it's not perfect. But what is? I mean you have to believe in something, right? Is it wrong to want to believe in something bigger than yourself? Is it crazy to want to be part of something? To be a part of something that's so much a part of you? Tell me! Is that crazy? Is it me?

KATRIN: No, of course it's not. I love this country too. As much as you do. No Rudy, it's not you. It's not you, honey. It's not.
(Fade to black.)

END OF PLAY

4 AM (Open All Night)
by Bob Krakower

CHARACTERS

MAN: A nice guy, semiregular at this diner.

JIM: The guy behind the counter, he knows Man and Woman.

WOMAN: A nice gal, a semiregular at this diner.

DOC: A regular. He is a little smashed but never violent. A dry wit, a big heart.

SETTING

An all-night diner.

Time: 4 AM an April evening.

NOTE

This play moves at a brisk pace. Pauses only where noted.

For Kathleen.

4 AM
(Open All Night)

Scene: One table, two chairs. A simplified counter, three stools.

MAN: I'm not hungry.

JIM: Coffee?

MAN: Ah, shit—

JIM: *(Pours coffee.)* What's the matter?

MAN: I'm outta smokes—

JIM: How many times I have to tell you, buy the carton—not the pack.

MAN: I know, but, and see, that's another thing—she hates that I smoke—

JIM: So—

MAN: Like lickin' an ashtray, she says, but I don't wanna quit—

JIM: So don't quit—

MAN: I'm gonna quit.

JIM: *(Offers cigarette.)* Here ya go.

MAN: Thanks.

JIM: *(Lights cigarette.)* So—

MAN: So anyway that's my point.

JIM: What is?

MAN: That we don't communicate—

JIM: No, you communicate—

MAN: No, we don't.

JIM: Oh, yes, you do pal. You communicate. You don't *agree,* but you communicate—

MAN: Hey, if she doesn't *understand* me, then how can you call that communication?

JIM: Look, do you understand the words I'm speaking?

MAN: Jim, your missin' the point—

JIM: No, I'm not. *(More coffee?)*

MAN: *(Yeah.)*

JIM: Do you understand what I am *saying?*

MAN: Look, we're just wrong for each other, that's all—

JIM: Do you?

MAN: Yeah—

JIM: Make sense to you?

MAN: Yeah—

JIM: Do you agree with me?

MAN: No—

JIM: So we disagree—

MAN: Yeah—

JIM: But you *understand.*

MAN: So?

JIM: So that's what I'm sayin'—You say—"I get up, I come down here for a burger, have a little bit of Joe, bum a smoke—no harm done."

MAN: That's right.

JIM: She wants you safe at home.

MAN: That's right—

JIM: She disagrees.

MAN: That's *wrong.* She doesn't *understand.* This is what I'm trying to tell you—Every fuckin' time. I get up. I can't sleep, right? I'm restless—wanna have a smoke, I don't know, just walk around or something, get centered or—no, I don't mean "get centered," I mean, well—you know?—I don't know—Anyway, the house feels stuffy, my head's a fuckin' wind tunnel, and I wanna be *outside,* ya know, in the air, I don't know—clear my mind, or something. Goddamn it, I can't pinpoint it, I just felt out of sync, I felt trapped—like, I don't know, I just don't belong there next to her and—

JIM: You wanna be with her or not?

MAN: Yeah, yeah, I *do*—I guess, she's great, it's just that I *got up,* ya know and I start tippytoeing out of the room—"Where you goin'?" she says. "Diner," I say ('cause that's where I'm going)—"For what?" she says—"I don't know, get a burger," I say—"No," she says. "No, what?" I say. "No," she says—"No, I can't go?" I say—"Nooooo" (and I hate the fuckin' way she says that, like she's got some kind of insight into the true meaning of my soul that *I* have yet to discover.) "Noooooo," she says "you're lyin'"—you ain't *just* 'goin'-to-get-a-burger.'" "I'm not?" I say, "Funny, that's what I *thought* I was doin'." *(Enter Woman with newspaper.)*

WOMAN: Hey, Jim.

JIM: Be with you in a second, kiddo.

WOMAN: Ya got change for cigs?

JIM: Yeah— *(Pause as Jim pours her a cup of coffee. Man and Woman notice each other.)*

WOMAN: Thanks.

MAN: Where was I?

JIM: You were leavin' the house.

MAN: Oh yeah, right, so—"Listen," she says, "We got chopmeat here. Stay, I'll *make* you a burger"—"But I wanna go *out*." I say—*(Woman exits, leaving coffee on table.)* "Stay and *talk* to me," she says, "What's on your mind"—"Honey, I'm going to the diner." "Liar."—*Liar?* I mean I'm here, aren't I? So then, I feel *bad*, see, 'cause I just want some air, but I don't want her to be *mad*, so I decide to *stay*—she then tells me I'm stayin' for the wrong reasons and yells at me to *go*. And the next thing I know *I'm* fightin' to stay in the apartment and she throws me out! I mean, help me out here— Can't a guy get into his car, roll down the window, turn up the radio, drive down to the local burger-hole (sorry, Jim), pop a quarter in the box, sing "Under the Boardwalk" (perhaps the greatest song ever recorded), and pound down on a burger without being accused of I-don't-know-what?

JIM: So you *do* communicate.

MAN: You *don't* understand.

JIM: Oh, I understand— She just wants you to *talk* to her. Have you ever had an affair?

MAN: What, cheated on her?

JIM: No, I mean ever, in your life?

MAN: Yeah.

JIM: Has she?

MAN: I think so.

JIM: So—

MAN: So what?

JIM: So she's working off a perception she has of this event based on life experience—

MAN: What event?

JIM: A man disappearing in the wee hours of the morning for seemingly no particular reason, you idiot. It's perfectly natural.

MAN: But I'm not *doin'* anything—

JIM: *I* know that.

MAN: Why doesn't she?

JIM: You tell me. *(Woman re-enters wearing Walkman, singing to herself.)*

MAN: So, what am I supposed to do?

JIM: I don't know— Find someone who likes to eat burgers and drink coffee at four o'clock in the morning.

MAN: Oh, yeah—Like who?

JIM: Like her— *(Woman lights a cigarette.)*

MAN: Oh, come on—

JIM: She smokes—

MAN: *(Looks at her.)* It wouldn't work.

JIM: How do you know that?

MAN: I can tell. Anyway—I'm not in the market.

JIM: You're happy where you are—

MAN: Yeah—

JIM: So what are you doin' down here at four o'clock in the morning? *(Pause.)*

MAN: She's taller than I am.

JIM: Everybody is.

MAN: Fuck you, Jim.

JIM: You haven't even met her—

MAN: *(Looks at her again.)* I got somebody—

JIM: Let me ask you something—you happy?

DOC: Unbefuckinlievable.

JIM: *(Overlapping.)* So what are you doin' down here at four o'clock in the morning?

MAN: I just want a fuckin' hamburger.

JIM: I don't see you eatin' anything. *(Pause.)*

MAN: What am I gonna say to her, I got nothin' to say. We got nothin' in common—

JIM: Well, for starters, you're both here at four o'clock in the morning for the same reasons—

MAN: You don't know that.

JIM: Bet ya a fin—

MAN: Forget it.

JIM: Then go home.

MAN: I don't want to go home.

JIM: Why not?

MAN: I just want a fuckin' hamburger!!!

DOC: You got chopmeat at home.

MAN: This is ridiculous.

JIM: Why did you come down here?

MAN: To be alone.

JIM: Take a look around you—

MAN: Yeah?

JIM: You alone?

MAN: Jim, let me tell you something—if you're really perceptive, you can tell within about ten seconds of meeting someone if the chemistry's there—

JIM: Yeah, I can tell it ain't there, I can tell by the way you can't help staring at her since she walked in the door.

MAN: Hey, I have *some* experience with this kind of thing…give me some credit.

JIM: You're full o' more bull, pal, than the chopmeat in your fridge. *(Man turns to stare at Woman.)*

DOC: Problems with your girl?

MAN: No.

DOC: Liar.

MAN: What is going on tonight?

DOC: You're lying, ain't you—you have problems with your girl.

MAN: Yeah, so?

DOC: I'd say that makes you a liar.

MAN: Who is this? Who the fuck are you?

DOC: I'm trying to communicate something to you here, pal—

MAN: I left my apartment and walked straight into the Twilight Zone—I just want a fuckin' hamburger!!! Jesus Christ, what is this, a goddamn conspiracy—what is going on here tonight? I just want a fuckin' hamburger!!!!! *(Gets up and goes to the men's room. Woman removes headphones.)*

WOMAN: Hey Jim, a burger and another cup of coffee, please—

JIM: A very popular item tonight.

WOMAN: What do you mean?

JIM: Nothin'. Anything else?

WOMAN: No, just a glass of water.

JIM: Sure.

WOMAN: And some more cream…

JIM: Okay…

WOMAN: …um, Jim *(Jim turns.)*

WOMAN: Who's the guy?

JIM: Which guy?

WOMAN: The guy—he was just sitting over there.

DOC: I think he went to relieve his conscience.

JIM: He had a fight with his future ex-girlfriend.

WOMAN: Oh.

JIM: Why?

WOMAN: I think I've seen him around, ya know—here and there, ya know?

JIM: Yeah?

WOMAN: Oh, I don't know, skip it. I don't know…I don't know. You got a light?—Thanks. I got this feeling like I've met him before, like I *know* him but I haven't, so—

JIM: So?

WOMAN: I can't explain it.

DOC: Explain what?

WOMAN: I don't know…Déja vu? Some *connection,* I don't know, skip it. Where's the paper?

DOC: Why is it I can sit here and look you dead in the eye and know exactly what you should do, but when I look at myself, I don't have a fuckin' clue?—nothing. Why is that?—Why is it that I'm smarter about your life than I am about my own—you ever think about that? I do—why is that—who am I talking to?? *(Pause—they stare at him.)*

JIM: So you think he's cute?

WOMAN: I didn't say that—

JIM: I ain't asking for a commitment—Come on, I'll introduce you—

WOMAN: No, that's okay.

JIM: Then why did you ask?

WOMAN: I don't know why—

JIM: Come on—I'll introduce you…

WOMAN: We wouldn't get along—

JIM: You haven't even met him.

WOMAN: Let me tell you something, okay? Intimate sexual relationships—

DOC: Excuse me?

WOMAN: —of course, it depends on the quality—distort your perceptions of time and space. You become irrational, single-minded, thick-brained and stupid, and tend to smile out of context occasionally. Articulation becomes a struggle. I can't get any work done—I'm absent-mindedly stroking my thighs in public and bruises appear on my body, and I wonder, "Where did those come from?" I eat less, smoke more, and drink by the bottle, not the glass. I become witty as hell—I mean, you feel so BLONDE. Man, *Cosmo* magazine becomes appealing and those little love quizzes take over

as the single source of outside information—and then before you know it
you start to feel pretty damn good about yourself —

JIM: Sounds terrible.

WOMAN: —and then you look up one day to find—he's gone. So, no.

JIM: No what?

WOMAN: I don't want to meet him—

JIM: So why did you come down here?

WOMAN: To be alone.

JIM: Take a look around you— *(Pause.)*

WOMAN: Let me ask you, what would I have in common with a guy like that?

JIM: A guy like what? You don't even know him—

WOMAN: He's shorter than I am.

JIM: Why do you do this to yourself?

WOMAN: Okay, just for argument's sake, let's say, I say hello—

JIM: Yeah—

WOMAN: He comes over—

JIM: Right.

WOMAN: We talk—

JIM: Hmm hmm.

WOMAN: Our eyes connect, he becomes vulnerable—

JIM: Now you're cookin'—

WOMAN: I start to care for him—

JIM: Go, baby, go—

WOMAN: He opens up and lets me in, my life starts to revolve around him—I
love him with everything I have—

JIM: Well—

WOMAN: —and wake up one morning to find that he doesn't *know* me.

JIM: Well, whose fault is that?

WOMAN: "I don't know, I don't have any idea who you are," he says, and he's
right, of course, because I've spent all my time holdin' *him* up and he gets
scared and pulls away—and then he's gone and here I am—

JIM: Whoa—

WOMAN: —right back down here at this damn little table—

DOC: Hey, kiddo.

WOMAN: —and I feel like I'm takin' my life in my hands just by sayin' hello,
ya know? I mean I've been around the block a few times, I think I can
save myself this one trip.

JIM: What if this *one* trip was the *right* trip? *(Pause.)*

WOMAN: Jim, let me tell you something—if you're really perceptive, you can tell within about ten seconds of meeting someone if the chemistry's there.

DOC: Unbefuckinlievable—if this was a movie, nobody'd believe it.

WOMAN: Look, I came down here for a burger and a cup of coffee. If I want a dating service, I'll go somewhere else.

DOC: It's amazing anybody meets anybody.

WOMAN: Please, I'm sorry, this whole thing, I don't know why I mentioned it—

JIM: I think I do.

DOC: Why is everybody so tense!?! Just say hello—

JIM: What are you afraid of?

DOC: It's not gonna kill ya!

WOMAN: Well, let's start with rejection and go from there.

DOC: You afraid he might *like* you? That it? *(Pause.)*

WOMAN: Okay, okay, okay—I'll tell you what—I'll make you a deal—

DOC: Okay—

WOMAN: I'll make you a deal—I'll count backwards from a hundred and if he turns around and says hello to me before I get to one, then I'll know it was meant to be, okay?

JIM: Okay.

DOC: Okay.

WOMAN: Okay. *(Breath.)* Now, may I please have a cup of coffee and the newspaper?

JIM: *(Smiling.)* One joe on the move—

DOC: Madam, your paper. I'll just keep the sports.

(Woman puts headphones on and tries to read the newspaper as she counts backwards. Man re-enters.)

MAN: So what's the answer?

DOC: What's the question?

MAN: What we were talking about *before*—

DOC: Two Hearts Are Better Than One.

MAN: What say?

DOC: Two Hearts Are Better Than One, at Belmont in the Eighth.

MAN: What are you talking about?

DOC: *(Nodding toward the woman.)* I got a gut feeling.

MAN: What are the odds?

DOC: A hundred to one.

MAN: A little high, wouldn't you say?

DOC: I got a gut feeling.

MAN: How does she run in the mud?

DOC: What's the difference?

MAN: You've got to take everything into consideration—You've got to figure—

DOC: Figure what?

MAN: Rain, odds, jockey—

DOC: No, too much trouble.

MAN: What do you mean?

DOC: Too much thinking.

MAN: You gotta *think* about it.

DOC: No, you think, you start to doubt...too much room for error.

MAN: And if you fail?

DOC: I fail. What are you, Mr. Perfect?

MAN: No—

DOC: You need to be right all the time?

MAN: You need all the information to help you figure it out.

DOC: All that shit does is keep you from laying down a bet.

MAN: But you gotta base your bet on something.

DOC: I do.

MAN: On what?

DOC: My gut.

MAN: And what does your gut say?

DOC: *Always follow your instincts.*

MAN: You bet on gut?

DOC: No, I bet on a horse, and I'm betting the bank on Two Hearts Are Better Than One.

MAN: *(To Jim.)* Come on, help me out here—

DOC: Hey, I'm trying to tell you something here, pal, and you ain't listening. You don't listen, is your problem.

MAN: I listen.

DOC: No, you don't, you *think*, but you don't listen.

MAN: Listen, I like thinking, okay?...you have to think through what you listen to.

DOC: I don't have to think of anything.

MAN: But what if you're wrong?

DOC: If I'm wrong, I'm wrong... *I'm* not afraid to be wrong—I *learn* from my experience, I'm still betting, my instincts get better, I'm *making* money, *losing* money, but I'm doing something. Every day I'm *doing* something, what are *you* doing? If I did it your way I'd never win, never lose, probably never lay a bet. I'd just be buried in the newspaper all day. You bet horses?

MAN: No.

DOC: Didn't think so. Ever think about?

MAN: Yeah—

WOMAN: Forty-seven, forty-six, forty-five… *(Etc.)*

JIM: I'll bet you a sawbuck you can't.

MAN: What? *(Jim points to girl.)* I can't.

JIM: Why not?

MAN: I'm not that kind of guy—

JIM: What kind?

MAN: The kind that, ya know, I'm not—I can't—I mean, I haven't. Listen, I don't want to bother anybody, ya know, EVER.

JIM: Listen, friend.

WOMAN: Twenty-nine, twenty-eight, twenty-seven, twenty-six…

MAN: I'm not equipped for this—

JIM: You know, you've given me lots of reasons why you shouldn't do this, except one.

MAN: What's that?

JIM: A good one.

MAN: What difference does it make to you?

JIM: I get tired of o' lookin' at lonely faces that don't need to be that way, come on—

DOC: Take a chance.

JIM: It's just hello.

MAN: Sayin' hello is like taking your life in your hands, ya know? It fuckin' scares me to death…

DOC: Every time.

WOMAN: Eighteen, seventeen, sixteen…

JIM: If it were me, you'd want me to ask her out—

MAN: Yeah. But what if I—

DOC: For Chrissakes, come on already!!!!

MAN: Okay, okay, okay, I'lla, I'll tell ya what I'll do—

JIM: Come on come on!

MAN: That's it, I'll count to ten, see—

DOC: Let's go, let's go!!

MAN: —And turn, I'll turn and if she's lookin' at me, I'll take my shot.

DOC: Count fast!

MAN: Okay, okay, okay. *(Closes his eyes, breathes.)*

MAN:

One	WOMAN:
Two	Six
Three	Five
Four	Four
Five	Three
	Two
	(The other men stand and lean in.)
	One

Six
(She stands, looks at him.)

Seven

Eight
(She crosses to the door.)

Nine
(She looks back at him.)

Ten
(He starts to turn, hesitates, takes a breath.)

(She leaves.)

(He turns, she's gone.)
DOC: Way to go, smart guy.
(Man slowly moves toward the door, looks around the window, and slowly waves goodbye as "Under the Boardwalk" begins to play softly. Lights fade.)

END OF PLAY

Just One Night
by Kim Levin

CHARACTERS

KATE, MARGARET, and LIZ: College students, early twenties, roommates.
DAVE: College student, early twenties.

SETTING

An apartment on a college campus.

Just One Night

Kate and Margaret pick up cups, bottles, and cans, the debris of a raucous party. On the couch, Liz is hunched over a stack of books and papers. "Respect" plays on the stereo.

KATE: Will you get another bag out?

MARG: They're any more under the sink?

LIZ: Bought some yesterday.

MARG: I feel like I'm gonna heave. Last night was insanity.

KATE: I can't believe how many people ended up here after the Beta party. Good thing we didn't get busted. We're only one warning away from being on social prob.

MARG: It was worth the risk 'cause guess who came over last night.

KATE: Yeah?

MARG: Mac Templeton.

KATE: He's a bad man.

MARG: Honestly Kate, you say that about every guy.

(Marg turns up the music. She and Kate dance. Liz, unfazed, flips through her papers. She does so automatically almost without thought behind her movement. Kate and Marg try to get Liz to dance. She refuses. Kate turns the music down.)

KATE: What's up with you, woman?

LIZ: I'm just trying to work.

KATE: You OK?

LIZ: Yeah. I have to get some stuff done. I have a make-up seminar tonight.

KATE: English?

LIZ: Yeah, it's my seminar on friendship.

MARG: *(To Liz.)* You have fun last night?

KATE: Well?

LIZ: It was fine.

MARG: Fine. I was out all night with my new boy and it was fine. Right! I saw you and Dave huddled in a corner, *whispering sweet nothings* to each other all night at the party. Glad to see you are finally doing something about your mutual attraction. Did you hook? *(The phone rings.)* So?

LIZ: Get the phone. It's probably for you anyway.

MARG: Get ready to dish 'cause I'll be right back.

(Marg goes out of the room to get the phone.)

KATE: Don't bullshit me, Liz.

LIZ: What?

KATE: I know when you're lying—

LIZ: I'm not ly—

KATE: Don't. What is it? Dave?

(Liz doesn't respond.)

KATE: Is it Dave? It is Dave.

LIZ: I don't want to…

KATE: It's OK. What happened?

LIZ: Dave and I were hanging out at the party. We were having a really good time. When everyone started to clear out, I figured you were inviting people to party late night at our place. I asked Dave if he wanted to. He said he wanted to stop by his room first to grab a sweatshirt. So we went to his room. While he was changing, I was looking through his CD collection. He had this great Neil Young import. I asked him if I could hear it. We were hanging out listening to the CD and we started to kiss… I don't know, I just, I feel like, I don't know…

KATE: Did you have sex?

(Liz nods her head reluctantly.)

KATE: Did you want to?

LIZ: No. I can't…but…no. No, I didn't want to.

KATE: Oh my God. I'm sorry.

LIZ: It's not—he didn't attack me or anything.

KATE: Did you tell him that you didn't want to sleep with him?

LIZ: Yes, yeah, but—

KATE: But nothing, Liz. He took advantage of you against your will.

LIZ: Forget it, Kate. I was feeling… I thought talking might help. I was wrong.

(Marg enters.)

LIZ: Who was it?

MARG: My mom. She was calling to see when—What's going on?

LIZ: Nothing.

KATE: Dave raped Liz last night.

MARG: Are you alright? What?

LIZ: I'm fine. *(To Kate.)* Why are you doing this? *(To Marg.)* Kate is exaggerating. This is getting completely out of hand.

KATE: Is it?

MARG: What the hell—

KATE: Since I have totally misinterpreted what happened to you Liz, why don't you go ahead and tell Margaret what did.

MARG: What?!

LIZ: I went over to Dave's room with him last night after the party. We hooked up and had sex even though I really wasn't into it. Alright!

MARG: You weren't really *into* it?

LIZ: We were listening to some music, talking and... I started to kiss him. I really wanted to. *Wanted to kiss him.* He took off my sweater and kissed my neck. He was gentle. We were both getting excited. I was enjoying it, him, but I knew I didn't want to have sex. He asked me if I wanted to. I told him I didn't think it was a good idea. He kept pushing it and I kept telling him no. I tried to explain it to him, that it wasn't him, I just didn't want to. Then he was on top of me...I don't know if he even realized what he was doing, that I didn't want to. I shouldn't have... I guess I had no business... I don't know.

MARG: I'm sure Dave didn't mean to hurt you. He is a good friend. He would die if he knew he upset you like this.

KATE: Give me a break. Ignorance is no defense. You're saying that because he didn't realize—

MARG: Kate, we all know Dave—

KATE: I suppose you're going to try to tell me that you can only be raped by a stranger.

LIZ: That's not what she's saying. He got a little carried away. We had both been drinking. He just wasn't thinking.

KATE: A person under the influence of alcohol cannot legally give consent to engage in sexual intercourse. So it doesn't matter if you said yes or no. He still had no right to have sex with you.

MARG: That means Dave could say Liz raped him. I'm sorry. *(To Liz.)* Theoretically.

LIZ: That's beside the point. We had both been drinking and I should have known better than to put myself in that position.

KATE: I'm not saying you shouldn't try to avoid bad situations. But that doesn't mean you should take responsibility for what happened. That doesn't mean that Dave didn't do anything wrong.

MARG: Kate, they're both adults. Both chose to go to Dave's room. I'm sure that both of them had a good idea they would hook up. I'm sure they both wanted to. I just think that if a person can't handle a situation then they shouldn't put themselves in it.

KATE: I see. Liz couldn't control the situation so she just got what she deserved.

MARG: I am saying that people should take some responsibility for themselves.

LIZ: Stop!

MARG: We're trying to help you figure this out.

LIZ: You're not... I was lying in Dave's bed last night. I was shaking. So much I was afraid he wouldn't fall asleep. I remember thinking, why did you have to mess things up. Everything was going so well. His leg was on top of me pinning me to the bed, but somehow I got out of his room without waking him. I ran home and went straight to bed. I didn't want to think anymore. When I woke up this morning, I couldn't help feeling that it was my fault too, that I was somehow responsible.

KATE: Liz, listen to me. You are no evil temptress. I understand how you feel, but don't let anyone try to make you believe that because you kissed Dave that you should see things through to his desired ends. You told him that—

(Interrupted by a knock at the door.)

MARG: Should I?

LIZ: It's fine. I'm fine.

MARG: Come in.

(Dave enters.)

DAVE: Hey.

MARG: Hey Dave, what's up?

DAVE: Nothing. Just riding my bike around. I thought I'd stop by and see what you guys were up to.

MARG: Trying to clean this pit up a little after last night. I'm gonna take this bag out.

(Marg exits.)

DAVE: I heard you guys were raging last night.

KATE: It was pretty crazy.

DAVE: Sorry I didn't make it by. I crashed pretty hard.

(Pause.)

LIZ: It's OK. I just came home and went to bed.

KATE: *(To Liz.)* If you need me, I'll be in my room.

(Kate exits.)

DAVE: Later Kate. What's up with you?

LIZ: Nothing. I'm tired… I was having trouble sleeping last night.

DAVE: I know what it's like living in the middle of the party. Good thing I'm a sound sleeper.

LIZ: Umm.

DAVE: When I woke up this morning, you weren't there.

LIZ: I had to take off.

DAVE: I was afraid something was wrong.

LIZ: *(Pause.)* We have to talk about last ni—

DAVE: Do we already have to start having long talks? *(Liz doesn't respond.)* Kidding. I'm joking. *(Pause.)* I had a really good time last night. I just wanted to say that. You have a lot of work. So do I. Tuesday night we could get some beer and hang out?

(Liz nods her head.)

DAVE: I'm gonna take off and let you get back to it.

LIZ: Okay.

DAVE: See ya later.

LIZ: Goodbye.

(Dave exits. Liz picks up the phone and dials.)

LIZ: Yes. Hello. This is Elizabeth Phillips. I need to report a rape.

END OF PLAY

What I Meant Was
by Craig Lucas

For Connie Weinstock

... but he would have us remember most of all
to be enthusiastic over the night,
        not only for the sense of wonder
    it alone has to offer, but also

because it needs our love.

—W. H. Auden, "In Memory of Sigmund Freud"

CHARACTERS

HELEN: Forty-nine.

J. FRED: her husband, forty-seven.

FRITZIE: their son, sixteen.

NANA: Helen's mother, seventy-seven.

PLACE

A dinner table in Columbia, Maryland, 1968.

What I Meant Was

Helen, J. Fred, Nana, and Fritzie are at the dinner table in their suburban kitchen. All but Fritzie are frozen, reaching for plates, mid-conversation. Fritzie looks front; he wears jeans and a flannel shirt, untucked.

FRITZIE: It's 1968 and we're at the dinner table in Columbia, Maryland—about 18 miles southwest of downtown Baltimore. Upstairs on my parents' dresser is a photograph inscribed to me from J. Edgar Hoover the year I was born. My mother has gone over the faded ink with a ballpoint pen so you can be sure to still read it. On this wall in another eight years will hang a letter to my mother from Gerald Ford thanking her for her letter of support. Right now we're in the middle of discussing the length of my hair and the clothes I have taken to wearing. The year before this I painted my entire bedroom black. Here then is everything we meant to say.
(The others unfreeze; they calmly eat their food and affectionately address one another throughout.)

J. FRED: What I think is probably at the root of our discomfort with your favoring long hair and denim is that for your mother and me and also for Nana, because we all survived the Great Depression and in some way feel we triumphed over that—coming from the working class and from immigrant stock, and because so much effort went into that struggle…

FRITZIE: Yes.

J. FRED: …and we know in a way that you probably never will know what it means to go hungry and to have to work with your hands…

FRITZIE: Probably not.

HELEN: Let's hope not.

J. FRED: …it seems an affront to our values to see you purposely dressing like a hobo. For that's what denim is, the costume of laborers, the unemployed. When we have seen so many people forced into that position very much against their will.

FRITZIE: I can understand that.

HELEN: And for dad's generation and mine, the idea of protesting a war which our own government has deemed to be necessary, much less desecrating our flag or burning your draft card, again flies in the face of so much we consider essential to our being.

FRITZIE: Yes.

HELEN: I know that a time will come when we will all look back and we'll say, "Perhaps this war was ill-advised," and, "Wasn't that quaint that we were so upset about the way Fritzie dressed," and we will recognize that we were probably as upset about the fact that you were growing up and we were going to have to let you go as we were about your hair, which, in the final analysis, is absurdly superficial.

J. FRED: Yes, and your mother and I were also trying to grapple, in admittedly inchoate fashion, with the subterranean knowledge that you were, and are, homosexual.

FRITZIE: I know.

HELEN: And we didn't want you to live a lonely, persecuted existence which, after all, is all we were ever told about the lives of gay people.

FRITZIE: And I know, Dad, that I most likely made you feel in some way personally culpable, as if my sexual orientation were some cruel whim of fate, implicitly criticizing you for having been a special agent of the F.B.I. which did so much to help contribute to our national perception of gays as threats to society.

J. FRED: Of course, I can see now with the benefit of hindsight, and the education which you have so patiently provided, that my activities in the bureau, though they may have added further burdens to the lives of many gays already freighted with discriminatory laws and at least one whole millennium worth of religious persecution, didn't actually make you gay.

FRITZIE: No.

NANA: But you know, what I notice in all of this: Fritzie is struggling with the normal tensions and fears any adolescent would be having, regardless of his sexual orientation.

FRITZIE: Thank you, Nana.

NANA: And he is also trying, since he knows he was adopted, and now also knows that he was an abandoned baby— *(To Helen.)* And though you didn't tell him that until you felt he could assimilate the knowledge in a way that wouldn't be destructive to his sense of self-worth—

FRITZIE: And I appreciate that.

NANA: —still Fritzie is searching for an identity, and that can't be a simple matter in a family which in many ways has hidden its own identity, and even fled from its roots.

HELEN: *(To Nana.)* Yes, by converting from Judaism to Christianity, you were effectively deracinating all your offspring and their progeny as well.

FRITZIE: But I can understand why Nana wanted to do that. Growing up Jewish in the deep South at the beginning of this century can't have been easy for her; and then the subsequent scorn heaped upon her by her sisters for what they considered to be cowardice.

HELEN: And you know Nana's brother was homosexual.

NANA: Well, we didn't call it that; we didn't call it anything back then.

HELEN: When I married your father, Uncle Julian told me he thought your dad was gorgeous. I was terribly embarrassed, and I wish to this day I could take it back and hug him and tell him that we loved him, no matter how he made love.

NANA: But I think we've made it difficult and confusing for Fritzie at times— and at this very table—by referring to some of my relatives as kikes.

FRITZIE: I guess it was hard for me to understand where all this animosity towards the Jews was coming from, especially from you, Dad, because you weren't hiding anything; none of your relatives are Jewish, are they?

J. FRED: No, but you know how illiterate and ignorant my mother was. Well, you didn't really.

HELEN: No, I made your father ashamed of her because I was; she was so uneducated, uncultured. Perhaps dad thought he could distance himself from the Jew he knew I was by—

J. FRED: My mother didn't want me to marry your mom.

NANA: I had called her up and told her we were Jewish. *(To Helen.)* Because I didn't want to lose you, I didn't think I should be alone.

FRITZIE: *(To J. Fred.)* Mom's having ovarian cancer and the burden of keeping that secret from her and from me when I was eleven must have fueled some of your anger as well. You must have wondered how you were going to manage if she died, and been looking for someplace to vent that rage and fear.

J. FRED: Yes, I think I was.

FRITZIE: I can't even imagine what that was like for you.

HELEN: You know, I think in a sense I must have known it was true. That I was sick. Because the doctor wouldn't give me any hormones, and sex was so incredibly painful. I begged him. *(To J. Fred.)* I thought if I didn't give you sex, you might leave me.

FRITZIE: Maybe that's another reason why you and daddy drank so much.

HELEN: Well, Nana drank. And my father.

NANA: *(To Fritzie.)* Everyone. And you will, too. And take LSD and snort cocaine. And risk your life by having sex with hundreds of strangers in the dark on the broken-down and abandoned piers of New York, even after the AIDS epidemic begins. You watched us losing ourselves over cocktails and cigarettes and thought, "That's what adults do." You wanted to justify our actions, make us good somehow, by emulating us.

FRITZIE: I think all that's true. And Mom, I want you to know I understand that the only reason you wanted to sleep with me and would crawl into my bed until the day I left for B.U. and snuggle up against me and kiss me and breathe your liquory breath so close to my face was that you yourself were molested by your dad.

HELEN: I was.

J. FRED: We've all seen and survived terrible things.

FRITZIE: In some ways I feel, because so many of my friends have died now—

J. FRED: Well your first lover.

HELEN: And your second.

NANA: And Tom is sick now, too.

FRITZIE: Well… I'm more prepared to face my own death than you'll be, Mom.

J. FRED: Well, we have thirty years before she gets lung cancer.

FRITZIE: But Nana already is senile. *(Nana nods.)* And all of us are alcoholics.

HELEN and J. FRED: Yes.

HELEN: Well, not Nana.

NANA: I'm not really. I wasn't.

(Fritzie kisses Nana on the cheek.)

FRITZIE: You were the first person I really knew who died.

J. FRED: No. My mother was the first.

FRITZIE: Oh, that's right.

J. FRED: I think you didn't say you were sorry the night we told you she was dead because I never held you or told you I loved you, and you had no idea how to relate to me emotionally.

FRITZIE: I really didn't. I didn't know what I was supposed to say. When I saw you cry at her funeral, I couldn't imagine what was wrong with you. I thought you had a foot cramp. Literally. It was so shocking—that contortion seizing your face in the middle of your walk back from the casket.

J. FRED: I do love you.

FRITZIE: I love you.

J. FRED: And I forgive you for saying it to me so often when you know how uncomfortable it makes me feel.

HELEN: *(To J. Fred.)* And I forgive you for never saying it in fifty years of marriage. For saying "Phew!" which, if you recorded it and slowed it down, might sound like "I love you." "Phew!" "I love you!" but to ordinary human ears sounds like "Phew, I don't have to say I love you!"

J. FRED: And I forgive you for not having children, for being afraid.

HELEN: And I forgive you for not magically knowing the doctors were wrong about my kidneys being too weak, and for not being able to take that fear away, or any of my fears, because you were in some ways more afraid than I.

NANA: I forgive you all for screaming at me when I couldn't remember anything. *(To Helen.)* When I picked up the knife and tried to stab you.

HELEN: I understood.

NANA: And for putting me in a home.

FRITZIE: Mom, I'm sorry I threw the plate of pasta at you and called you a cunt.

HELEN: I'm sorry I said your therapy wasn't working.

FRITZIE: *(To J. Fred.)* I'm sorry I embarrassed you by doing the cha-cha in the outfield and being so disinterested in and poor at sports.

HELEN: *(To Fritzie.)* I'm sorry we didn't let you know it would be okay if you turned out to be gay.

NANA: And an atheist.

J. FRED: And a Communist.

HELEN: And I'm sorry I told you your father hated homosexuals when it was me, and it was only fear and ignorance.

FRITZIE: *(To J. Fred.)* I'm sorry I asked if I could touch your penis the only time we ever took a shower together, when I was four. I know that freaked you out.

J. FRED: *(To Helen.)* And I forgive you for getting lung cancer.

FRITZIE: I do, too.

NANA: I'll be dead by then. *(To Fritzie.)* I forgive you for calling me a racist pig when I said Martin Luther King was an uppity nigger.

FRITZIE: It's the way you were raised. *(To Helen.)* I forgive you for telling me that my career was more important than going to the hospital in Denver with Tom when he had AIDS-related TB and that was the only place he could get treatment, and for suggesting that I should let him go by himself.

HELEN: *(To Fritzie.)* I forgive you for lighting the woods on fire. And for making me feel like such a failure as a mother up until and even including this very instant.

J. FRED: *(To Fritzie.)* And I forgive you for what you and I both know you did once and I can't say, or you'll probably be sued.

FRITZIE: Thank you.

HELEN: *(To Fritzie.)* And I forgive you for trying to kill yourself and leaving that awful, long note saying your father and I were NOT TO BLAME over and over. I forgive you for pretending you didn't know me when I walked into the wall of plate glass at your grade school and broke my nose.

FRITZIE: I forgive you for not being the parents I wanted—articulate and literate and calm.

HELEN: People who knew how to use words like "deracinate."

J. FRED: "Inchoate."

NANA: "Emulate."

J. FRED: I forgive you for being ashamed of us, for telling us that you were going to look for your natural parents; I forgive you for not finding them and being so horrified at whatever you found you had to come begging our forgiveness.

HELEN: I do, too. And for telling everyone that I pushed you onto the stage and saying to Deborah Norville and Bryant Gumbol that you were gay when I asked you not to. When I said I would lose all my friends if you did.

J. FRED: Well…it was important.

FRITZIE: And you didn't. Did you? Is that why you seem so alone now?

J. FRED: No.

FRITZIE: Did I do that?

(Helen looks at him for a moment. She gently shakes her head.)

J. FRED: Love is the hardest thing in the universe. Isn't it?

(Pause.)

NANA: No.

(They stare, lost in contemplation. Fritzie gently kisses each of his parents on the cheek.)

END OF PLAY

Stones and Bones
by Marion Isaac McClinton

CHARACTERS

MISTER BONES: A young black man.
SISTUH STONES: A young black woman.
BONE: A black man.
STONY: A black woman.

TIME

The ever-present now.

SETTING

Very minimal. Should be all done with light and sound. No furniture, no props, nothing save the imagination of the artists is necessary. This will make the piece very stylized, but that is the way it should be. Mister Bones and Sistuh Stones are dressed in the primary colors of hip-hop fashion, but they wear a minstrel's black face in all its blatant big-lipped caricature. If they have dreads, it should look more pickaninny than Bob Marley, but MOVE is an option for the look as well. They should be very colorful, like cartoons, and they should be trying to fight through the image of the role they have been designated to play. Stony and Bone are buppies to the max. Both groups of couples are on stage the entire play. It should not be played for the psychological subtext, but rather the effect they have on each other. They can notice each other as seems fit.

Stones and Bones

There will be no other stage direction until the end of the play except for this:
Music starts. Lights up.

MISTER BONES: Yo, baby.

SISTUH STONES: Hello.

MISTER BONES: Yo baby, yo baby, yo baby, yo.

SISTUH STONES: (Shit.)

MISTER BONES: What's up, you fine cutie, honeybear-looking thing you.

SISTUH STONES: Uh huh.

MISTER BONES: What you got going on with this fine motherfucking day, and shit? Man, fine as this motherfucking day is with all that sunshine and shit, the bitch ain't no kind of ways finer than your sweet motherfucking ass, I know that. What I don't know is if you're wearing the sunshine, or if that sunshine is wearing you. You know what I'm saying?

SISTUH STONES: Yeah.

MISTER BONES: So fuck all the dumb shit, you know what I'm saying?

SISTUH STONES: I wish we would.

MISTER BONES: Yeah, move over and let me sit next to your fine motherfucking ass. I'm the number one nigger, ain't a motherfucker bigger, who make your body all a quiver, and find your soul's motherfucking trigger. I'm the true for real dope motherfucker on time with all the hype rhymes, you know what I'm saying?

SISTUH STONES: Look... I just changed my seat...okay?

MISTER BONES: Yeah... so?

SISTUH STONES: I would rather not have to move again. There's too much ignorance perpetrating itself on this bus, and not enough seats to go around...you hear what I'm saying?
(Pause.)

MISTER BONES: You saying I'm a counterfeit motherfucker? Is that what you saying?

SISTUH STONES: As a three-dollar bill with Whoopi Goldberg's picture on it... my brother.

MISTER BONES: Oh, it's like that now, huh? You just gonna front my manhood all off and shit like I'm some kind of bust-out punk, and shit?

SISTUH STONES: Yeah, well, you know what they say?

MISTER BONES: No, what do they say?

SISTUH STONES: If your shit is to the curb, you gonna wind up in the gutter.

MISTER BONES: Yeah? Well, fuck you, bitch!

SISTUH STONES: Not in this life, junior.

(Mister Bones leaves. A moment. Mister Bones returns.)

MISTER BONES: So, you busy tonight or what?

SISTUH STONES: I can't believe you…

MISTER BONES: Believe it, baby. I'm for real.

SISTUH STONES: This goes beyond all the normal boundaries of stupidity into something truly weird.

MISTER BONES: Whatever…so you busy tonight?

SISTUH STONES: Nigger, drop dead.

MISTER BONES: So what about tomorrow?

SISTUH STONES: Nigger, I wouldn't accept a glass of ice water from you if I was on a roasting spit in hell for a thousand motherfucking years! A thousand years, you hear me!

MISTER BONES: That's all right, baby. I'm a nineties nigger. I'll just wait for the next millennium to make its way by here. You worth waiting a thousand years for. Shit, the devil will quench his motherfucking thirst before I'm done waiting on you. Shit, baby, I'm a nineties nigger. I ain't got nothing promised me but time. You know what I'm saying?

BONE: Something wrong?

STONY: You tell me?

BONE: What?

STONY: Can't you talk?

BONE: I don't know what you're talking about.

STONY: You are a lie and a half. I can smell the truth stinking all over your tongue. Tell me the truth, and get your taste back.

(Pause.)

BONE: How do you know? I thought I was… I don't know…

STONY: Careful? *(God, I hope you were careful.)* I have danced with you inside of my heart and with my soul, Bone. Who did you think I was? Come on…speak. You were always such a good talker. So good with words. Tell me something true, Bone.

MISTER BONES: Miss me much, baby?

SISTUH STONES: You... shit.

MISTER BONES: Where you been?

SISTUH STONES: I'm mourning my life.

MISTER BONES: I knew your ass missed me. You missed me, didn't you?

SISTUH STONES: I'm sorry, brother...

MISTER BONES: Mister Bones.

SISTUH STONES: Whatever...you put too much pressure on somebody. Hard to remain a lady if I listen to you, do what you want me to do. Understand. You need to chill down. You too psychotic about it.

MISTER BONES: Why I gotta be all of that? I just think you and me could be fantastic together. I see you, and I see my whole life stretched out before me, and I get excited. I don't usually get excited about my future, so I gotta grab that motherfucking ring when it swings on by, you know what I'm saying? I talk shit, but I ain't a not-about-shit-Motherfucker...shit... I want the motherfucking finer things in life my own damn self, and you, sweet honey in the rock, is one of them kind of things.

SISTUH STONES: That's exactly what I feel like when I talk to brothers like you, Mister Bones. Some kind of thing for some coonshow nigger who think he got some kind of rap that got something to say to me. All you rough-neck gangstuh brothers been hitting on me so hard I'm a serious TKO behind all that mess you talk. You all done hit on me until your words got tired, and your mouth got sore. I ain't even here anymore.

MISTER BONES: Look, I walk through the world like I got some kind of right of way in it. I'm loud because nobody gives enough of a shit about nothing to do with me to pay attention to whatever I'm saying. I ain't like y'all sistuhs. Y'all done bought that white girl chickenshit about being victims so long lately you become addicted to victimization. I don't tear you down. You do a good enough job of that your own self. To tell you the truth, I hate to look at it. Breaks my motherfucking heart.

SISTUH STONES: You might not be trying to tear me down, but you sure as shit ain't trying to help build me up. Ask me what's on my mind outside of do I want to do the nasty with you. You hate to look at it? Good. I wish you would quit looking here, and take your twenty-twenty somewheres else. I need a mate, not a date...you know?

BONE: So you wanna know anything else?

STONY: No.

BONE: About whether they married, or have children, or anything?

STONY: No.

BONE: Their age, weight, height, the color of their eyes, whether they remind me of you or not?

STONY: If they got children, and are married, and unsatisfied with their life, then I already know what about them reminds you of me.

BONE: I still want us to be together.

STONY: I don't believe this chickenshit bullshit.

BONE: Look, I don't take them out, never fucked them through the night, and ignore you in our bed, I don't buy them things, I don't call them every chance I get in the day free and clear, I never said anything about them being better loves, or finer women than you, or that being unhappy with you was the reason I was with them. You know what I'm saying? I didn't, don't, and won't love them period. It's me! OK? I'm just wrong! I'm all of everything you was afraid I was gonna be! I'm wrong, down and dirty, no good to the motherfucking bone! OK! I don't know why! What else you want me to say? How many more ways can I say it?

STONY: There is one thing you could tell me. Something you neglected to mention.

BONE: What, Stony, damn?

STONY: Whether or not these bitches are white. You can talk about that.

MISTER BONES: Well...this is where I hang. The motherfucking crib in all its glory.

SISTUH STONES: Yeah. Charming, or something.

MISTER BONES: So you like?

SISTUH STONES: It's all right.

MISTER BONES: I tried calling you, you know, all afternoon and shit, and like you weren't never around, or nothing.

SISTUH STONES: Yeah? So?

MISTER BONES: Look, this shit ain't easy for me either, you know what I'm saying? It's hard to get next to somebody on the real tip. This shit hurts my gut it's so bugging, you know what I'm saying? I'm trying to touch another like motherfucking human being and shit. I mean, like fuck the dumb shit, you picked up on me, and I want to deliver. Not just that physical thing, but I mean I want to thaw out your soul, raise you up, I mean, I don't even know why you even are up here with my black ass this minute, you know...

SISTUH STONES: Just be all right with me being here, that's all you gotta do, and I'll be cool with it.

MISTER BONES: No, fuck that, I gotta know! Why here, why with me, why… any of it, why?

SISTUH STONES: You need something? All right…because you brush your teeth three times a day, put some deodorant under those funky armpits, and every other world out of your mouth ain't "bitch" or "ho." *(Pause.)* Because you said I was beautiful, and meant it. Said it sweetly, and smiled with a smile looked like it was full of French champagne when you said it.

MISTER BONES: I ain't that kind of motherfucker. I wish I was, but I truly…

SISTUH STONES: I don't need to hear it from your lips, baby. I know all of that already. Besides I didn't come up in here to talk to you anyways. You promised me something else, some other kind of time. I'm here for that. I don't want to talk about it anymore. I want to taste all that sweet champagne you got behind your lips. I want to drink my fill. *(Pause.)*

MISTER BONES: You better go home, honeybaby. You know too much, and you too thirsty.

SISTUH STONES: What…you kidding me, right? A round-the-way fellow with the funky fuck of the ages up inside of your pants? I thought…

MISTER BONES: I ain't got that much champagne in me. I'll call you tomorrow.

SISTUH STONES: Jesus will have come back, and gone by then. I can't wait that long.

MISTER BONES: I'm scared, Sistuh Stones.

SISTUH STONES: I knows the feeling, Mister Bones. We sitting chin deep in some blackfaced, shit-stomping, low down blues, baby, and we can't get up out of it without each other. *(Pause.)* This shit is supposed to be scary.

STONY: You know…

BONE: No, what?

STONY: When I'm breathing, when my heart is flying all around up in my mouth screaming, all I can do is think about it…

BONE: Think about what?

STONY: You touching them with your smile all wide open, slipping all of that champagne that be all mine by right of birth, all turned around, turned out, and your smile.

BONE: Enough, baby. You gonna lose your mind behind all of this. I just better go.

STONY: Yeah, well enough is never enough… I ain't thinking about that. That what is stealing my sleep away from me all through the night. Something else.

BONE: What, Stony?

STONY: If I could take my nose, and cut it, pull my flesh from off of my bones and put on a skin made of peaches like was a new winter coat, if I could look at you like you were a criminal all the time, cross to the other side of the street every time I see you coming my way, never wait on you first when it's your turn in line, never sit next to you on the bus even if it's the only seat, make you forget you had a mama that always looked old, and a daddy that always seemed broken, if I could make you forget the manhood that supposed to be in between your legs, make you dream in black and white, and turn the black to gray, if it were true that I had more fun, and knew what Clairol knows, and make you feel it's all right and cool with me if you take every last bit of black that was passed down to you from every African hanging from your family tree, and trash it like it wasn't never there, and wasn't never anything worth keeping no how. If I can get you to change how you talk, if I can refine all the loudness from out of your soul...if I didn't know nothing about nothing worth knowing about you...If I was white would I stop intimidating you so you could hold me through the night clutched to your chest? Would you be scared of me then? Would you stop being scared of yourself then?

(Silence.)

BONE: I don't know. I don't know.

(Beat.)

STONY: Oh.

SISTUH STONES: God dammit...that was the best... I hoped you was something special...

STONY: Okay.

MISTER BONES: Shit, baby, I knew I could rock your world.

BONE: I do know it wouldn't change anything. I been trying to fuck myself into a new life. I ain't got that much juice in me.

SISTUH STONES: This shit is frightening, ain't it?

STONY: Well.

BONE: I don't recognize my own voice anymore.

MISTER BONES: Seem like I know myself so well when I'm inside of you.

STONY: I know you.

SISTUH STONES: I know.

MISTER BONES: Just gonna get better and better.

BONE: I don't know.

SISTUH STONES: Ain't nobody else supposed to make me feel like you do. Maybe that's it.

STONY: Maybe you just plain can't…

BONE: Love you? Maybe I never did.

MISTER BONES: Shit, baby, you with the jam master blaster of ceremonies hisself.

STONY: You love me. Probably always will. It'll be the only thing that will keep you alive in the end. But until you can love yourself and we can take each other in hand, neither of us will ever live.

MISTER BONES: We gonna be getting busy, and swapping spit full of Dom Perignon, and being happy forever and a day. For ever and ever and ever and ever…

MISTER BONES and SISTUH STONES:…and ever, forever, and ever, and ever, and ever…until death do us part…amen.

(Lights go down to black as Mister Bones and Sistuh Stones are in an embrace, and Stony and Bone are far apart, as we hear the sound of love-making, mingled with the sound of crying.)

END OF PLAY

An Evening Crossword
by Kimberly Megna

CHARACTERS

KERRY

RENEE

MAXIE

JACKIE

An Evening Crossword

The social area of a dorm room suite. There is a doorway to the bedroom up-stage and a doorway to the common hall downstage. A radio can be heard from the back bedroom playing a country rock ballad, perhaps on repeat. The sound of a hair dryer.

At start we see two women, Kerry and Renee, enjoying some postdinner relax-ation. There is, however, an air of tension in the room directed toward and emanating from, the third woman, Maxie. Maxie enters at start of play, look-ing for a barrette; she doesn't acknowledge either girl before going back to the bedroom to resume getting ready.

KERRY: I need a three-letter word for being.

RENEE: Exist.

KERRY: THREE letters?

RENEE: Are.

KERRY: R? That's a letter I need a word.

RENEE: Are. As in you are.

KERRY: Oh, right. So now I need a five-letter word for: the devil once was… third R.

RENEE: Angel.

KERRY: There is no R in angel.

RENEE: It has to be angel put it down.

KERRY: But then Are is wrong.

RENEE: You know, if you didn't insist on doing these in pen you wouldn't be so touchy about changing the answers.

MAXIE: *(As she passes through the room with her robe on and a towel on her head, makeup bag in hand.)* If you didn't insist on doing these stupid puzzles every evening you wouldn't be too tired to go out.

KERRY: I do not insist on anything, first of all and secondly I happen to have a paper to write tonight.

RENEE: Oh, come on, I thought you were going to come down to the Brewery for a pint tonight. We told Patrick we'd pick him up around…

KERRY: *(Interrupting.)* I don't know, I have to see how much time I have. Now what is a three-letter word for being with the second letter G?

JACKIE: *(Entering from outside door.)* Ego.

KERRY: Damn.

RENEE: Hey Jackie.

KERRY: It's *always* ego.

JACKIE: You're welcome.

KERRY: Now what's a seven-letter….

JACKIE: *(Overlapping.)* Ask me another one of those clues and I will impale you on that pencil.

RENEE: It's a pen.

KERRY: Fine. Fine.

RENEE: Jackie, tell her to go start her paper so we can go to the Brewery tonight.

JACKIE: Where's Maxie?

KERRY: In the other room.

RENEE: Grooming.

JACKIE: Close the door.

KERRY: She's got her Garth on.

JACKIE: She might lower it.

RENEE: We should be so lucky.

JACKIE: I'm serious.

KERRY: What? Did she leave another written ultimatum on the kitchen counter about someone devouring her Breakfast Bars? Ooh ooh, I'd be glad to take the fall, just to be witness to another of her "Personal Responsibility Lectures."

RENEE: An oxymoron if you think about it.

KERRY: Really, I just thrive on Maxie-Wisdom. Like last night's treatise on sunburns.

JACKIE: Sunburns?

KERRY: While we drove to Indianapolis, her right arm suffered quite a burn.

RENEE: Through the closed car window.

KERRY: Apparently it's possible.

JACKIE: That's ridiculous.

RENEE: I am sure it had something to do with my driving.

KERRY: Well, you did insist on heading south while she was in the passenger seat.

RENEE: That's right, next time, I'll just circumvent the state to avoid putting her in any medical or cosmetic danger.

JACKIE: Alright, enough. Where is she?

KERRY: We just said she is in the other room getting ready.

JACKIE: For what?

RENEE: I try not to ask questions I might get an answer to.

KERRY: I'm pretty sure she is going to the Gamma house. They're having some invitation-only party. Maxie can get us all in of course, but we would have to realize that it is going to go really late, and most people are going to stay over, so we won't be able to bring our highlighted copies of *Moby-Dick*.

JACKIE: Shit.

RENEE: Did you want to go?

JACKIE: No, I just. Is the door closed?

KERRY: Yes already! What is your deal?

JACKIE: While I was at the computer lab I heard the two guys sitting—

KERRY: Who?

JACKIE: I don't know, from the Gamma house, you know the one with the floppy brown hair—

KERRY: Trevor.

JACKIE: And the one who plays the guitar sometimes at the café—

KERRY: David. What about them?

RENEE: How do you know these people?

KERRY: I pay attention.

JACKIE: Girls.

KERRY: Alright!

RENEE: What?

JACKIE: I heard them talking about their party tonight and, well…they are such assholes.

(Renee and Kerry exchange a look.)

RENEE: Whatever.

JACKIE: What? She should not go to that house tonight. They're planning something.

RENEE: Jackie, what were they saying?

KERRY: Keeping in mind that Maxie goes to these parties with the intention of seeing how many people she can alienate herself from through personal contact.

JACKIE: This is different.

RENEE: What did they say?

JACKIE: Apparently the graduating seniors get some sort of present from the junior class officers.

RENEE: Present?

JACKIE: Sex.

KERRY: Sex? That doesn't make a party dangerous for Maxie, just more enticing.

JACKIE: The guys sounded seriously deranged. They were talking about special invites that went out to the women. The women who they knew would, would respond "agreeably" to heavy drinking.

KERRY: Jackie—when was the last time you were at a party where there wasn't heavy drinking?

RENEE: Seventh grade.

JACKIE: That's not what I mean.

KERRY: You're overreacting—

RENEE: They must've been kidding, those guys aren't that—

JACKIE: What?

RENEE: Did they really sound, serious?

JACKIE: Worse.

KERRY: Please—

JACKIE: They are dangerous assholes.

KERRY: Trevor and David are players but they aren't dangerous.

JACKIE: How can you say that? You've never even talked to them.

KERRY: Come on.

JACKIE: They're disgusting.

RENEE: Hello? Women?

KERRY: Look, Maxie knows—

JACKIE: The girls aren't going to have a choice.

  (Pause.)

RENEE: Well?

KERRY: She does fit the description.

RENEE: So are we going to say something?

JACKIE: I don't know.

RENEE: Shouldn't we?

KERRY: Definitely, so that way I can hear all about how I don't understand the ways of sexually liberated people on campus.

JACKIE: Do you think that she'd listen if we told her?

KERRY: *We? You* heard the guys talking.

(*Suddenly the music stops and the girls stop talking. Maxie opens the door more dressed and enters the room.*)

(*Pause.*)

MAXIE: Girls. Jackie.

JACKIE: Hi.

MAXIE: Have you guys seen my tapestry purse?

RENEE: Is anyone picking you up?

MAXIE: I'm supposed to meet Carolyn downstairs in like five minutes.

KERRY: The purse with the black ties?

MAXIE: Yeah.

KERRY: I think I saw it hanging up in the closet.

MAXIE: Huh. I don't remember putting it there. Maybe someone borrowed it.

(*Goes back into the other room.*)

RENEE: So?

KERRY: What?

RENEE: Are we going to say something or what?

JACKIE: I don't care.

KERRY: Wait a minute, I thought you said we should? I'm certainly not going to if you aren't.

JACKIE: What? I didn't say I wouldn't.

KERRY: Call her in then.

JACKIE: OK. I mean, yeah, OK.

MAXIE: (*Entering.*) It's not there, Kerry, did you say in my closet?

KERRY: What?

MAXIE: The purse?

RENEE: Where are you going tonight?

MAXIE: What? The Gamma house.

RENEE: Is it going to be OK there? Do you know the guys well?

MAXIE: Are you kidding? Of course I do. We went out with a bunch of them last weekend.

RENEE: I know, we just. I don't know.

MAXIE: What?

RENEE: Jackie just said, I mean she heard…

KERRY: I'm sure it's going to be fine. They're nice guys.

MAXIE: What? Jackie? Did someone say something about the guys?

JACKIE: No. Not really.

MAXIE: Not really?

    (Beat.)

JACKIE: No.

MAXIE: Look, the Gammas are awesome guys. If someone is saying something, they just don't know…

KERRY: We know. Forget it.

MAXIE: Besides, they love Carolyn and I. If anything ever got out of hand, the guys would take care of us.

KERRY: We know.

    (Intercom rings.)

MAXIE: Shit that's Carolyn. Tell her I will be right down. *(Goes into the other room.)*

    (Pause.)

KERRY: See. She's fine.

RENEE: We didn't say anything.

JACKIE: We tried.

KERRY: She doesn't want to hear it.

RENEE: Fine.

JACKIE: Forget it.

KERRY: Trust me, she'll just twist it around and go anyway so just forget it.

RENEE: Fine.

KERRY: What?

RENEE: Nothing.

KERRY: What? Say something.

JACKIE: Shhhh.

RENEE: It's your call. *(Indicating Jackie.)*

JACKIE: No it isn't.

KERRY: Look let's just forget it OK?

    (Maxie enters.)

MAXIE: OK I'm leaving. I'd appreciate, if you don't go out tonight, you trying to remember where my purse was left and returning it to my desk.

    (Pause, girls look at each other.)

MAXIE: What? Did you want to come?

KERRY: No.

MAXIE: OK. *(Beat.)* I'll probably crash there tonight. One of the guys will drive me home in the morning. *(Beat, she shakes her head.)*

KERRY: What?

MAXIE: You guys are just…you need to calm down.

KERRY: We are very calm.

MAXIE: You know what I mean. If you went out more you would…well, you would understand people better.

JACKIE: Yeah.

MAXIE: Whatever. I have to go.

KERRY: Bye.

JACKIE: Bye.

MAXIE: Bye.

(She leaves. Pause.)

KERRY: What?

RENEE: Nothing.

KERRY: What?

RENEE: I just think we should have told her.

JACKIE: We tried.

KERRY: You know Maxie.

(Renee moves toward bedroom.)

KERRY: Why are you so mad?

RENEE: I'm not mad I'm just…

JACKIE: Forget I said anything.

RENEE: You didn't.

JACKIE: Did you? *(Beat.)* Just because I don't like confrontation—

RENEE: Forget it. *(Goes into other room.)*

KERRY: Look guys, we tried. She'll probably be fine so just don't worry. Now let's get down to business here, we have a crossword to finish.

JACKIE: No, I refuse to be partner to your sick obsession.

(Renee returns with her sweatshirt on and a Walkman.)

KERRY: Where are you going?

RENEE: For a walk.

KERRY: I thought you were going to the pub.

RENEE: Maybe later.

JACKIE: It's dark out.

RENEE: Don't worry, I'll be fine. *(She leaves.)*

(Pause.)

KERRY: Forget it. We did as much as we could, the guys didn't say anything wrong anyway. Renee is just tense and has an overactive guilt complex. She hates Maxie just as much as we do.

JACKIE: I don't *hate* her.

KERRY: Whatever, I don't want to talk about it anymore. Seven-letter word, clue is blank-aggressive. I think there might be an S in the fourth space… come on…

JACKIE: *(Overlapping at "seven-letter word, clue.")* No, no no no. *(Then ignoring her as she gets her stuff together and goes into the next room.)*
(Lights fade to black.)

END OF PLAY

Going Nowhere Apace
by Glen Merzer

CHARACTERS

JUDD
FRANCESCA
CECILIA
MARY

Going Nowhere Apace

Francesca, Judd, Cecilia, and Mary are all riding their exercycles at a good clip. Judd pedals along between Francesca and Cecilia; Mary is to the other side of Cecilia. There are no other exercycles. The women stare straight ahead as they exercise; Judd steals a few glances to either side, as if his mind is on other things than fitness. Finally he smiles at Francesca.

JUDD: Maintaining eighty?

FRANCESCA: Excuse me?

JUDD: Are you maintaining eighty RPM?

FRANCESCA: Yes.

JUDD: Me too. *(Pause.)* How's your pulse?

FRANCESCA: Fine.

JUDD: Not me. *(Indicating dial on his bike.)* According to this, I'm legally dead. No pulse at all. I'm not just getting in shape, I'm confronting my mortality. *(Pause.)* That's all right by me. People don't think enough about death, anyway. In my opinion. *(Pause.)* You don't mind that I'm talking to you, do you?

FRANCESCA: No.

JUDD: What's your name?

FRANCESCA: Francesca.

JUDD: Pretty name.

FRANCESCA: Thank you.

JUDD: I'm Judd.

FRANCESCA: Hello.

JUDD: Sometimes you start a conversation with a woman, you don't know if she thinks you're a creep just because you're a man.

FRANCESCA: I don't. Think you're a creep just because you're a man.

JUDD: Good. *(Pause.)* I was saying…

FRANCESCA: You were saying?

JUDD: People don't think enough about death.

(A moment.)

FRANCESCA: What makes you say that?

JUDD: Just making conversation. (Pause.) Now if people thought more about death, what do you think would happen?

FRANCESCA: They'd get depressed.

JUDD: No. Happier.

FRANCESCA: Why?

JUDD: They'd realize, hey, someday I'm going to die, so while I'm riding my bike here going absolutely nowhere, I might as well smile at the person next to me, say hello, pass the time pleasantly. And then that would cheer a person up. I know some very morbid people—happiest people I ever met. One of them, for example, real bright lady, philosophy professor, with a huge gap between her front teeth, she could french-kiss with her mouth closed, she's totally obsessed by the image of her own burial. Never stops giggling. Another guy, he reads the obituaries every day, gets a big kick out of sending sympathy cards that rhyme to the widows and signing them "Elvis."

FRANCESCA: How do you know all these morbid people?

JUDD: Can't tell you.

FRANCESCA: All right.

(A long moment.)

JUDD: A therapy group. I belong to a therapy group for morbid people. I'm not supposed to talk about it.

FRANCESCA: All right.

(A moment.)

JUDD: Another guy, a bank teller, fat, jolly type, he looks at you, he sees your skeleton. Can't get it out of his head. Looks at a pretty face, sees a skull.

FRANCESCA: That's awful. Are you like that?

JUDD: No. I see a pretty face. I'm attracted.

FRANCESCA: Why do these people go for therapy if they're so happy?

JUDD: Guilt. Guilt is the major drawback to morbid living. No one feels good about death perkin' him up.

FRANCESCA: Is that your problem?

JUDD: No. My problem is... I shouldn't discuss it.

FRANCESCA: All right.

(A moment.)

JUDD: I think of death during sex. I'll be fondling a breast, I'll imagine worms gnawing away at it.

FRANCESCA: Yeech.

JUDD: Yeah. I actually have thoughts like that.

FRANCESCA: And does that—does that make you happy, too?

JUDD: No. But it does keep me from coming too soon. *(Pause.)* Am I being too vulnerable with you?

FRANCESCA: Not at all.

JUDD: I don't confide in people easily. Do you?

FRANCESCA: Yes.

JUDD: I wish I could.

FRANCESCA: I figure otherwise I'd have to go to confession. And I'm a very tactile person. I don't see the point in confiding in someone without touching. Do you belong to any organized religion?

JUDD: No, I'm Jewish. *(Pause.)* Could I maybe take you to dinner sometime?

FRANCESCA: No.

JUDD: How's your speed?

FRANCESCA: Fine.

JUDD: Pulse?

FRANCESCA: Good.

   (A moment.)

JUDD: Why not?

FRANCESCA: I don't know how to answer that question.

   (A moment.)

JUDD: Why not?

FRANCESCA: I'm not attracted to you.

JUDD: No, I meant why don't you know how to answer that question.

FRANCESCA: It's hard to do tactfully.

JUDD: Then forget it. Don't even try.

   (A long moment. Francesca once again stares straight ahead as she pedals. Judd slowly turns to Cecilia, smiles at her.)

JUDD: Hi.

CECILIA: Hi.

JUDD: Are you maintaining eighty RPM?

CECILIA: Ninety-five.

JUDD: Very good. How's your pulse?

CECILIA: Oh, that does not matter to me. I don't look for that really.

JUDD: Where are you from?

CECILIA: Sweden.

JUDD: I thought so. You've got just a little bit of an accent.

CECILIA: Oh, I have very much an accent!

JUDD: No, just a little one. What's your name?

CECILIA: Cecilia.

JUDD: Pretty name. I'm Judd.

CECILIA: Nice to meet you.

JUDD: Nice to meet you. *(Pause.)* I hear people commit suicide a lot in Sweden.

CECILIA: Well, yes, too much.

JUDD: *Too much* is a value judgment; the point is you have a very high rate over there. Why do you think that is? I mean, you have everything in Sweden, don't you? You're all filthy rich, absolutely stunning people, the state looks after your welfare, you have a peaceful society, not even a prayer of racial antagonism, the Volvo is a terrific make of car, why do you suppose your people go around killing themselves the way they do?

CECILIA: It's not so many people. It's only a...minority.

JUDD: I should hope so. But it's a silent minority, wouldn't you say? I mean, it's not your noisy, American breed of suicider, who generally uses a shotgun and takes a few innocent bystanders with him sort of as chasers. No, your people just down a few extra pills and go to sleep, and if they leave a note it's undoubtedly short, considerate, and typed on nice letterhead. Am I right?

CECILIA: Some scientists say it's because the nights. We have very long, dark nights in Sweden.

JUDD: Still, you don't have to kill yourself. You could turn a light on.

CECILIA: It has a biologic effect, they say, the long nights. On the brain.

JUDD: Could be.

CECILIA: But nobody really knows why.

JUDD: Have you lost many friends to the dark nights?

CECILIA: No. One person I hardly knew at university—

JUDD: I lost more than that. I lost a girlfriend.

CECILIA: I'm sorry.

JUDD: Well, she wasn't technically a girlfriend yet. But I was really looking forward to a relationship with her. And I think she was looking forward to a relationship with me. *(Pause.)* Although I suppose she might not have been as gung ho.

CECILIA: I'm sorry, what is *gung ho?*

JUDD: What is *gung ho?* For example, I'm enormously attracted to you, Cecilia. Could I take you to dinner tomorrow night?

CECILIA: No.

JUDD: Okay, you see, *you* are not gung ho. You see?

CECILIA: I'm sorry, I am married.

JUDD: Dammit, Cecilia! Why did you withhold that information? Jesus!

CECILIA: I did not—

JUDD: You're not wearing a ring—

CECILIA: I don't like to—

JUDD: You knew I was interested—

CECILIA: No, I—

JUDD: The proper thing to do—maybe you're not aware of American customs—the proper thing to do, Cecilia, in a situation like this is to mention your husband in conversation. For example, we were chatting about suicide in Sweden, you could have said, *my husband* attributes this phenomenon to our long, dark nights. You could have said that and spared my feelings.

CECILIA: I'm sorry but—

JUDD: Is it mainly the men who kill themselves in Sweden? I'll bet it is. I'll bet it's the men who dive headlong into those long, dark nights. I'll see you around.

(Judd hops off his bike, and jogs behind Cecilia's bike and Mary's bike. He runs in place next to Mary, who tries not to notice him. Mary is wearing headphones; a cassette player is strapped to her belt. Judd mimes removing the headphones as he runs in place. He has to perform this mime several times before Mary notices and removes her headphones.)

JUDD: Hi. *(Pause.)* Are you maintaining eighty RPM?

MARY: Yeah. Why?

JUDD: *(As he jogs in place.)* Me too. How's your pulse?

MARY: Why?

JUDD: Just interested.

MARY: Fuck off.

(A silence. The three woman keep pedaling away, facing straight ahead. Mary puts her headphones back on. Judd jogs in place, then turns and jogs away, then suddenly turns again, jogs back towards Mary, rips her headphones off her ears, and, choking with emotion, explains himself.)

JUDD: Look forgive me I'm a human being, I'm reaching out, please, I'm only asking, I need to talk to someone or I may I may lose my—please, the world beats down on you and down on you and I'm, I'm, help me, I don't know if I can take people's cruelty anymore, all I'm asking is to have a little simple talking interaction token of human kindness! I'm losing my breath.

(He takes a long, deep breath. Mary is frozen, stunned by this onslaught. Judd looks at her, feels that he has won his point, and slows down to a walking pace.)

JUDD: Do you mind if I just walk while we talk? *(Judd smiles, walks in place.)* I'm perfectly harmless, I really am.

(A moment, as Judd walks in place, and Mary, still stunned, stares at him.)

JUDD: I'm sorry. I'm sorry. *(He reaches over to put her headphones back over her ears.)* Forget it. Have a good day.

(He turns to walk away, but just as he does so, Mary removes her headphones.)

MARY: What do you want to talk about?

JUDD: *(Smiles. He will continue to walk in place throughout his conversation with Mary.)* What's your name?

MARY: Mary. *(A moment.)*

JUDD: Pretty name. Where are you from?

MARY: Cincinnati. *(Pause.)* And you?

JUDD: I'm from Lexington but my ancestors go back to Long Island. On the East Coast. *(Pause.)* Well, tell me something about yourself, Mary.

MARY: What do you want to know? I'm a word processor.

JUDD: High-stress occupation.

MARY: I know.

JUDD: I was reading there are a lot of strokes among word processors. A lot of early deaths. They don't know why. Either the stress or else some kind of radiation they haven't discovered yet emanating from the terminals.

(A moment.)

MARY: What do you do?

(A moment.)

JUDD: I'm currently between transitions. *(Pause.)* What's your most embarrassing memory?

MARY: Why?

JUDD: I'll bet you've got some good ones.

MARY: I can think of one but it's personal.

JUDD: Tell me.

MARY: I don't even know you!

JUDD: My name is Judd.

MARY: What's your problem, Judd? I mean, what got you so upset a minute ago? You sounded desperate.

(A moment.)

JUDD: Oh. Oh, *that.* That was nothing really. I was just feeling a little low for a moment there. *(Pause.)* All right, all right, I'm denying. *(Pause.)* I'm scared to leave myself open. I don't confide in people easily, do you?

MARY: Yeah, my friends.

JUDD: Well, I wish I could. I wish I could be as open as you. You know what it goes back to? It goes back to, little girls are allowed to cry in our society and little boys aren't. Which is sick. Either *we* should be allowed to cry, too, or else girls shouldn't be. *(Pause.)* The fact is, Mary, I'll be honest…I haven't been happy lately. I've been unhappy, in fact.

MARY: Why?

JUDD: Let me ask you this, Mary: Where did you meet your current boyfriend or husband?

MARY: I don't have a current boyfriend or husband.

JUDD: Okay, most people meet them at work. Studies have verified that the work environment facilitates flirtation and courtship far better than other environments such as leisure environments in which people are generally preoccupied. Consequently I find myself at a strategic disadvantage.

MARY: I don't follow you.

JUDD: It's a chicken-and-egg problem. Can I get motivated to work or will I just get more mystified by the aloneness that develops from interpersonal confusion?

(A moment.)

MARY: What does that have to do with a chicken and egg?

JUDD: I'm not presently employed. I can't seem to choose an area of…I can't concentrate long enough to…I'm on S.S.I. I had to fill out a form. *Tell in your own words why you can't earn your living. (Pause.)* I made up my own words. *(Pause.)* I used to work, moving shit back and forth, but working made me think of death, which was the last thing I needed to think about given the type of worker I was.

MARY: What type of worker were you?

JUDD: Slow. I was too slow. *(Pause.)* The problem is, I don't work, so I only get to meet people when they're out in the world and being unfriendly… because people don't talk to people who they can't be sure who they are, whether they're stable, solid citizens, see—they're scared of them, so what happens is…what happens is…I can't break through…it's a vicious cycle…I never get *taken in* by anybody, you know? I'm like a dog that's always out on the stoop. I never get *taken in.*

(A long moment.)

MARY: My roommate walked in on me once while I was having sex.

JUDD: WHAT?

MARY: My roommate walked in on me once while I was having sex. You wanted to know my most embarrassing moment. That was it.

JUDD: You just tell me a thing like that out of the blue? Your roommate—why are you telling me this? Christ Almighty, Mary, are you trying to make me jealous?

MARY: No, I'm—

JUDD: I never realized you had this uninhibited side to you!

MARY: I was just—

JUDD: What a story! Your roommate walks in and—bam! That's unbelievable! That's a fucking unbelievable story! *(Pause.)* Could I maybe have your phone number and take you out sometime?

MARY: No. No, I don't think that would be a good idea.

JUDD: What was your roommate's reaction? What did your roommate say?

MARY: She said excuse me.

JUDD: Unbelievable! She really said *excuse me?* And what did you do?

(A moment.)

MARY: I was busy.

JUDD: You didn't stop?

MARY: Well…she excused herself and left right away.

JUDD: Did you laugh? Did you and the guy laugh about it?

MARY: No.

JUDD: Really? You really didn't laugh. You just kept going?

MARY: Yes.

JUDD: Like nothing happened?

MARY: I got rid of my roommate, though. For being so inconsiderate.

JUDD: That's amazing. Did you ever discuss the incident with your roommate?

MARY: Not in so many words.

JUDD: But you evicted her?

MARY: Yes.

JUDD: Am I the first person you told about it?

(A moment.)

MARY: Yes.

JUDD: Well, I'm just bowled over. I am bowled over by the trust you've placed in me! I don't know what I've done to earn it. *(Pause.)* Why did you choose me? Why did you choose me as the first person you'd confide in? *(Pause.)* Well, let me tell you, Mary, I will think of that story every time I see a word processor. I will think of that story, and I will remember how oblivious people can be, and it'll put a smile on my face! *(Pause.)* You really kept going just like nothing happened?

(Mary is not even looking at him anymore; her face is set in a determined mask and she is pedaling furiously.)

JUDD: *(Smiles.)* You really did, didn't you?

(Chuckling to himself, Judd jogs away and exits. The three woman, looking straight ahead, keep pedalling away. Very slowly the lights fade to black.)

END OF PLAY

Marred Bliss
by Mark O'Donnell

CHARACTERS

JANE

DINK

JEERY

ALAS

SETTING

The front porch of Jane's family home.

Marred Bliss

At rise: Jane arranges roses in a vase. Dink sits on the glider, reading the paper or just enjoying the evening. It's a typical midwestern scene. Jane is a pretty, prissy, inhibited young woman, wearing starched, modest clothes. Dink is a regular lug who's been talked into marriage but is willing to turn himself over to it.

JANE: Darkling?

DINK: *(Looking up from his paper.)* What is it… Dulling?

JANE: I thought we'd have ruses for the centerpieces. For us and for all the guest tables. Ruses *are* traditional.

DINK: Ruses it is. *(He returns to his reading.)*

JANE: *(After a restless pause.)* Oh honey, just *sink!*

DINK: What do you want me to sink about?

JANE: In less than forty-eight horrors, you and I will be moan and woof! *(Grins.)* Isn't it amassing?

DINK: It *is* amassing. *(Lowers his paper thoughtfully.)* So much has harpooned in just a few thief years!

JANE: It steams like only yesterday that you were the noise next door.

DINK: And you were that feckless-faced cod sitting up in the old ache tree!

JANE: And now we're encaged! I can hardly wait till we're marred!

DINK: Oh, Hiney! *(Makes to enfold her in his arms.)*

JANE: Now, now! I'm sure the tame will pass quickly till our hiney-moon! *(Eases out of his grasp.)* I'll get you some of that nice saltpeter taffy that Smother brought back from A Frantic City. *(Jeery, a sexy, slouching sailor, appears at one corner of the stage.)*

JEERY: Hello?… Any him at home? *(He carries a tiny bouquet.)*

JANE: Oh my gash! It's Jeery, my old toyfriend!

DINK: Jeery! That bump! What's *he* brewing here?

JANE: Oh, Dueling! Try to control your tamper! I'm sure he means no charm! Don't do anything you might regress! *(Jeery approaches.)*

JEERY: Hollow!—Revised to see me?

JANE: Hollow, Jeery.

DINK: Hollow. *(Pause.)*

JEERY: I'm completely beware that I'm out of police here. But— *(Looks to Jane.)* —for old climb's sake—Jane—I brought you this little bunch of foul airs. A token of my excess steam. Lots of lack to you. And much lack to you too, Dink.

JANE: *(Unsurely.)* Wail... *(Decides to accept the flowers.)* Spank you, Jeery.

DINK: Spank you very much.

JEERY: My shaft is at rancor in the harbor, and they gave me whore leave. I heard you were engorged, and I just wanted to slop by and pave my regrets.

JANE: *(Uncomfortably.)* Well, blank you!

DINK: Blank you very much.

JANE: *(Uneasy with this stand-off.)* I think you two have already messed, haven't you?

JEERY: Oh, we've thrown each other for years!

DINK: We went to the same cruel... Till Jeery dripped out to join the Nervy.

JANE: Of course. I remainder all that now! *(She is eager to lessen the awkwardness.)* Um—Do you haunt to sit down?

JEERY: Well, only for a menace. *(He sits with them on the glider.)* I'm hooded over to Pain Street. There's a big trance at the Social Tub. I'll probably go and chick it out. *(Awkward silence as they sit on the crowded glider.)* Wail, wail, wail... So when do you two tie the net?

JANE: The day after temerity!

JEERY: That soon?

DINK: *(Curtly.)* We've been enraged for over a year.

JEERY: Well, concatenations!

DINK: Rank you very much... *(Tense pause.)* ...Jeery, it's getting awfully lout! You don't want to miss the trance! *(From the other entrance comes Alas, a provocatively dressed woman with elaborate hair and a loose manner.)*

ALAS: Hell's own? Hell's own?

JANE: *(Aside.)* Oh no! Is that who I slink it is? Why won't she let us align? *(Alas advances.)*

ALAS: Hell's own, every burden! Hello's own, Dink!

DINK: *(Uncomfortable but heated.)* Hell's own, Alas!... Fantasy seething you here!

JANE: *(Tartly.)* I thought you'd be at the Social Tub trance, Alas. Aren't you on the degradation committee?

ALAS: *(Offers a gift-wrapped bottle.)* I may stoop by there later. I sinfully wanted to winch you both all the beast. Let icons be icons. Here's a battle of damn pain for you—I hype you enjoy it.

JANE: *(Suspicious.)* How sweet of you. *(Takes bottle, puts it aside.)* You know Jeery, don't you, Alas?

ALAS: Yes, we mated years ago. How's the Nervy, Jeery?

JEERY: Great! I was born to be a soiler. *(Another awkward silence as they regard her.)*

DINK: *(To Alas.)* Um—Would you like to hit with us, Alas? Jane, you don't grind if Alas hits with us, do you?

JANE: Well, the glider's getting awfully clouded!

ALAS: *(Airily.)* I'll just loin against the railing! *(She poses against the pillar seductively.)*

DINK: No, here, have my seed! *(Stands.)*

JANE: Dallying! *(Pulls him back into his seat.)* I think she'd rather remain stunning!

DINK: *(Getting agitated.)* Jeery, you could awful her *your* seat! Don't they teach you manners in the Harmed Surfaces? *(Jeery bristles.)*

JANE: *(To avoid a scene.)* Look, qualm down! Maybe we should admit this is an awkward saturation! I have complete face in you, Dink—But I think it's in power taste for your old street-part to come around so soon before our welding!

ALAS: *(Offended.)* I can't bereave this! There's no reason to be sub-species, Jane!

JANE: *(Affronted.)* No?

ALAS: This is a Good Wall visit, that's all! You're just high-stung!

DINK: *(Chiming in his objections.)* And what about Jeery here! I don't luck having him luring at you!

JEERY: *(Contemptuously.)* Oh, relapse, Dink! Afraid she'll realize her Must-Ache before the Sorrow-Money? *(To Alas.)* He's in debt, it's a mortgage of convenience!

JANE: *(Frightened by this sudden passion.)* Toys, please! Clam yourself! *(Earnestly, to Dink.)* Dink, don't drought yourself this way! Where's the strong, stabled man I'm taking to be altered? You know I lug you, I'll always lug you. *(Puts her arms around him maternally.)* I want ours to be a beautiful cremation-trip. But it has to be based on *truss*. *(Hugs him even more suffocatingly, and not erotically.)* I want to be able to *truss* you.

DINK: *(Too independently to suit Jane.)* All I did was offer Alas my seed. You act like I rammed off with her!

JANE: *(Feels dressed down before company.)* Well, maybe you'd rather ram off with her! She's been trying to reduce you since she got here!

ALAS: *(Angry.)* Don't spike like that to me! I bitter go.

JANE: *(Her insecurity making her hysterical.)* Stew where you are, you're the claws of this! You *slot!*

ALAS: *(Sneering at Jane.)* —What a little squirrel! I have nothing but potty for you!

(The women suddenly slap each other; the men must intervene.)

JEERY: *(Restraining Alas.)* The whole tissue is ridiculous! Fighting over a man who's in doubt up to his ears!

DINK: At least I'm not diddled with funereal disease, you bellow-jellied bull-bottomed sin of the beach!

JEERY: You sod-damned cowbird!

(The men fight; now the women must intervene.)

ALAS: Boys! Stomp it! Stomp it this minute!

(There is momentary silence as they all recover from their wounds.)

JANE: *Why are we having such trouble trying to communicate?*

DINK: *(Taking the lead.)* …Look. Alas… I heave nothing but harpy memories of our time together. I depreciate your good winces, but Jane and I are to be marred, and that's that. *(He looks to Jane to match his definitive renunciation.)*

JANE: *(Taking Jeery's hand briefly.)* And…Jeery…I leave you very much. You know that. But that's all winter under the fridge. *(Turns to Alas.)* Alas, I'm sorry I lost my torpor.

ALAS: *(With dignity.)* I understand. And I axe-up your apology. Anyway, I'm getting marred myself. To Henry Silverstone.

JANE: *(Impressed.)* The banker! But he's rather old for you, isn't he?

ALAS: Luckily, he's in very good wealth. *(A car horn honks from offstage.)* There's my chauffeured limbo now. I'd better get golden. Conglomerations, and gall the best!… Goad bye!

DINK: *(Feeling bested.)* Bile!

JANE: *(Feeling outdone.)* Bile!

(Alas exits. Jeery now feels superfluous.)

JEERY: Her own limbo!… Well, I guess I should leave you two lifeboats alone!

JANE: Thanks for the foul airs, Jeery! Enjoy the trance!

JEERY: Maybe I'll meet my future broad!

DINK: *(As if to a buddy.)* That's the right platitude!

JEERY: So long! Have a lot of skids!

DINK: Bile!

JANE: Bile! *(Jeery goes.)* He's a good spore, isn't he?

DINK: *(Reluctantly.)* I gas so.

JANE: *(Hugging him consolingly.)* But you're the *uphill* of my eye!

DINK: Oh, hiney! *(He holds and tries to kiss her, but she resists him.)* Oh come on! Plead? Pretty plead? *(She relents and gives him a peck, then quickly raises Alas' gift bottle between them.)*

JANE: Oh look! A vintage battle of damn pain! Let's celibate! *(She pops it open and pours some of it into two empty lemonade glasses on the porch table. She raises her glass.)* I love it when those little troubles get up your nose!— Here, let's test each other! *(They toast.)* To *ice!*

DINK: To *ass!* *(They drink.)*

JANE: Oh, galling! Our life together is going to be *blitz!*

(Blackout.)

END OF PLAY

Pillow Talk
by John Pielmeier

CHARACTERS

DOCTOR TIFFANY HEAVEN: Twenty-five, a marriage counselor.

MARK BLOOMER: Twenty-four, a young newlywed.

DOCTOR ROGER CREOSOTE: Twenty-six, a marriage counselor.

JAYDEEN BLOOMER: Twenty-three, a young newlywed.

TIME AND PLACE

The marriage counseling room of Creosote and Heaven—no chairs, just lots of big pillows.

PROPS

A battaka.

Pillow Talk

The marriage counseling office of Creosote and Heaven. There is no furniture, just several large pillows suitable for lounging. A battaka, looking like a base-ball bat covered in thick cotton batting, lies nearby.

As the lights rise we see Mark Bloomer pacing the floor. Tiffany breezes in.

TIFFANY: Mark? Hi, I'm Doctor Tiffany Heaven. Welcome to Creosote and Heaven. We're so sorry for your pain. Doctor Creosote will be along any moment. Have a pillow. Where's your wife?

MARK: She should be here by now, I'm surprised, she's usually...

TIFFANY: Is that a noogie?

MARK: What?

TIFFANY: A noogie. A little something she does that gets on your nerves.

MARK: Well, she's usually on time, but for some reason...

TIFFANY: Use the battaka.

MARK: What?

TIFFANY: *(Handing him the battaka.)* Here. Whenever we encounter the noogies of this life, it's always best to deal with them in a violent and aggressive manner. Hit the pillow and say, "Damn you..." What's your wife's name?

MARK: Jaydeen.

TIFFANY: Jaydeen. "Damn you, Jaydeen." Say it.

MARK: I don't really...

TIFFANY: Of course you don't. But you *do*. Inside you *do* want to say it. That's the secret to a happy, healthy, mature relationship. Confront the noogies and slaughter them. Now hit the pillow and say it. "Damn you, Jaydeen."

MARK: Look, this really wasn't my idea, I only came...

TIFFANY: She made you come to see us, is that what you're saying?

MARK: Well, not exactly *made*, but...

TIFFANY: Feeling a little castrated, aren't you, Mark? Go with it. Let it out. Hit the pillow and say, "I *do* have balls."

MARK: Well...

TIFFANY: *(Tough as a coach.)* Hit the pillow, Mark! Come on! You want to save this marriage, don't you? Hit the pillow!

MARK: Look, I...

TIFFANY: You're afraid, is that it? You're basically a coward. At bottom you're nothing but a yellow-bellied castrated coward.

MARK: Look, why don't we wait until Jaydeen...

TIFFANY: Angry, Mark? Does my saying that make you angry? Hit the pillow, Mark! Show me you have balls! Hit the pillow and say, "Damn you, Tiffany!"
(Mark hits the pillow limply.)

TIFFANY: Say it! "Damn you, Tiffany!"

MARK: Damn you, Tiffany.

TIFFANY: Damn you, Jaydeen!

MARK: *(Hitting the pillow.)* Damn you, Jaydeen!
(He continues hitting the pillow as she shouts.)

TIFFANY: That's it! That's it! Oh, that's wonderful! You *do* have balls! You *do* have balls!

MARK: *(Hitting the pillow.)* Damn you, Jaydeen! Damn you, Jaydeen!
(Jaydeen enters.)

JAYDEEN: What the hell did I do now?!
(Mark stops, nonplussed. Tiffany is not in the least flustered.)

TIFFANY: Hi. I'm Doctor Tiffany Heaven. Welcome to Creosote and Heaven. We're so sorry for your pain. Does this bother you, what you just heard? Take the battaka, Jaydeen. Hit the pillow and say, "Damn you, Mark." Mark, give her the battaka.

MARK: No.

TIFFANY: Give her the battaka! Don't be hurt by what she's going to say.

MARK: Tell her to get her own battaka.

TIFFANY: *(The angry coach.)* Mark!
(He surrenders the battaka to Tiffany, who hands it to Jaydeen.)

TIFFANY: *(Sweetly.)* Now remember what he said, Jaydeen. He damned you. In front of a total stranger. When he was hitting that pillow he was hitting you. What do you say to that, Jaydeen?

JAYDEEN: Damn you, Mark.

TIFFANY: That's right. Now use the battaka.

JAYDEEN: *(Hits Mark, not the pillow.)* Damn you, Mark! Damn you, Mark!

TIFFANY: The pillow, not your husband!
(Jaydeen whacks Tiffany with the battaka, knocking her backward into some pillows, then continues her attack on Mark, bringing him to his knees, then to

the ground. Breathless, she stops, throws the battaka onto the ground, then collapses onto some pillows, exhausted. Silence.)

TIFFANY: *(Sweetly, as if nothing has happened.)* Now…what seems to be the problem?

(Jaydeen breaks into sobs, unable to speak. Tiffany clucks her tongue in disapproval.)

TIFFANY: You did this to her, didn't you, Mark? Oh my.

MARK: I…

TIFFANY: *(Sadly, sweetly.)* Don't deny it. No one's blaming you. What did you do? Abuse her mentally? Physically? Emotionally? Did you force your big ugly body on her when she didn't want it?

MARK: Look, I…

TIFFANY: Or was it just the opposite, Mark? Are you incapable of giving her the physical pleasure she so desperately needs?

MARK: No, I…

TIFFANY: *(Understanding, kind.)* Admit it, Mark. You're a cold-hearted, selfish, shallow individual. Once you admit *that*, your relationship can be saved.

MARK: She's not like this *all* the time…

TIFFANY: *(Sweetly at first, but the anger of her memories soon overpowers her.)* I used to have a relationship like this too. My first husband chained me to the kitchen stove. Do you believe that? I thought it was normal. I wrote my dissertation on the open oven door. I got a degree in marital counseling and my own personal relationship was a sham. I would have committed suicide if the stove had been gas. I tried to stick my head in the microwave but the chain wouldn't reach. And then I met Roger and I realized that all men weren't like that Neanderthal Hitler I lived with. Just some of them. But *you* can't be helped, Mark. This marriage must *never* be saved. Men like you should be put in jail for what you do to women! You disgust me! Now get out of here! Get the hell out of here before you make me vomit!

MARK: Please, I…

TIFFANY: *(In an hysterical fury.)* GET OUT! GET OUT!!!

(Roger enters, breezily.)

ROGER: Sorry I'm late. I'm Doctor Roger Creosote. Welcome to Creosote and Heaven. We're so sorry for your pain.

(Roger holds out his hand. Mark hesitantly takes it.)

TIFFANY: He's sick, Roger! Sick! Sick! Sick!

ROGER: I see you've met Tiffany.

TIFFANY: Get him out of here!

ROGER: And this must be your lovely wife.

JAYDEEN: *(Looks up at him.)* Roger…

ROGER: Oh my God…

TIFFANY: Roger, did you hear me?!

> *(Sobbing, Jaydeen runs to Roger, nearly tackling him.)*

TIFFANY: What? What is it? Roger, what is she doing?

ROGER: I don't know.

JAYDEEN: Of course you know. Why won't you return my calls? Why won't you answer my letters? I only married him because I thought he had your eyes. But on our wedding night he took them out! They were colored contact lenses! And he doesn't make love the way you do! He says the bathroom spigot hurts his back!

TIFFANY: Do you know this woman?

ROGER: Just an old acquaintance, dear.

JAYDEEN: Roger! I love you!

> *(Jaydeen kisses him fully on the mouth. Roger breaks the kiss with difficulty.)*

MARK: Uh, Jaydeen why didn't you tell me he was…

TIFFANY: Oh my God! Roger! How could you deceive me like this?!

ROGER: Honestly, Tiffany…

> *(Jaydeen is sobbing, clinging to Roger like poison ivy, kissing his chest, his back, his hands, while Roger tries to extricate himself.)*

MARK: Jaydeen…

TIFFANY: You set this whole thing up, didn't you?

ROGER: *You* made the appointment.

MARK: Jaydeen, please…

TIFFANY: You did this just to humiliate me!

ROGER: I swear I didn't know…

MARK: For better or worse, Jaydeen, remember?

TIFFANY: Oh my God! Throw her out! Kick her out!!!!

ROGER: Tiffany, she's hurting.

TIFFANY: She'll be hurting even more when I'm through with her!

> *(Grabbing the battaka, Tiffany lunges for the sobbing Jaydeen. Mark grabs the business end of the battaka, trying to restrain her.)*

MARK: No!

TIFFANY: You stay out of this!

> *(She wrests the battaka from his grasp and hits him, knocking him back onto the pillows. Roger gets between her and the sobbing Jaydeen.)*

ROGER: Tiffany, be reasonable. She's never done anything to hurt you. *She's* the one who's suffering. I loved her for a time, and then I met you. We all know that love is a momentary and ephemeral thing. Love changes. She's got to learn that. You do too. We all do.

TIFFANY: What do you mean?

ROGER: Love is a wisp on the wind. It blows here, then it blows there…

TIFFANY: You don't love me anymore? Is that what you're trying to say? You don't love me?!

ROGER: Well, I wouldn't put it quite like that…

TIFFANY: *(Begins to sob.)* NO!!! No. No. I don't believe this. I don't believe this nightmare!

ROGER: I'm sorry, Tiffany. I'm so sorry for your pain.

TIFFANY: I'll show you pain!

(She raises the battaka and beats Roger several times over the head with it. Jaydeen screams. Roger screams and collapses. Mark tries to pull her back.)

MARK: Hold it! Let's be sensible here!

TIFFANY: You stay out of this!!! *(She delivers a couple of battaka blows to Mark, beating him back.)*

JAYDEEN: *(Nurses Roger.)* Oh Roger. Roger.

MARK: *(Warding off the blows.)* Please! I don't mean to get involved here but that's my wife who's…

(In an instant Tiffany throws down the battaka and is on Mark, kissing him passionately on the mouth, the eyes. Mark struggles valiantly with her.)

MARK: What are you doing?!

ROGER: Tiffany! Don't!

TIFFANY: *(Breaks the kiss.)* What? Are you jealous? Do you want these kisses, Roger?! He's more of a man than you'll ever be!

(Tiffany kisses Mark again. He pries away.)

MARK: No, please…

JAYDEEN: Leave her, Roger. Let's run away.

TIFFANY: You don't need to leave me. *I'm* leaving *you! We're* running away, him and me.

MARK: Don't you think we should talk this over…

TIFFANY: *(Slapping his shoulder.)* You stay out of this! *(Then desperately, clinging to Mark, speaking to Roger.)* He loves me, Roger. I'll do anything he wants. I'll be his slave. He'll chain me to the stove and I'll love it!

ROGER: *(Leaping to his feet…)* Stop it! *(…and pulling Tiffany away from Mark.)* Stop it!

(Tiffany is pleased. For a moment, all is calm.)

ROGER: You're trying to make me jealous, Tiffany, aren't you? Well, it worked. But not the way you think. I don't love you. And I don't love you, Jaydeen. I don't love anybody. I'm a sad, pathetic, despicable human being. We all are. All except this man. *(Putting his arm around Mark.)* The three of us are searching for love and we love no one but ourselves. But this man…he's good. I sensed it as soon as I walked into the room. He's capable of great affection, great feeling. Aren't you?

MARK: Well, I…

ROGER: And I'm not. I look at a man like this and I am *consumed* with jealousy. *(Fighting emotion, to Mark.)* I could hate you, I could murder you, I could tear you into little pieces and feed you to the dogs, but you know something else? I could also love you. I know I just said I don't love anyone, but if I *could* love anyone, I could love you. *(Roger falls to his knees sobbing, laughing, clinging to Mark's knees.)* Yes. Oh yes. I want to love, I want to love *you* and I don't even know your name. I am such a fake! I make money teaching people how to love and I don't even love myself! Help! HELP ME!!! *(Roger is sobbing, kissing Mark's feet.)*

JAYDEEN: He can't do it, Roger.

MARK: I'm really not that good at loving anyone myself…

JAYDEEN: He's boring, he's unimaginative…

TIFFANY: The spigot hurts his back.

JAYDEEN: He's pathetic, he's weak…

TIFFANY: He's one big noogie.

MARK: I don't love you, Roger!

(A beat. Roger looks up.)

MARK: No offense. Don't take it personally. I can't teach you anything about love because I really don't love *you.*

(Silence.)

ROGER: *(Sits back, wipes his eyes, gathers his wits again.)* Well. All right. At least *that's* cleared up.

(Another moment, and then Roger grabs the battaka and attacks Mark, shouting angry primal screams, beating him to the ground. Tiffany and Jaydeen finally succeed in prying Roger away from Mark.)

JAYDEEN: Leave him be, Roger. He's bad for you.

TIFFANY: He's a cold-hearted, selfish, shallow individual. He can't appreciate you, Roger.

(The women are holding Roger down.)

JAYDEEN: But *we* can. *We* can love you.

TIFFANY: We *do* love you, Roger. And in time, perhaps you can grow to love us.

JAYDEEN: Together.

TIFFANY: We're yours.

> *(Roger calms, quietly sobbing. The two women comfort and coo over him, kissing him, loving him, oblivious of Mark.)*

MARK: Well…goodbye then. *(No response.)* I won't be coming back, you know. *(No acknowledgement.)* It's all my fault, I know. And I *do* feel guilty. I guess I just fell in love with the wrong person. *(Nada.)* Life goes on. Right? *(Nope. He picks up the battaka and playfully hits himself on the head.)* Well…goodbye.

> *(No response. Their three heads are close together, the women lying on either side of Roger, soothing him. Mark leaves. After a moment he runs back on, screaming…)*

MARK: NOOGIE!!! *(…battaka still in hand, and brings it down soundly on their three heads. Blackout.)*

END OF PLAY

If Susan Smith Could Talk
by Elaine Romero

CHARACTERS

SUSAN SMITH: The young South Carolina mother who drowned her two children in the family car.

CARRIE: A judge.

STEPH: Susan's white, feminist defense attorney.

JERRY: A male African-American prosecuting attorney.

TIME

An appeal to change Susan Smith's sentence to death.

PLACE

A court room/execution room.

SETTING

An electric chair sits in the center. The judge sits to one side. The attorneys sit at tables on opposite sides of the electric chair.

AUTHOR'S NOTE

It seems only fitting that Susan Smith's story would resonate with me after growing up in the Southwest, hearing the legend of *La Llorona* who drowned her children in the Rio Grande. Doomed forever to roam the land, mourning her lost children, they say when the wind howls at night, it is she, crying for them; she can never find peace, not even in death.

If Susan Smith Could Talk

Lights up on Steph who sits far to one side, facing the audience.

STEPH: When I first saw Susan Smith—when I very first saw her. I saw the face of an angel. And with those gold-rimmed glasses, it was like she had some kind of vulnerability 'cause her eyes didn't work right.

(Jerry sits across the room.)

JERRY: When I first saw Susan—Susan Smith. The first thing I didn't like was the way she said "black man." And that picture she had the cops draw up. He didn't look like any real black man to me, but a lily white woman's vision of a black man—one speck human, most part gorilla. No, not human at all.

(Carrie, the judge, sits off-center behind a podium. A gavel rests next to her hand.)

CARRIE: I was driving home from court in my car, listening to one of those talk shows on the radio, and this woman called in to say Susan had confessed. She had just watched it on *A Current Affair*.

JERRY: I knew she was guilty the first time I saw her on the TV. She kept averting her eyes from the camera, and grasping her stomach. Didn't anybody see the meaning behind that? Like she was trying to reach back inside her body and find something in that empty womb.

STEPH: Here was a woman who was realizing for maybe the first time that men weren't gonna want her. I think that's what made her snap, knowing she was young, and beautiful in her own way, but she was already soiled goods because of those two kids.

CARRIE: I thought, we've got a little Medea on our hands. You know the story of Medea, don't you? She went out to destroy somebody else, but she destroyed herself instead.

JERRY: Like she was trying to find something in that empty womb.

CARRIE: I saw her there on the TV, saying, "Bring my babies…back to me," and it's the way she slowed down before she said "back" that I knew she'd done it.

STEPH: Her eyes didn't work right.

CARRIE: And then, she added, as she stood next to that handsome ex-husband of hers, she said, "Bring them back to us, so we can be a family again."

STEPH: I saw the face of an angel.

CARRIE: That told the whole story for me. Here was a woman, abandoned by her husband, raising two kids alone. And I thought, this is perfect. She brought her husband back by saying some strange man had driven off with their children during a carjacking. But our modern Medea, I knew her story. She hated that husband of hers as much as she loved him, and this was the only way she could get revenge.

STEPH: When I first heard she'd done it. I thought, it must be because of a man. There's only one reason women do these kinds of things. They do them for love.

(Lights down. Lights up. All freeze, except Susan, who paces around the courtroom and stops.)

SUSAN: *I knew what they were thinking. They'd made up their minds about me before I'd said anything. (Susan sits in the electric chair, moves her hands into leather wrist wraps, strapping herself to the chair. Her hair falls in her eyes. To the audience.) You all had, too. You all held judgments against me in your hearts. How can anyone living or dead get a fair roasting anymore? (Carrie hits the gavel lightly on the podium.) I keep replaying the trial in my head, trying to figure out what I really said. (Wistfully.) I have dreams. I have things I want. (Carrie hits the gavel on the podium more loudly. Susan looks up. Tough.) Crack me like an egg and let me pour.*

CARRIE: *(Not hearing.)* Are you clear on what's at stake?

SUSAN: I've been sentenced to life imprisonment. I understand.

JERRY: If she were black, she wouldn't even have the luxury of appealing for life or death. You all would have fried her up long ago.

STEPH: My client would like to make her case.

CARRIE: This is an appeal to change your sentence to death, Susan. Do you understand that?

SUSAN: Decisions have been made, I understand. I understand that decisions can be…

STEPH: Challenged.

SUSAN: *I don't like my sentence. My sentence is fucked. It doesn't let me run. Into*

the cracks of the asphalt. It doesn't let me seep into the holes in the earth. This
sentence does not keep me fluid.

CARRIE: So, you have nothing to say?

SUSAN: I would like to die, your Honor. I'm looking forward to it. I made a pact with my children. I freed them from the pain I would have caused them, and now I'd like to be freed from mine. I don't care what anybody ever thinks or says about me. I saved those two little souls from everything. From the disappointment of love. I know I've done the right thing. *(Beat.)* You may do the same for me.

(A moment. Carrie looks at Susan. Carrie nods. As the lights dim and flicker, Susan's body jolts slightly. Her head drops. Steph looks at Jerry with disgust. Carrie looks between them, unsure. Jerry starts clapping.)

JERRY: Bravo and it would have been so easy. *(Susan jolts her head up.)* All satisfied?

SUSAN: *I have dreams. I have things I want.*

JERRY: Your Honor. She rejects your leniency.

CARRIE: Life imprisonment is lenient?

JERRY: *(Simultaneously; sarcastically.)* Or was that cruelty?

SUSAN: *(As if she has said it before.)* People don't understand. There was this man that I really loved with all my heart. But when it came time for us to get married, he said, "I can't do it. I'm not ready to take on the responsibility of being a father."

JERRY: *(Simultaneously; as if he has heard it before.)* "I'm not ready to take on the responsibility of being a father."

SUSAN: No man fathers another man's children without some resentment in the heart. And when he said that, it just shattered me because I'm beautiful, aren't I? And I don't deserve this.

(Susan drops her head.)

JERRY: You think you're beautiful?

(Steph stands.)

STEPH: Let's not forget that Susan is a symbol first, a woman second. *(Catching herself.)* I mean—

SUSAN: *I stand for something else. Other than being me.*

STEPH: Her mistake is a cry—a cry from a whole society of young women who feel like Hester Prynne. Well, Susan Smith ripped that scarlet letter right off her chest.

JERRY: Your Honor, literary allusions aren't gonna save her face. She killed two innocent children. They had no choice. All those kids knew was that they were goin' on a drive with mommy, and mommy dumped them in a lake.

SUSAN: What people don't understand is that I was trying to kill myself.

JERRY: We all understand that really well. *(Beat.)* But you failed. You drowned your kids and left precious Susan alive.

CARRIE: Mr. Johnson.

JERRY: It's just so obvious—this woman never had a brain.

SUSAN: I made a mistake. *I have most of a brain. I can think the same thought every day for the rest of my life. (A mantra.) I killed them. I killed them.*

JERRY: You didn't breathe a word until you knew you'd been caught, and the press announced on national television there were holes in your story.

SUSAN: *The press announced on national television there were holes in my head.*

CARRIE: *(Simultaneously.)* Mr. Johnson, that's enough.

STEPH: It's really easy for Mr. Johnson to be self-righteous. But we all know that Mr. Johnson will never know what it's like to be a young and scared single mom.

SUSAN: *Mr. Johnson will never know what it's like to be your step-dad's favorite…*

JERRY: *(Simultaneously.)* I know what it's like to be a black man. She accused all of us, you know.

SUSAN: *His favorite* daughter. *(Retreating.)* If I'd committed suicide, I would have left them motherless and that wouldn't have been right.

JERRY: So, it's better to kill them?

SUSAN: *(Venom.) His favorite fuck.*

STEPH: *(Loudly.)* Your Honor, the death penalty.

(Carrie pounds the gavel.)

CARRIE: Order in the court.

SUSAN: *My stepfather is not on trial here. He is not on trial. (Beat; catatonic.)* Children can't live without their mothers. It's a known fact. *I know I wouldn't be who I am today if it weren't for my parents.*

CARRIE: Susan.

SUSAN: I loved my babies more than anything. I never wanted anything bad to happen to them, and nothing ever will. 'Cause I've spared them. And you don't know how that makes me feel as a murderer—I mean, a mother.

JERRY: Your Honor, Susan suffers from delusions. No matter what anybody tells her, she sees this whole thing through her own twisted eyes. And in those eyes, she's always the heroine.

STEPH: She feels she has saved her children because something about this world has been too painful for her.

SUSAN: *My stepfather chomped me down bit by bit. He was a criminal that way. He liked to eat people.*

STEPH: Say something. Describe your pain.

SUSAN: *My stepfather swallowed my tongue. If he hadn't, you'd hear me.*

CARRIE: Susan, don't you want to say anything in your defense? Something that will help us understand?

SUSAN: *(Not a response.)* I've been talkin' to my babies. They've forgiven me. I've talked to God and he's forgiven me, too. *Every day.* People from the world yell at me through their TVs. They'll never feel anything for me but hatred.

JERRY: Your Honor, Susan Smith does not have a repentant heart. I doubt Susan Smith has a heart at all.

STEPH: I ask that my client be put to death at her request. To stop the pain.

JERRY: Life imprisonment. Let her count the days.

SUSAN: *Have you ever cried and no one listened?*

STEPH: Listen to her words.

SUSAN: *No one hears me.* A couple days before I sank to that lowest point, my oldest was playing, hanging from my neck. His hands felt like ropes around me.

JERRY: Your Honor, this is preposterous.

SUSAN: My oldest lived a happy two years and my youngest, a blessed fourteen months. Nobody's gonna take that time from us. Sure, I could have killed them bit by bit. But I did it fast and quick and without a lot of pain.

JERRY: Your babies suffered. You watched your eldest try to get out of the car seat.

SUSAN: I was crying too much to watch, sir.

JERRY: You were so tearful you went on national television going on about some black man when all the time it was you.

SUSAN: I know.

JERRY: You lied to every sympathetic heart in this country.

SUSAN: I wanted to live.

JERRY: I thought you wanted to kill yourself.

SUSAN: *(Stronger.)* I wanted to live.

JERRY: So, you lied to save your ass.

SUSAN: I lied to start over. With him. I'm giving you my second chance.

STEPH: My client wants to be free. She wants to die.

JERRY: This young woman is a murderess. *(Short beat.)* This whole death penalty thing is just a complicated suicide. She wants to get us to kill her because she never had the courage to do it herself.

SUSAN: You're right. I never had the courage.

(A pound of the gavel.)

CARRIE: Sentence stands. Life. No parole.

SUSAN: No! *(Beat.) Sacrifices made for love are never understood by the people inside the TV who pound the gavel loud and hard, especially human sacrifices made for helium balloons who want to live in castles on the hill. (Beat.) I was going to be his princess—I was going to be his queen. Put a pin in me, so I'll pop.*

(Carrie crosses to Susan and frees Susan's hands from the wrist wraps. Steph looks at Jerry with disgust. Carrie looks between them, unsure. Blackout.)

END OF PLAY

The Guest of Honor
by Richard Strand

CHARACTERS

KAREN
LYNN
JASON
DAVID

The Guest of Honor

KAREN: So, what's he like?

LYNN: See, that's the thing about him: he's really no different from, say, you or me.

JASON: Exactly. That's how I feel. He's like, you know, just a person. That's the only thing that matters. Just a person. No different, really, from any other person.

KAREN: How marvelous. A person. Uh, what's wrong with him?

LYNN: Nothing. That's the point. In a very real sense, there is nothing wrong with him.

JASON: Exactly. And that is very well put. There's really nothing wrong with him. That's how we should always look at it.

KAREN: How wonderful. Uh, is there some reason I might *think* there was something wrong with him?

LYNN: No. That's the amazing thing. There is really no reason you would ever think that there is something wrong. Because of his attitude. He's got a great attitude.

JASON: Exactly. We have these prejudices and fears, but they are all unfounded. They are meaningless. And he, maybe more than any man I know, is proof of that.

LYNN: A shining example, really. A shining example of the indomitable nature of the individual.

KAREN: Wow. That's great. Uh, forgive me for seeming a bit thick here, but what prejudice and fears should I have about him?

JASON: None. That's the point.

LYNN: Exactly. For all intents and purposes, he is a man like any other man.

JASON: And that's how he likes to be treated.

KAREN: Yes. Yes. I understand, and, of course, I'm sure you're right. But, you know, if I *were* to have a prejudice or fear about him, what would that prejudice or fear be?

JASON: Karen, the whole point is that you should feel no such thing.

LYNN: Yes. That's the point we're trying to make.

KAREN: Oh, I understand. And I agree with you. Absolutely. Down the line. All the way. Believe me, I'm in your corner. Only, I was sort of hoping that you might give me a clue, you know, of what sort of prejudices and fears I might, if I were less sensitive, be tempted to have so that, you know, I could sort of push those aside as soon as I felt them rearing their ugly little heads. You know.

JASON: Karen, believe me, you will be so comfortable with him that you won't be tempted, even for a second, to think of him as anything other than a person, a human being, one of us, a friend, a colleague, and a wonderful guy.

(The doorbell rings.)

LYNN: That's him. Okay, now, Karen, don't say anything embarrassing.

KAREN: Like what?

LYNN: You know. Just don't say anything that shows you're self-conscious.

JASON: Because, really, there's nothing to be self-conscious about.

LYNN: Exactly. He's just a person. That's really the only important thing. That he's a person.

KAREN: Well, of course. That is the important thing. Only, do you think you could give me an example of something embarrassing I might say so that I could have a solid hold on what I shouldn't say?

LYNN: Say anything you like, Karen. He's a man, that's all. And no different from you or me. Not in any way that matters.

KAREN: That's certainly good news. Only I'd still like one example of a truly embarrassing thing that I might say so that I could avoid saying it.

JASON: You're worrying too much. Relax.

(The doorbell rings again.)

LYNN: I better let him in.

KAREN: NO! Not yet! I'm not ready!

LYNN: Ready. Ready for what? Karen, you're making way too much out of this.

KAREN: *(Grabbing Lynn.)* You can't open the door. Not yet. Not until you give me an example of an embarrassing thing that I might say.

JASON: This is just silly.

KAREN: Tell me. I mean it. Tell me.

JASON: He's at the door. We have to let him in.

KAREN: TELL ME! TELL ME SOMETHING I MIGHT SAY THAT WOULD BE REALLY EMBARRASSING. TELL ME NOW!

LYNN: Jason, can you think of something?

JASON: Well, sure. Uh, let me think…

LYNN: Oh. I know. You know, just as an example, don't say something like, "Master, I found a letter for you at the institute this morning; it was addressed to Arbois."

JASON: Sure. That's a good example.

LYNN: You know, it might make him feel self-conscious.

JASON: Right. Just a little sensitive.

(The doorbell rings again.)

KAREN: Why would I say that?

LYNN: Well, frankly, I can't imagine that you would which is why this whole conversation is so ridiculous.

JASON: I agree. You're becoming obsessed by this. When the whole point is, he's no different from anyone else.

LYNN: Exactly. *(The doorbell rings again.)* I can't continue to leave him out there, Karen. You have to let go of me so I can open the door.

(Karen lets go. Lynn answers the door and David enters. As advertised, he is, in no important way, different from you or me.)

(In the following dialogue, Lynn, David, and Jason all speak simultaneously.)

LYNN: *(Taking a bottle of wine from David.)* David! Thanks for coming and what's this? You brought wine? That's wonderful! Thank you. Thank you so much.

DAVID: *(Giving Lynn a bottle of wine.)* Here. I brought this for you. It's not a real expensive...you know, just a little gift. For you. And Jason.

JASON: Take your coat? Oh, sorry. You're not wearing one. Well, thanks. Thanks a lot.

(Continuing normally.)

LYNN: And David, this is our very good friend, Karen. Karen, this is David.

DAVID: Hi. It's a pleasure to meet you.

(Karen is conspicuously staring at David, looking for the problem. David becomes quite self-conscious. So do Lynn and Jason. Lynn nudges Karen.)

KAREN: Oh! Uh, uh, of course... *(Karen looks to Lynn, very afraid she will say something wrong. Her next words are very stilted. Everyone is staring at Karen, hanging on each word.)* It's, uh, a-pleasure-to-meet-you-too.

(Everyone heaves a sigh of relief. David is smiling broadly.)

LYNN: Let's sit down.

JASON: I'll get wine glasses.

(Jason exits to get wine glasses. Lynn manipulates Karen into sitting next to David on the sofa.)

LYNN: So, David, Karen writes shareware.

DAVID: Really!

KAREN: Yes. Yes I do.

DAVID: That's fabulous.

KAREN: It's okay.

DAVID: What is shareware exactly?

KAREN: Well, it's nothing really. It's just software. Only it's marketed differently from software that you might buy at a computer retailer.

DAVID: How so?

KAREN: Well, instead of buying a program for tens, or sometimes hundreds, of dollars, you pay a nominal price and try it out on your computer.

DAVID: I see.

KAREN: Then, if you like it, you send money to the programmer. Usually something like ten or twenty dollars.

DAVID: I see.

KAREN: And, if you don't like it, well, you just delete it from your hard drive and you don't have any further obligation.

DAVID: *(Taken aback.)* I beg your pardon?

(Lynn looks mortified. Jason comes running back into the room to smooth things over.)

(Jason, Lynn and Karen all speak the following lines simultaneously.)

JASON: I don't think she really meant that you would just delete it from your hard drive…

LYNN: What Karen means…

KAREN: Did I say something?

LYNN: Right. Or that there would really be no further obligation…

JASON: Right. Not in the sense of, you know, an obligation…

KAREN: Oh no. I didn't mean…

(They continue normally.)

LYNN: I think what Karen meant was …

JASON: Karen can speak for herself, dear.

LYNN: Of course. I'm sorry. Karen, why don't you just clarify what you meant.

(All eyes are on Karen.)

KAREN: I…uh…I can't really even remember what it is I said that I didn't mean.

JASON: Well, you *said* that you could delete it from your hard drive…

KAREN: Oh, right. And what I *meant* was, uh, you could, uh…*erase* it from your, uh, *data storage device.*

DAVID: *(Relieved.)* Oh. Oh, I see.

JASON: And, Karen, you also *said* that you wouldn't have any further obligation.

KAREN: Right. Right. I *said* that. But what I *meant* was that you, you know, wouldn't have any *subsequent commitment*.

(Everyone relaxes and feels better.)

DAVID: Oh! Oh! Of course. I see now.

JASON: Subsequent commitment.

LYNN: *(Laughing.)* Makes all the difference, doesn't it?

DAVID: *(Laughing.)* Well, sure. Subsequent commitment.

JASON: *(Laughing.)* She just *said* further obligation. She *meant* subsequent commitment.

KAREN: Right. And all I was really trying to point out is, that the whole thing is on the honor system.

(Everyone abruptly stops laughing. Lynn kicks Karen's ankle. David is again taken aback.)

DAVID: I beg your pardon?

KAREN: Um, um…

JASON: Uh, again, I don't think Karen really meant to say, honor system.

KAREN: Well, no. Of course not. Not, honor system.

LYNN: No. She meant to say…

JASON: Dear! Let Karen say it.

KAREN: Sure I can say it. I meant, uh, not honor system, but, uh… integrity… scheme.

(David is even more taken aback. Lynn kicks Karen's ankle again.)

DAVID: I beg your pardon?

KAREN: And, really, I didn't even mean integrity scheme, as much as I meant, uh…morality…structure.

(David is even more taken aback. Jason shakes his head in disbelief. Lynn kicks Karen's ankle again.)

DAVID: I *beg* your *pardon?!*

KAREN: And, actually, I didn't even mean morality structure, because what I really meant was, uh, uh… *(She is pretty sure she's going to get it wrong again.)* scruple…strategy.

(In a preemptive strike, Karen kicks Lynn's ankle. As anticipated, David is even more taken aback.)

DAVID: Excuse me?!

JASON: I think what Karen means…

KAREN: I CAN SPEAK FOR MYSELF, JASON! *(Everyone is silent, waiting for Karen to do just that.)* I found a letter for you at the institute this morning; it was addressed to Arbois!

(Karen makes a grand exit. Everyone else is left shell-shocked.)

DAVID: *(After a reflective moment.)* You know, I hate to admit this, but I had that coming.

END OF PLAY

Let the Big Dog Eat
by Elizabeth Wong

CHARACTERS
TED
BILL
MICHAEL
WARREN
(Ages forty to seventy)

PLACE
A prestigious golf course. At the first tee.

TIME
The present.

PLAYWRIGHT'S NOTE
The men are avid golfers. They are impeccably attired in tasteful clothes befitting their status. They take their golf game seriously. Golf is precision.

Hierarchy, competition, alliance, and realignment of power and position are a necessary part of the play's subtextual infrastructure, and need to be reflected by actors, spatially. Golf is stillness.

The play is neither a cartoon nor a caricature, but a fun fraternity—full of good-natured teasing, roughhousing, and school-boy antics. But make no mistake—they are powerful, confident, deferring to none, including each other.

In the Actors Theatre of Louisville production, thanks to Michael Dixon, the play began with a "rain shower" of over-sized money of various denominations, floating onto the playing area, augmented by a subtle green strobe, to a sound mix of cash registers and the song, "For the Love of Money" by the O'Jays. This special effect worked sublimely as the golf course.

Let the Big Dog Eat

A golf course. At the first hole. Warren and Michael, Bill and Ted—four cap-
tains of industry at play, about to tee off. They are relaxed, convivial, fraternal.

BILL: *(To Ted.)* Geez, that's kinda hard-core, Ted. We cannot be *the* lousiest
golfers in the Fortune 500.

TED: We suck. In God we trust, and in golf we suck. That's why I'm taking up
flyfishin', and you are taking the honor. After you, my friend.

BILL: No way, I really suck.

WARREN: *(To Michael.)* The Shark handed me his driver, I swing, I hear a
whoosh, I look up. I don't see it. That's because the ball is four inches
from my left foot. In front of Greg Norman, I dinked! Twice! It was so
humiliating. Dink!

MICHAEL: You wanna talk humiliation. I'm at the shotgun start of my own
tournament on my own network, I whiff. From coast to coast in living
color, from Epcot to Anaheim. Whiff. The sound of empty air. That's
embarrassment!

TED: *(Interrupting.)* Hell Mikey, that's nothing. I was at Kapalua with Arnie
and Jack, couldn't hit it past the goddamned ladies tees, and those guys
invoked the goddamned rule. Had to play the rest of the hole with my
dick hanging o.u.t.

(Bill emits a loud raspberry.)

MICHAEL: That's it. I declare a winner. Show us your big swing, Ted. We've
already seen your big wallet!

BILL: First on the first tee, and first in charit-TEE!!!

WARREN: You win Ted! Let the big dog eat!

BILL/MICHAEL/WARREN: Chomp! Chomp!/Arrrooooo!/Woof woof!

TED: Now, that's it. I'm sick of being just a big growling stomach. A gigantic
digestive tract, with dollars dripping from my maw. Chomp chomp
chomp. Hell, I'm no poorer than I was nine months ago, and the world is
maybe a lot better off. *(Beat.)* Okay, all right, what do you say, we play a
penny per hole, greenies get a nickel, par gets a dime. High score buys a
round of milk at the 19th.

BILL: Whew! For a minute there, I thought I'd have to pledge a billion to the Red Cross just to play this round.

TED: Okay! Now you're talkin'.

WARREN: Don't worry Bill, I'll spot you. Better yet, I'll take a few million shares of Cap Cities, if Mike here doesn't mind. That should make a nice, sizeable contribution to the Mickey Mouse Fan Club.

MICHAEL: Come on Ted, face it, you turned us into measly cheapskates. Bill here gave some 135 million away last year, and now it sounds like chump change. Hell, you're making us all look bad. Right Warren?

TED: Redeem your immortal soul! Now, one of you slackers tee up!

WARREN: Well, Mike, I know how you can redeem your *immoral* soul. Sell off your hockey team. Disperse the funds in ten-year increments, $100,000 per annum to Greenpeace or Save The Rain Forest.

MICHAEL: Not my team! I love my team. Ted got to keep his team. I'll sell off the Magic Kingdom first.

BILL: Oh nooooo! Not Mickey! Don't liquidate Mickey!

WARREN: Next thing you know, Mickey and Minnie will be living out of a cardboard box, sellin' shares of Disney in front of Mr. Toad's Wild Ride.

BILL/MICHAEL/WARREN: *(Harmonizing beautifully.)* M.O.U.S. Eeeeeeeeeeeee… for sale!

TED: Hell, that sounds all right. Let's pass a law! Lobby! Make *that* the national anthem.

MICHAEL: Now that's a good idea. I'll have my people get some people to hire some people to work on that.

WARREN: Gentlemen, nothing wrong with a little strategic philanthropy. Few things lubricate power faster than a well-placed seven-figure check to the right hospital or university.

TED: That's right, T-bone. Turn over a few shares of Time Warner every year. I feel good about that. Nothing wrong with working for a more humane world.

BILL: *(To Warren.)* But Brother T-bone, Brother Ted has fallen from the pure of faith. He no longer takes joy, as we do, in the pleasure of sheer accumulation. *(To Ted.)* Blasphemer!

TED: Sure it's fun making money, watchin' it grow. Making so much money, you never have to write a check or carry cash in your wallet. So many damned zeros and commas to make your mamma proud.

WARREN/BILL/MICHAEL: Amen/I heard dat/*Watch it grow!*

TED: Sure, money is a measure of success. I won't deny that, heck, we all have lived by its dipstick.

WARREN/BILL/MICHAEL: Whoever has the most! *Biggest dip wins!* That's right, uh huh!/Winner take all.

TED: But boys, I'm upping the ante. I'm playing a new game, with a new scorecard. Who's in with me? It's not how much you make, but how much you can give, give, give.

WARREN: Bill…

BILL: Yup.

WARREN: I think Ted not only wants to top the Forbes' 400 list, but he wants to be tops on the list in that *American Benefactor* magazine too. We all know how photogenic you are Ted, and you too Michael.

MICHAEL: Thank you Warren, you are so kind. True, I'm happier donating to my own foundations since most nonprofits are lousy with money management and…it gives my wife something to…

BILL: *(Interrupting.)* Move over George Soros! George is running scared, Skipper! The Ted wants to run with the big dogs—Feeney, Getty, Annenberg, Carnegie, Rockefeller. *(Bill runs in place.)* You know, Ted, when Warren isn't eating steaks, he's a real shark at bridge. King of the trump. He's so addicted, in one night, I bet he could win a billion easy.

TED: A billion *is* a nice round number.

WARREN: *(Raising right hand.)* I pledge to donate all my winnings to… Gamblers Anonymous.

BILL: Ohmigosh T-bone, you have to give up cigars! The money you spend on Cohibas you could finance a small war.

WARREN: But I love my Cohibas. I can't give 'em up. Don't make me. They are so delicate.

MICHAEL: Well, Warren, you could roll your own. I've been rolling my own since…

BILL: *(Interrupting.)* Mickey, you spoiled my surprise. Tee, I brought you this old wooden cigar thing from Cuba, been in Castro's family for years. But sssssshhh. Don't tell Ted. Or he'll make me take it back and donate the money to the *(Pointedly.)* American Lung Association.

TED: If you boys are through. We got 382 yards from the black to the pin. And we're burning daylight.

MICHAEL: I was saying, my buddy Schwartzenegger got me into packin' and rollin' my own stogies. Okay, I admit the first few I rolled were a bit bumpy and lumpy…

TED: *(Interrupting.)* Dopey, Sleepy, Bumpy, Lumpy! Sounds like the goddamned seven dwarfs. Hell, maybe some of those good ol' boys want to play some golf!

WARREN: Now, gentlemen, the dwarfs are a pivotal variable. Huge valuation disparity relative to the market. Balance sheets haven't looked better in thirty years, they are awash in cash flow. Maybe the dwarfs should turn over their stock outright, claim 30 percent of their adjusted gross income in deductions. Avoid capital gains on any increases in value. Of course, Ted knows all about those juicy tax deductions, right Skipper?

TED: Tax nothing! It's a third of my net worth! This is going to cost me!

BILL: Nah, I see your game, old boy. You give it to the UN, and the UN lets you broadcast TBS, CNN, and the Atlanta Braves home games to the nice people of Timbuktu! Rumor has it, he may also buy out Barry and send 'em The Home Shopping Network, you sly dog!!! Arrrroo!

MICHAEL: Not at all, gentlemen, I heard through very reliable sources, the poor man had to get his wife off his back! Jane wanted him to help her open up an acting school in Hanoi AND a health club in Ho Chi Minh City!
(They congratulate Mike, with pats on the back and handshakes. Mike beams.)

BILL/WARREN: You win that one, Michael! Arrrrooo!/Good one, Michael! Let the big dog eat! Arrrrooooo!

TED: It's about compassion, boys. I gotta believe when you give from your heart, you got yourself a win/win situation.

MICHAEL: Speaking of heart, what about you, Bill? Not everyday we have a tri-zillionare among us. Ready for that win/win scenario? When are you gonna ante up? Ted's waiting for you to fold, call, or raise.

BILL: Well, Michael, I was thinking about that. Gee whiz, well, I could sell my house, it's worth about $40 million, but then my wife would really be mad at me.

MICHAEL: It's a good thing, Bill, you added that trampoline before The Ted here put us all on the hot seat.

WARREN: A man's castle isn't complete without his trampoline room.

BILL: Hey, it's great. I'm serious, you should all try it. It's really a good work-out! I like to bounce. *(Bill bounces!)* Helps me think when I'm bouncing. I got the idea to start up MSNBC with a front-twisting somersault and landing on my butt. It's fun! Maybe when I'm bouncing, I'll think of a way to trump The Ted. Outdoing a billion-dollar giveaway takes some considerable bouncing.

TED: Well boys, maybe y'all should bounce on it. *(Ted bounces, leads all in a lively bounce fest.)* Belly up to a man's game. Stop playing that tired two-dollar table. Shake loose something more than measly pocket change.

MICHAEL: *(Coyly.)* By God, I think he's right. Compared to you guys, all I got is pocket change. I'm just a lowly billionaire in waiting. Boo Hoo.
(Michael cries.)

WARREN: There. There. You are catching up fast, that's what counts. But you better hurry it up, because the future makes me feel like an over-sexed guy in a whorehouse. The future is ripe for making more money. It's like this beautiful green manicured golf course. The fairway of opportunity, lots of hazards, but we know where they all are, and when we hit the green, we drain that bad boy for a million, ten million! My boy, the future is bright.

MICHAEL: The future is bright.

BILL: And ripe.

TED: It sure is.

(All look dreamily down the fairway, relishing the idea of a lucrative future.)

BILL: *(Gently.)* You know Ted, it's not like we don't give. We give. Right Michael?

MICHAEL: That's right. And Warren is going to be the biggest of the big-time givers. *Beyond* big. Don't be modest, Warren. Some $21 billion, after you-know-what happens, croak city, then BAM, everybody wins. Everyone goes to the bank.

BILL: It's cosmic the amount he'll leave behind. Beyond cosmic!

TED: *After*, Warren? But then you'll be dead. Give a billion right now, T-bone, you can make it back, then give a billion more. Enjoy the smile on some poor kid's face. Hell, put a thousand smiles on a thousand faces. You can't get that kind of pleasure from *worms*, six feet under.

BILL: Warren and I talked long about this. Even my kids won't get a big piece. I want them to understand the value of hard work. Make their own opportunities. I'm giving it all away, *after*.

WARREN: Right! You could say, we are working and saving for the future. It's a long-term thing, that's how we are doing it. Not before, AFTER.

BILL: After.

TED: Boys, what we got here is a dogleg right, with the green trapped left. Best line is straight out from the tee. There is our future, boys. Who's it gonna be? *(All back away from tee mound.)* This is gonna sound crazy. But Warren, I had this dream. It was like that movie *Road Warrior*. Chaos everywhere. Everybody starving. People resorted to cannibalism. I think about that all the time. People eating each other to survive. Chomp chomp. It was terrible. The worst-case scenario. But I refuse to be a cannibal. I would rather starve.

BILL: A billion dollars to feed the pigeons!

TED: I refuse to eat my fellow human beings. I would rather starve to death than be a cannibal…

BILL: A billion dollars to feed the ducks!

MICHAEL: A billion for the battle of the bulge! A billion for the war on pimples! Come on Warren, it's fun!

(Warren waves him off. He keeps his eyes on Ted.)

BILL: A billion to feed the hungry.

TED: Exactly.

MICHAEL: A billion to heal the sick.

TED: Exactly.

WARREN: Ted, you are so full of shit.

*(Ted's next speech ** overlaps with the following chant by Bill, Michael, and Warren.)*

BILL/MICHAEL/WARREN: *(One-upping each other.)*

A billion to house the homeless.

A billion to shelter refugees.

A billion.

A billion to educate children.

A billion for a cure for AIDS.

A billion for a cure for cancer.

A billion for human treatment of animals.

A billion to teach people to read.

A billion for national health care.

One billion.

A billion to end suffering.

A billion to end pain.

A billion to buy peace.

A billion to spread luvvvv.

TED: ** Very funny. Who's gonna tee off first? Warren? Bill? Michael? Okay, all right, you had your fun. You guys are doing this because you don't want to go first. Cowards. I'm onto your game. You'll do anything as long as some other sucker tees off first. Cowards! Pansies! We came to play some golf. I'm onto your game. Let's play. Let's go! You selfish bastards! *(Bill, Michael, and Warren have all ended their chant, and Ted continues.)* Move aside. I'll show y'all how it's done! Here it is—for a penny!

(Ted swings his drive. Whoosh. He freezes at the end of his follow-through. Blackout.)

END OF PLAY

Plays
for
Five Actors

The Problem Solver
by Michael Bigelow Dixon and Val Smith

CHARACTERS

MEGAN

PHIL

TINA

KURT

JER

The Problem Solver

Transcendent morning sounds. This punctuated by muttered curses and the occasional loud discordant bashing of metal. Lights up. A patio with an ocean view. In one area of the patio, five large rectangular boxes with the word "chair" stenciled on their sides are stacked. Downstage is a pile of metal tubing of various lengths, plastic baggies with nuts, bolts, etc. Each is prominently marked with different letters of the alphabet. Phil stands, back to the audience, inhaling the ocean breezes. Occasionally he turns his head to look in the direction of the noise which occurs more frequently, increasing in volume. Megan enters.

MEGAN: There you are. What time is it?

PHIL: Six forty-three.

MEGAN: What is all this stuff?

(Offstage grinding of a circular saw is heard.)

MEGAN: And what on earth is that racket?

PHIL: I thought it was road construction. Now I'm not so sure.

MEGAN: A relaxing vacation, Phil. Our escape from the kids. No yelling, no crying, no squabbling. No car puzzles with the pieces missing. No traveling computer games beeping and farting in our dreams. Just the whoosh-boom of the ocean. The lonely cry of the gulls, caw-caw.

(High-pitched whine of a drill is heard.)

MEGAN: Natural sounds.

PHIL: Hon, it'll be fine. Tina and Jer invited us here, and they promised us peace and quiet. And Kurt will be back to his old self. Once he unwinds.

MEGAN: I hope so. I don't know if I can take another day like yesterday.

PHIL: Hon, I'm sorry. He's a friend. I thought a break would help him out.

(Tina enters with a kitchen towel and apron. She seems edgy, on the verge of tears, but puts on a good face.)

TINA: I thought I heard voices. You two are up early. How did you sleep?

(Sound of frenetic hammering on metal.)

PHIL and MEGAN: Fine.

TINA: Is your friend feeling better?

MEGAN: We haven't seen him yet this morning.

TINA: I hope Jer didn't upset him last night.

PHIL: Oh no no no. Now that we're here, Kurt'll be fine. Normally he's a quiet accountant-type guy.

MEGAN: Normally he wouldn't throw up in the car.

PHIL: But he's been under a lot of pressure lately, Tina. What with the audit, trying to reconstruct the missing records and everything. You understand.

TINA: I understand.

MEGAN: Failing the lie detector test didn't help.

PHIL: Well, the whole thing has made him a nervous wreck. I hope you don't mind us inviting him along, Tina. Kurt's a good friend.

(Offstage clanging.)

MEGAN: Tina, what is that noise?

TINA: That? Oh, that's Jer. He's in the garage putting together the patio furniture. He wanted it to be a surprise. Wants everybody to have breakfast out here so they can enjoy the view. He's been up for hours. You know what a perfectionist he is.

(Tina suddenly wells up, wiping her eyes with her apron.)

PHIL: Tina?

JER: *(Offstage.)* TINA—A—A!

TINA: Better see what he wants. Coffee's on the stove. I'm so happy you're here. *(Tina exits in tears.)*

MEGAN: Coffee?

PHIL: I think so.

(Megan starts to exit. Kurt enters, red-eyed, rumpled.)

PHIL: Morning, Kurt.

KURT: *(Steps on a screwdriver.)* Ouch! Ouch ouch ouch! Get away, you nasty thing. *(Kicks screwdriver.)*

MEGAN: Kurt?

PHIL: He stepped on a screwdriver.

MEGAN: Let me see. Oooo, just a minor puncture. Can't hardly see it.

KURT: Well it's the blood that gives it away, Megan.

MEGAN: I'll get a Band-Aid.

PHIL: Kurt, you've got to take things a little easier, buddy.

(Megan exits as Tina enters.)

TINA: *(Offstage.)* All right! All right! I'll find it. *(To Phil and Kurt.)* Oh my. Everybody's up early. Isn't that nice?

KURT: Like my stigmata?

PHIL: Kurt stepped on a screwdriver.

TINA: Where?

KURT: Here. Sliced into the instep. The most painful part of the foot.

TINA: *(Picking up the screwdriver.)* AHA! *(To offstage.)* Found it! *(Tina exits with the screwdriver.)*

KURT: Thank you for your concern.

(Megan enters with coffee and Band-Aid which she gives to Kurt.)

KURT: This is all wrong, Phil. I should have stayed at home and faced the music.

PHIL: Kurt, everything is going to be okay. You just need to rest. Then you can go back fresh, alert, and straighten everything out.

KURT: *(Wincing.)* You're right. You're right. Relax. Rest.

(Sudden sound of offstage drill.)

KURT: And we've certainly come to the right place to do that.

MEGAN: Calm down, Kurt.

KURT: You said this place would be quiet.

PHIL: It will be. Okay, so we got off to a rough start. A few more hours in the car than planned. Jer and Tina are really nice people though, Kurt. Jer just says things in a funny way sometimes that's all.

KURT: Funny?!!? Like calling me an imbecile for not being able to read his stupid map.

MEGAN: Kurt, Jer did not call you an imbecile and you know it. All he said was he thought that the turn-off next to the gas station was pretty clearly marked on the map.

KURT: Did it or did it not look like the Big Boy with a hamburger platter? *(Assuming the Big Boy pose.)*

PHIL: Well, it could have been a little man with a gas hose like Jer said.

KURT: I don't care. It's a stupid way to indicate a gas station.

(Sound of frenetic hammering.)

KURT: I'm going to crucify that moron with his own Black and Decker!

(Agonizingly high-pitched sound of tearing metal under chain saw.)

MEGAN: I'm sure the noise will stop soon.

(Jer enters behind Kurt near end of following speech, disheveled, with drill and hammer in hand, and numerous twisted aluminum tubes under his arms. Tina follows.)

KURT: Oh, I know what you're thinking. Kurt's working himself into another fit. But high-pitched sound waves have been recognized as a form of torture since the Geneva Convention. And people who do this on Saturday mornings are sadists. They're the sick ones. They deserve to die!

MEGAN and PHIL: Mornin', Jer!

> *(Jer walks to the pile of tubing downstage and drops everything. He then takes an instruction diagram from his pocket and thrusts it in Kurt's face.)*

JER: Tell me. What does this say?

KURT: Oh boy, more little pictures. A little screwdriver. Little parts sliding into other little parts. What is it? A little sex manual?

JER: Little pictures. Little, tiny pictures.

TINA: Jer's been working since four. There's been some snags. Don't worry about it sweetheart. Leave it for now.

JER: Little pictures of things that don't happen.

TINA: We can have our breakfast out here anyway.

MEGAN: Right! We use the barstools from the kitchen.

PHIL: Shove some of those boxes together for a table.

JER: Because these are little pictures of things that doesn't exist.

MEGAN: Ah.

JER: That NEVER existed!

PHIL: Ha! I had the same problem when we bought the gas grill. Remember, Megan?

MEGAN: Yes. Terrible. We finally took it back and exchanged it for the floor model.

TINA: There's an idea. We'll have breakfast out here on the barstools. Then we'll go get the one *they* put together.

JER: *(Retrieves a twisted piece of chrome and waves it around dangerously.)* See this? See it? I had to cree-ate this. No such piece existed in reality. Yet on the diagram. Look. There it is. See-eeee…

PHIL, MEGAN, and TINA: Hmmmmmm.

KURT: Looks like another Big Boy.

JER: Ex-cuse me! I didn't mean to inflict anything on *anyone.* It WAS going to be a surprise. So we could sit out here comfortably. Watch the waves, the birds. Relax.

MEGAN: It was a lovely thought, Jer. Really sweet.

PHIL: It was. And we'll still do it. Jer. Together. What are friends for? Right? We'll whip this pup. Yes, sir.

TINA: Right after breakfast.

KURT: Yes. Food would be nice.

PHIL and MEGAN: Good idea!

JER: You all go on. I'll manage.

TINA: I've made Tina's Special Eggs Benedict. Jer? Your favorite.

JER: I'll have some later.

TINA: It won't be any good later! It's already congealing. Later it will be concrete! Just like last night with that stupid map. And this morning with this stupid, stupid, stupid patio furniture, which is ruining everyone's vacation!

MEGAN: Now, Tina, nobody's vacation is ruined.

TINA: Yes it is! It is! You're having a terrible time!

PHIL: No, now really, it's fine, Tina.

KURT: Well, *I'm* having a terrible time.

PHIL: Tell you what. You go warm up breakfast and we'll all pitch in here. Kurt can *relax* and Jer and I and Megan can snack and assemble. A group effort. Just like the old days. Huh? It'll be fun. Okay?

MEGAN: Tina? Okay?

TINA: Well.

PHIL and MEGAN: That's the spirit!

TINA: Can I reheat mayonnaise?

MEGAN: Sure. It tastes better that way. Phil loves his mayonnaise reheated.

PHIL: Hmmmmmm! Yum! I sure do!

KURT: I just tasted my stomach.

TINA: Oh, I'm really, really glad you two are here. *(Tina exits, sniffling.)*

PHIL: Okay. Jer, where are we?

(Jer hands Phil the diagram in disgust. During the following exchange, Kurt should, in the process of finding a box to sit on, also locate a piece of metal tubing wedged underneath, remove it, and twirl it absentmindedly.)

MEGAN: You labeled the parts very nicely, Jer.

PHIL: A real professional. No mistaking those parts, eh, Jer? No, sir. Very clear. We have two A's.

MEGAN: Check. There should be two B's.

PHIL: Yep! Two B's.

MEGAN: And one C.

JER: YOU! *(Notices Kurt's piece of tubing, jumps up, and points at it.)*

KURT: ME?!

JER: THAT!

PHIL and MEGAN: WHAT?

JER: WHERE? WHERE DID YOU GET THAT?

KURT: I didn't do anything. It was just laying under the box.

JER: I looked under the box. Over, around, and inside that box. With a microscope. That wasn't there before. I know it wasn't.

KURT: It was right here.

JER: Oh? Really?

KURT: It was. Megan, Phil, you believe me, don't you?

MEGAN and PHIL: *(Dubiously.)* Well…

JER: That was the piece that was missing. That piece. Right there.

KURT: Oh, well. I confess! I snuck out here in the moonlight and hid it when your back was turned. I've always wanted a bent piece of aluminum tubing. I collect them! And then I sell them to other collectors! For thousands of dollars!

PHIL: Kurt! Jer! Everybody stay calm.

KURT: I'm not ashamed. I saw my opportunity. I took it.

JER: I knew it!

MEGAN: Phil, this is getting out of control.

KURT: He's accusing me of stealing this…this…this…thing! First the audit! Then those idiots with their deceitful little machine. Now this! I don't believe it! Where's the blindfold and cigarette?!

PHIL: Time out! Everybody's tired. Tempers are flaring. Kurt, you go help Tina in the kitchen. We'll get the chair together. Then we'll all go for a nice swim, and everything will be wonderful.

KURT: I didn't steal it!

MEGAN: We know that, Kurt. No one's accusing anyone of stealing anything. Okay? In fact, it's a marvelous thing that you did here. That you, Kurt, found this, the missing piece, because now everything's bound to work. The chair should practically assemble itself now. Right, Phil?

PHIL: Absolutely. Right, Jer?

JER: I suppose.

PHIL and MEGAN: There! You see!

KURT: All right. I'm going. But I'm not a thief!

TINA: *(Enters, tearfully, with smoking frying plan.)* Who borrowed the carving knife?

KURT: This is unbelievable! Give me till noon and I'll have every piece of metal in the house!

TINA: All I said was the carving knife was missing. Why is everyone yelling at me! I can't do anything right! Look at the eggs! Ruined! *(She begins to cry.)*

KURT: Any ninny knows you can't reheat mayonnaise!!! *(Limps off.)*

MEGAN: Kurt! Please!

TINA: Megan, you said it could be reheated!

(Megan exits with Tina following.)

MEGAN: *(As they go.)* It's OK. Tina, we can scrape away the burnt parts and there's still enough mayonnaise for everyone.

JER: He's wound kind of tight, isn't he?

PHIL: Well, Jer, it looks to me like EVERYBODY is wound a little tight.

JER: I looked for that piece, you know.

PHIL: Jer. There's no point continuing here. Let's just call it a day, okay?

JER: You mean give up?

PHIL: Yes.

JER: I'm no quitter, Phil, I'm an engineer. Have been for six years. And during those six years, I've put a lot of things together. Big things. Massive things. With massive problems. And my job has been to solve 'em. It's what I do. What I like to think I do best. So, you want to help me here or not?

PHIL: Okay. But look. Maybe we could just start fresh. A whole new box. A different chair. Come on.

JER: Well…okay.

(Throughout the following speech, Phil opens a new box and proceeds to check off various components against the diagram as before.)

JER: See, Phil, we're different. You work with people, and there's nothing wrong with that. But sometimes, well, it keeps you from seeing a problem clearly. See, there's a certain Zen process to solving a problem, even a simple problem like a patio chair. The trick is to give it all your attention, to block out distractions. Concentrate. Concentration allows you to visualize first the problem, think it through thoroughly and logically so you can arrive at a complete solution.

(Offstage, the sounds of a door slamming. Tina's hysterical crying, a frying pan ricocheting off a wall.)

MEGAN: *(Offstage.)* TEE-NA! That's ENOUGH! Now no more throwing! Give that to me.

TINA: *(Offstage. Simultaneous with above.)* Stupid! Stupid! Stupid!

PHIL: That's great, Jer, but there's no part E in this box.

JER: No E?

PHIL: Or K.

JER: You looked under the box?

PHIL: It isn't here.

(Carrying his luggage, Kurt crosses from the house to garage.)

JER: Do you think Kurt… *(took them?)*

PHIL: Jer!

MEGAN: *(Appears from house.)* Kurt! Stop acting like a child. Put your suitcase back. Tina, now where are you going? Tina! *(Megan exits in direction of house.)*

PHIL: Look. How about we use parts K and E from the first chair to finish this one?

JER: Hey-y, fella! That's using the old noggin.

MEGAN: *(Enters from house and exits into the garage. While passing through, an exasperated whisper.)* Phil!

JER: I wish I hadn't cut and bent that other K.

(Offstage a car engine coughs, sputters, and then dies.)

PHIL: Well, maybe we don't need a K!

JER: Oh, we definitely need K, Phil. We can't put it together without K. K is vital, see? Sit on this chair without K, and you'll need a proctologist.

MEGAN: *(Offstage.)* Kurt! Unlock the door! Well, then roll the window down! Just listen to me for a minute.

(Sound of car engine trying to start but sputtering out.)

PHIL: Then maybe we *can* go get the floor model. We put all the pieces back in the box. Wrap 'em up. Take 'em back to Sears and tell 'em it came this way. And then we *make* 'em give us the floor model. Okay?

MEGAN: *(Offstage.)* Kurt!

JER: Nah. Sorry. Can't do that Phil.

(Offstage, sound of car engine trying but failing again.)

PHIL: Why not, for God's sake? Why can't we do that?

MEGAN: *(Offstage.)* Kurt! Come on!

JER: Because that's the same as quitting. And like I said I'm a problem solver, Phil. It's in my blood.

(During this next speech, Megan enters from garage and walks toward house where she meets Tina, who enters from house with a knife in her hand.)

MEGAN: Oh, Tina. Good. You found the carving knife.

(Tina marches past her and exits to garage. Megan turns and follows.)

MEGAN: Now Tina! Kurt! Phil! PHIL! *(Exiting.)* PHIL! PHIL! GET OUT HERE! QUICK!

(Phil and Megan exit, leaving Jer alone to examine the diagram. He picks up one piece of tubing, compares it to the little picture.)

JER: Nope. I'm definitely not a quitter.

(Jer pulls out masking tape and begins to tape the pieces that wouldn't fit together with screws. Sounds of argument. Sound of car revving and peeling out.)

MEGAN and PHIL: TINA! LOOK OUT! *(Assorted screams.)* OH MY GOD!

PHIL: Is she okay?

JER: Yup. I'm gonna lick this baby, yet.

(Phil and Megan enter, supporting a wounded, bedraggled Tina between them.)

PHIL: JER!

MEGAN: JER!

TINA: Jer—RY!

JER: One moment. Almost done. Ah. Ah. Ah-ha! *(Triumphantly holds up piece taped together.)* This is gonna be one great weekend!

END OF PLAY

Bed & Breakfast
by Richard Dresser

CHARACTERS

SARAH: A young American woman.

ALICE: An American woman of any age.

EVELYN: A British woman of indeterminate age.

CHUCK: Sarah's husband, a thug.

CLAUDE: Alice's husband.

SETTING

The play is set on a spring morning in a modest bed and breakfast establishment in England. The time is the present.

We see the dining area, which includes perhaps three or four tables for the guests. A door leads to the kitchen, another door leads to the rooms.

Bed & Breakfast

A bed and breakfast in England. Morning. Several tables with red and white checked tablecloths. At one of them sits Sarah, American, young, nervous, vulnerable, and terribly sad.

Alice enters. She is very self-possessed, brisk, and efficient. Sarah smiles at her hopefully. Alice barely acknowledges this with a cursory nod. She sits down at the other table and snaps open a newspaper with great authority. Sarah stares at her, trying to get up the nerve to speak. Alice suddenly bellows toward the kitchen.

ALICE: I'm not going to sit here all day waiting! I want my coffee and I want it now! This is your last warning! *(Under her breath.)* Lazy good for nothing bastards.

SARAH: *(Full of wonder.)* Oh! You're an American!
(Alice glances at her briefly.)

SARAH: I feel like I'm seeing an old friend even though we never met. Just the sound of a good old American voice, I must confess it warms my heart. I have such problems with the language here. Could you say something else? I don't care what it is, I just want to hear the sound of your voice.

ALICE: *(Yelling at the kitchen.)* Bring the goddam coffee! I refuse to be treated this way!

SARAH: Thank you. My name is Sarah Greenwell. Well, actually, as of last week it's Sarah Greenwell Pitkin, due to the occasion of my marriage, my very first. What's your name, or maybe I should just sit quietly and mind my own business?

ALICE: Alice. *(To the kitchen.)* I'll give you till ten. Then I will not be responsible for my actions. One. Two. Three. Four.
(Evelyn enters. She is a very morose British woman.)

EVELYN: *(Heavy British accent.)* Me mum is sick, Miz Madison. I'm all alone in the kitchen trying to feed and clothe the twins for the day ahead—

ALICE: Oh, for God sakes, Evelyn, your mother's drunk and the twins are eighteen years old. I'd like my coffee now.

EVELYN: Right away, right away. *(An afterthought.)* If I had the courage I'd end it all. There's nothing left for me to live for, nothing at all. I'm nothing but a burden to myself and those around me. All I live for is my Final Reward.

ALICE: I'm still waiting on that coffee.

(Evelyn exits.)

SARAH: See what I mean about the way they talk? They all sound like they're on Public Television. *(Tentatively.)* What's it like over there now? In America, I mean. Where I'm from it's the first blush of spring. The time of year when I met Chuck Pitkin. I think about home all the time. The people are so friendly, and the television is better and they cook things right. Sometimes I think if I wished hard enough I could actually be there. Even if it's just for an instant. Isn't that silly?

ALICE: How long have you been over here, anyway?

SARAH: We got in Tuesday. It seems like forever.

ALICE: No wonder you're homesick.

SARAH: And lonely. Terribly terribly lonely.

ALICE: I was under the impression you just got married.

SARAH: Oh, yes, but, well, it hasn't been easy. You know, the silly little differences that don't seem so important until you get married. See, Chuck and I are from different backgrounds. My family owned the factory in town. We were almost like royalty. People would practically bow down to us on the street. And Chuck, well, he came from a large family. They had nothing. They lived in a shack in the woods and sometimes they tried to sell things beside the road. Mainly useless junk or things they'd stolen. In the evening, all fifteen or sixteen of them would ride around in his daddy's pick-up, searching for roadkills. There was a barbecue in the back, and they'd grill them up, right there next to the road. He still thinks it's a luxury to eat an animal with no fur on it. Do you see what I'm up against?

ALICE: Well, I'm sure you can get used to each other.

(Evelyn enters with coffee. She's just about to put it down when Alice stops her.)

ALICE: Wait! This coffee is terrible! Isn't it!

EVELYN: Yes, Miz Madison. I'm sorry.

ALICE: Take it back and make me a fresh cup, do you understand?

(Evelyn whimpers and exits.)

SARAH: How could you tell?

ALICE: It's always terrible. It saves time if I don't taste it.

SARAH: I don't like this place. Chuck is restless. He wants to move on. He says there's nothing here.

ALICE: There's Stonehenge.

SARAH: Oh, have you been?

ALICE: Every day.

SARAH: Really? Because we went and it was okay, but nothing moved or anything. It was just these rocks. I liked the gift shop. *(Gets out little rocks.)* See? I got my own little Stonehenges. Fourteen dollars, or maybe it was pounds. *(Beat.)* Why would you go every day?

ALICE: My husband likes it.

SARAH: Your husband! You must be married! Congratulations! *(Beat.)* Oh, God, what a stupid, stupid thing to say. Of course you're married if you have a husband.

(Evelyn enters with coffee for Alice, then starts to leave.)

SARAH: Oh, excuse me, miss. I'd like to order breakfast? This is breakfast-inclusive, isn't it?

EVELYN: What would you like?

SARAH: I'd like two poached eggs, with sausage on the side, a grapefruit, and two coffees. My husband likes his coffee first thing.

EVELYN: Toast?

SARAH: Whole wheat.

EVELYN: Very good. *(Evelyn exits with a smirk.)*

SARAH: Isn't that dear? She didn't even write it down.

ALICE: Why should she? We all get the same thing every morning, no matter what we order. I used to believe it made a difference, but it doesn't.

SARAH: Why do they—

ALICE: They think it's polite to pretend you can have whatever you want.

SARAH: How long have you been here?

ALICE: A long time. A very long time. Years.

SARAH: Why would you stay if this is the way they treat you?

ALICE: Stonehenge. My husband likes Stonehenge.

EVELYN: *(Entering with two bowls of porridge.)* Porridge?

ALICE and SARAH: Here!

EVELYN: *(Giving them the porridge.)* If I weren't around any longer, the twins would have to take over the place. Make something of themselves. As long as I'm here they do nothing at all. I'm holding them back something terrible, and they're quick to tell me. I can hardly see through the black cloud that surrounds me. Oh, it's constant misery in my little corner of the world. *(Evelyn exits.)*

SARAH: I feel so much better the more I know of that woman's life. My little problems don't seem near so bad. *(Starts to sob.)*

ALICE: What is it?

SARAH: Nothing. Just… I think Chuck is trying to kill me.

ALICE: No! Really?

SARAH: He refuses to drive on the left side of the road. He says he's been driving since he was ten and he'll be goddammed if a bunch of foreigners will tell him what to do. He just grits his teeth and barrels ahead and the other cars have to swerve out of the way. Everywhere we go we leave a trail of vehicles on their side next to the road. It's so embarrassing.

ALICE: You don't say anything?

SARAH: He won't listen. He says this is why we fought the war, so we can have personal freedom. What should I do? I think he wants to bump me off for my money. These odd things keep happening. I'm lucky to be alive. I don't know what to do. I promised to spend the rest of my life with him, but I didn't think it would come so soon.

ALICE: *(Gets out pills.)* Put this in his coffee.

SARAH: What is it?

ALICE: My husband's medication.

SARAH: For what?

ALICE: To calm him down. He has this condition. He can only remember what's happened in the last fifteen minutes. Then it's all gone. Life begins all over for him every quarter hour.

SARAH: How awful!

ALICE: We prefer to think of it as a challenge. *(Looks at watch.)* If he isn't here soon, then he'll forget how to find the dining room. He'll forget that we're married. That's why we always have to stay together…so he'll remember.

SARAH: I wouldn't want to be you for anything in the whole world!

ALICE: Oh? Well *my* husband is not trying to kill me.

SARAH: I'm sorry. I'm not myself this morning. I'm not even anyone I know. *(She takes the pill from Alice as we hear Chuck coming.)* What will this do to him?

ALICE: Loosen him up, break through his defenses, and help him get to the truth. *(Sarah tosses it in the coffee. Chuck enters and sits down with Sarah. He's a grim man who should be incarcerated.)*

SARAH: Good morning, honey!

CHUCK: Yeah? Is that what it is?

SARAH: Would you like some porridge?

CHUCK: Sure, that's what I'd like. Some goddam porridge. Maybe then we can eat some cement. *(Loudly.)* What I want is a freaking cheeseburger!

SARAH: I'll tell the girl.

CHUCK: We coulda gone anywhere and we come to this lousy little dump where all they speak is English. For Chrissakes we coulda gone to Florida, and you push this on me. Like it's going to make me a better person. No TV, no *USA Today;* let me tell you one thing, babe, you got your way now, but I'll get my way in the end.

SARAH: Chuck! Please.

(Sarah gets up and goes to the kitchen. Alice is reading the paper. Chuck looks around, then furtively drops some pills in Sarah's coffee. Sarah comes back.)

SARAH: So…what would you like to do today?

CHUCK: Maybe we can find some more funny rocks to stare at.

SARAH: Ssh! My friend Alice goes there every day!

CHUCK: *(Looks at her.)* That figures. *(Beat.)* I think I'll take the car, try to find a pub with a big screen TV. Maybe catch some bowling or something. Get drunk on my ass. Pick up some wench. Come back and wreck the room and puke on your clothes.

SARAH: What about me? This is my honeymoon, too.

CHUCK: I don't think you need to worry about planning your day.

SARAH: Why?

CHUCK: Let's just say I planned it for you.

ALICE: *(Looks at watch.)* Damn! I don't think he made it.

(Just then Claude enters. He looks a bit confused.)

ALICE: Hi, Claude. Over here.

(Claude takes another table. He nods at Alice without recognition.)

ALICE: It's me, honey. Alice.

(Claude gets out a newspaper.)

CHUCK: *(To Alice.)* Give up, sister. He isn't interested.

(Evelyn enters with a bowl of porridge.)

CHUCK: I had the cheeseburger, medium rare.

EVELYN: Very good, sir. *(She puts the bowl of porridge in front of him.)* Me doctor says I'm in excellent health. "Miranda," he said, confusing me with my late sister, "you have the body of a young woman and the mind of a small child. I predict you live to one hundred and twenty." Don't be puttin' your curses on me, I replied. It's all I can do to drag myself through the afternoon. If I were nimble enough I'd leap in front of a speeding bus. *(Evelyn exits.)*

CHUCK: *(To Sarah.)* Does this look anything like a cheeseburger to you? Does it?

SARAH: I'm sorry, Chuck.

CHUCK: I need some male companionship. All this girl-talk is making me angry.
> *(He goes over to Claude's table. Sarah is alone with her porridge, which she tries to eat.)*

CHUCK: Hey, bud. On your own?

CLAUDE: I think so.

CHUCK: You wanna raise some hell today? Drink too much, drive too fast, buy some guns, see what happens?

CLAUDE: No thank you.

CHUCK: *(Shrugs.)* It's your life. *(Chuck takes a big swig of coffee. The medication starts to hit him.)*

CLAUDE: *(To Chuck.)* Hey, do you know that woman over there?

CHUCK: Alice something. Frankly, I think you're wasting your time.

CLAUDE: I think she's a beauty. Would you mind introducing me?

CHUCK: Hey, Alice! Mind if this twerp talks to you?

ALICE: Not at all.
> *(With great ceremony, Claude goes over to Alice's table. He brings a flower that was in a vase on his table. Sarah watches this, envious.)*

CLAUDE: My name is Claude.

ALICE: Hello, Claude. Won't you join me?

CLAUDE: I'd be delighted. *(He sits down with her.)* I couldn't take my eyes off you from the time I walked in here. There's something about you. Something special.

ALICE: There's something special about you, too, Claude.

CLAUDE: Are you traveling with someone?

ALICE: I'm all alone.

CLAUDE: You're the most beautiful woman I've ever seen. I hope you don't think I'm too forward, but I was wondering if you'd like to take a trip with me today. I got a brochure in the lobby. There's this place not too far from here. An ancient place, full of mystery. Stonehenge. I'd like to see it …and I'd like for you to go with me…if you could.

ALICE: I'd love to. Thank you for asking. I think we should leave right away. I've heard it's better in the early morning, before all the tour busses show up.

CLAUDE: There's so much I want to know about you, Alice. I feel as though I've been looking for you my whole life.

ALICE: We've got all the time in the world, Claude.
> *(They smile at each other. Then they get up and leave, with Alice taking his arm. Sarah is watching them.)*

SARAH: Remember when it was like that, Chuck? Whatever happened to us?

CHUCK: *(Dreamily.)* I don't know. I don't know anything anymore. *(Chuck sees Sarah about to drink her coffee.)* Sarah! Stop!

SARAH: What is it?

CHUCK: Don't drink that coffee!

SARAH: *(Puts the cup down.)* Chuck? Are you all right?

CHUCK: I feel so strange. So calm. Like I'm seeing things for the first time. There's poison in the coffee, Sarah. I put it there myself.

SARAH: You've been trying to kill me this whole honeymoon, haven't you?

CHUCK: Yes. But now I see it's something else I'm angry at. How hard my life has been, having to eat small animals, that kind of thing. It makes a man nasty. And you having everything. I start to hate you for loving me. And then I think "would I hate her less if she didn't love me so much?" And then I start to get confused. And when a man gets confused, he has to take immediate action. I'm sorry, Sarah. *(Beat.)* Why am I talking this way? I could be on any number of daytime talk shows.

SARAH: I put something in *your* coffee, Chuck.

CHUCK: What?

SARAH: It wasn't poison. Just some medication that Alice gave me when I told her you were trying to kill me.

CHUCK: Whatever it is, I want to hold onto this. I want to hold onto everything I know right now. I've spent my whole life trying to avoid what I now feel. *(Beat.)* Would you like to go to Stonehenge today?

SARAH: Stonehenge? You really want to go?

CHUCK: I think today I might understand it.

(They stand up.)

SARAH: Will you promise me one thing, Chuck?

CHUCK: Anything.

SARAH: Will you drive on the right side of the road?

CLAUDE: Yes, darling. For you I will do that.

(They leave, very much together, just as Evelyn enters from kitchen. She sees the full cup of coffee on the table where Sarah was sitting. She picks it up.)

EVELYN: Coffee's still no good?

(No response, as Chuck and Sarah leave. Evelyn shrugs, drinks the coffee, piles up the dishes, and goes into the kitchen. A beat, then an enormous CRASH. Blackout.)

END OF PLAY

Telephone
by Ginna Hoben

CHARACTERS
DANNY

J.T.

SAM

KELLY

CHRIS

Telephone

The stage is split. The action is simultaneous, but spaces separate. On left, Danny and J.T. are seated at a table playing cards. On stage right is Kelly. There are boxes around her. She has been packing to move.

DANNY: So, you wanna go do something?

J.T.: Sure.

DANNY: What do you wanna do?

J.T.: I dunno.

DANNY: Well, where you wanna go?

J.T.: I don't care.

(Sam enters on stage right; pause, she gives Kelly a hug.)

KELLY: We broke up.

SAM: What happened?

KELLY: It's kinda a long story. Wanna drink?

SAM: I'll get 'em. What do you want?

KELLY: All I have is vodka and diet coke. Does that go together?

SAM: It does tonight.

(Sam searches around in some boxes for the vodka. Then she rummages around in a tiny refrigerator for the diet coke. They continue to fix the drinks and "chat" silently during the stage left exchange. Chris enters into the stage left scene. He walks straight to the fridge, grabs a beer, and walks off to his room.)

DANNY: What the hell was that?

J.T.: I dunno.

(Door slam.)

DANNY: Shit. He just went to see Kelly.

J.T.: She's leavin' tomorrow, isn't she?

SAM: Ooh, you have tonic way in the back!

KELLY: Okay, but take it easy on the vodka. Tomorrow's gonna be a long day as it is.

DANNY: I think he was gonna try and talk her out of it.

J.T.: Good fucking luck! She is the most stubborn girl I know. You can't reason with her.

KELLY: He couldn't be reasoned with. He just kept saying that what I'm doing is wrong. And I said, tell me you don't like my choice, or you don't understand, but don't tell me I'm wrong.

SAM: And what did he say?

KELLY: He said, "I think what you're doing is wrong. I think it's selfish and I think it's wrong." Basically, he can't stand the thought of my living with another man.

SAM: But, Scottie's gay.

DANNY: Yeah, but did you hear about this gay guy she's living with?

J.T.: That's fucking crazy. I don't blame him. I'd be pissed too.

SAM: So, what's the big deal?

KELLY: It's not a big deal! Which is why, during this argument, all I can think is, "Who is this guy in front of me?"

DANNY: Well I don't think it's such a big deal.

J.T.: That's because you, Danny-boy, are a little light in the loafers yourself.

DANNY: Shut up!

SAM: So, what are you gonna do?

KELLY: What do you mean? My car is loaded, I signed a lease...I...I...I'm moving, that's what I'm doing.

SAM: Just like that? I mean, will you call him before you go?

KELLY: No. *(Pause.)* Do you think I should?

SAM: I don't...I mean, yeah. Do you?

KELLY: I...I...

(*Chris comes back in the room, throws the beer away, grabs another, sits down at the table.*)

CHRIS: I'm in. I'll deal. *(Picks up the cards and starts to deal.)* Where are we goin' tonight?

J.T.: I don't know who you're kidding. It's already midnight. I gotta work tomorrow.

DANNY: I'll go out.

(*Beat.*)

CHRIS: Never mind. Let's just play cards.

(*They play in silence.*)

J.T.: So, Kelly all packed up and ready to go?

CHRIS: *(Shrugs.)* I guess so.

J.T.: Well, didn't you just come from there?

CHRIS: Yep.

J.T.: I thought you were gonna help her with the move.

CHRIS: She doesn't need any help. She's got the homo to help her move.

J.T.: Oh. Was he there?

CHRIS: Not while I was there.

J.T.: Oh.

DANNY: So, you're not goin' to Chicago this weekend?

CHRIS: Nope.

DANNY: Is she pissed?

CHRIS: I don't know.

J.T.: What the fuck happened?

CHRIS: We broke up.

KELLY: I can't believe we broke up.

DANNY: Shut up.

CHRIS: She wanted it.

KELLY: *(Overlapping.)* It's what he wanted.
> *(J.T. laughs, shakes his head.)*

CHRIS: What are you laughing at?

J.T.: Because that phone is gonna ring within the next ten hours and your ass is goin' to Chicago to help your girlfriend move. That's why.

CHRIS: The fuck I am.

J.T.: That phone is gonna ring.

CHRIS: I'll bet you $500 it won't be her.

J.T.: Whatever. We'll see.

CHRIS: Dude, she's moving in with another guy. She doesn't give a shit what I think about it. She wouldn't even hear me out. I mean, you should have seen it, she literally put her hands over her ears. I've never see her act so selfish. *(Beat.)* I support her, but I'm just not gonna sit here while she's livin' with another dude, whoever the hell it is.

J.T.: Man, I can't blame you. That's fucked up.
> *(They play cards. Silence. The phone rings. Chris continues to play cards. The other two look at one another. The phone rings again. No one moves.)*

J.T.: *(Stands to answer the phone.)* $500?
> *(No response. He answers the phone.)*

J.T.: Chris and Danny's house. *(Pause. He hangs up the phone.)* She hung up.

CHRIS: It wasn't her.

J.T.: Do you have star-sixty-nine?

CHRIS: Just sit the hell down and play.

J.T.: I want my five hundred bucks.

CHRIS: Fuck you.

(Phone rings again.)

J.T.: Hello? *(Hangs up.)* She's quick.

(Back to the girls. They're both a little drunk. Kelly is on the phone. She hangs up.)

SAM: Well?

KELLY: They don't deliver this late.

SAM: No! AAH! I'm starving! This is a crisis. We need Doritos.

KELLY: The crisis is over. I have tortilla chips.

SAM: Not the same.

KELLY: I know, but I have salsa.

SAM: Is it hot, though?

KELLY: Medium.

SAM: Heartburn.

KELLY: *(Softly.)* Heartburn.

SAM: Forget it, we'll take Pepto. Bring out the chips!

(Kelly fusses in the fridge and brings out the food. They sit on the floor in front of the couch.)

SAM: All right. I'm making a toast.

KELLY: To salsa?

SAM: Yes, and to Kelly, because she's getting out of this stupid town and doing what she wants and leaving a crappy boyfriend.

KELLY: Ex-boyfriend.

SAM: Yes, as of two hours ago, ex-boyfriend.

KELLY: He's a jerk.

SAM: You said it!

KELLY: He's oppressive and closed-minded!

SAM: There she goes…

KELLY: And he mixes up subject and object pronouns. I hate that.

SAM: I do that.

KELLY: Well… he's much worse.

SAM: Right, and he… he…what about the time he kicked your cat?

KELLY: *(Shocked.)* He kicked my cat?

SAM: Yeah! Remember?

KELLY: No, but that's good, now I'm really getting mad!

SAM: Yeah!

KELLY: He's a shit!

SAM: …and…

KELLY: And…and I love him.

SAM: *(Quietly.)* I know.

KELLY: I love him, I do, and I can see his point. He doesn't want me to live with another man because he wants to be the first one. He wants to be the one who sees me first thing in the morning and who hears about my bad days and what groceries I buy and what's my favorite midnight snack. He wants to know that stuff and he doesn't want to share that with anyone else.

CHRIS: I shouldn't have to share my girlfriend, right?

DANNY and J.T.: What?

SAM: Did he say that?

KELLY: Yeah.

SAM: *(Impressed.)* Damn.

CHRIS: It's really fucked-up, isn't it?

KELLY: I know. It's really sweet, isn't it?

SAM: Yeah, when you look at it that way. But, on the other hand...

KELLY: He kicked my cat!

(They laugh.)

SAM: Yeah, and all that stuff he said to you about being selfish. Kelly, that's crap.

KELLY: I know! I know, if all I'm missing is his fifth fucking year of college, after I promised to come back and follow him...

CHRIS: ...after our last breakup?

KELLY: ...after I agreed to basically sacrifice my entire career...

CHRIS: ...to watch her kissing other people on stage...

KELLY: ...to be an Army wife.

CHRIS: ...All I want is loyalty.

KELLY: ...All I want is one year!

CHRIS: She's gonna be in a totally different city...

KELLY: ...in a real city, just a year! And he can't even give me that.

CHRIS: She couldn't just wait for me. Why would you leave someone you supposedly love? I just don't think we'd make it if we were that far apart. She obviously disagrees, but what am I supposed to do?

KELLY: What am I going to do? Maybe I should reconsider the whole move...

CHRIS: I don't know, maybe I'm overreacting. I mean, is it worth it?

KELLY: *(Overlapping.)* I mean, is it worth it? It's all a gamble. I could totally fail.

J.T.: Who knows, man.

SAM: I don't know what to say. Of course I want you to stay. I want someone to stay up late and eat nachos with me. But, *you*...you gotta do what's best for you.

J.T.: But you gotta take care of yourself first.

CHRIS: I just figured we'd do all the stuff we wanted to do together.

SAM: Well, I think he thought you two were the perfect couple. I mean, everyone did. And if you're a perfect couple, then you stay together and you have to not do some of the things you want to do because you make the other person a priority.

KELLY: But what if going our separate ways is what makes us the perfect couple? It seems to me that if we stay together, he won't have his dream or I won't have mine and one way or the other, we'll be living with a hell of a lot of resentment. And maybe in a few months, or a year, or two, we will have gained the proper perspective on the whole thing and it will make sense to us, to me, hopefully, why two people so obviously in love are so not together.

(Beat.)

SAM: Get your ass on the phone and tell him that! Kelly, this is about timing. If you don't call now, you'll come back someday and find out that he's in freakin' Korea or something.

KELLY: I can't. I can't. I think I'm having an anxiety attack.

SAM: You are not. Here, have a drink.

KELLY: *(Drinks.)* Damn, Sam. Ever heard of adding a little tonic to a vodka and tonic?

SAM: Sorry. Look, anxiety is natural at this point. It's like we get to this age and feel like we're done with college and so we have to start our real lives and we're all just scared. Scared little pseudo-adults. We all just want something to hang on to. Some people hang on to their jobs, some people stay in school as long as they can. And some people get married.

KELLY: Married.

SAM: You are doing the right thing.

KELLY: I know, but don't think for a second that I won't wish every day that I had my someone perfect to come home to.

(Phone rings. They look at each other. Kelly goes to answer it.)

KELLY: Hello?

(Chris hangs up the phone.)

DANNY: Who was that?

CHRIS: None of your business.

J.T.: It was Kelly. You don't have to be embarrassed. I know you're gonna call her as soon as I leave, anyway.

CHRIS: It wasn't her.

DANNY: Then who else would you call? It's like, one A.M.

J.T.: Danny, pick up the phone and hit the redial button.

CHRIS: Don't do it, Danny.

J.T.: Danny, I'll pay you $20.

DANNY: *(To J.T..)* You do it.

J.T.: And I'll buy your beer tomorrow at Dooley's.

DANNY: All night?

CHRIS: Don't do it, Dan. You'll wish you hadn't.

DANNY: I won't say anything. I'll just wait to hear her voice.

CHRIS: Don't do it, man.

J.T.: All your beer…

(Danny picks up the phone and dials redial. Waits a second. The smile leaves his face. He hangs up the phone. Chris shakes his head.)

DANNY: It was his mom.

J.T.: Shut up!

CHRIS: I told him not to do it.

(Danny picks up the phone and hits redial again.)

DANNY: *(Into phone.)* Mrs. O'Reilly? Hi, it's me, Danny. Sorry 'bout that last call you got. It was me. It was an accident. I just didn't want you to worry. Okay. Uh-huh. I will. Okay, you take care now. Bye. *(Danny sits back down. He feels bad.)* She said to tell you to get some sleep.

(Pause. They all laugh.)

CHRIS: Aww shit. I wish I could.

(They are quiet.)

DANNY: Maybe you should just call her.

CHRIS: I can't. We've done this before. She's got to do what she's wants. I mean, I *want* her to do what she wants. It's why I…you know…that's what I liked about her in the first place. *(Beat.)* And you know what? I think we are meant to be together, but the time just isn't right, you know?

J.T.: Or maybe you're meant for each other, but you're both so bull-headed that you fucked it up.

CHRIS: That could be it too.

(Beat.)

DANNY: I gotta go to bed.

J.T.: Yeah, I gotta go home.

(They stand up from the table.)

J.T.: *(On his way out. To Chris.)* Tell her I said hi.

(Danny punches J.T. on the arm and mouths the words "shut up." J.T. hits him back. They leave. Kelly hangs up her phone. Chris takes his phone off the wall and places it in the center of the table. He puts his chin on his folded arms and stares at the phone.)

KELLY: My mom said to tell you hi.

SAM: Your mom is the best. She gets so mad at these boys when they make you cry.

KELLY: I know.

SAM: Okay, I gotta go. We'll talk all night if I don't leave this instant. Besides I'm eating all your food. Hug?

KELLY: I'm gonna miss you.

SAM: We're not gonna do a big good-bye, okay?

KELLY: I know, I know. I'll see you in a couple of months anyway.

SAM: Right. Call me soon.

(She leaves. Kelly walks over to the phone and speaks at it without picking up the receiver.)

KELLY: Call me, you jerk. I don't want to leave you.

CHRIS: I don't want you to go.

KELLY: How did this happen?

BOTH: Is this what you want?

KELLY: I'm miserable.

CHRIS: I'm miserable.

KELLY: Call me, you jerk.

(Chris picks up the phone receiver, shakes his head, hangs up.)

CHRIS: I can't.

KELLY: You're not gonna call. I know you. You are being proud.

CHRIS: *(Overlapping.)* I have to have some pride.

KELLY: Fine. I'll be the mature one.

(She picks up the phone receiver.)

CHRIS: Why am I always the one to call?

(Kelly dials six digits.)

CHRIS: She can call me.

BOTH: *(Exasperated.)* I'm too bull-headed.

(Kelly hangs up the phone.)

KELLY: I can't.

BOTH: I hate this.

CHRIS: The timing…

KELLY: Why is it like this…?

CHRIS: …with you and I…

KELLY: …with you and *me*…it's not…

CHRIS: The timing…

KELLY: …right.

CHRIS: Damn! This isn't how it was supposed to go.

BOTH: This is all your fault!

KELLY: It's my fault. I hate you so much.

CHRIS: *(Overlapping.)* I hate you.

KELLY: I wouldn't hate you this much if I didn't love you. *(Beat.)* And now I have to move all this shit alone!

CHRIS: I'm never falling in love again.

KELLY: I'm never gonna get married.

CHRIS: And fuck marriage.

KELLY: We were gonna have kids.

CHRIS: Good thing I didn't buy the ring.

KELLY: *(Overlapping.)* You shoulda just bought me a ring.

BOTH: It's all about timing.

CHRIS: She still woulda left.

KELLY: I wouldn't have left.

(They stare at their phones.)

KELLY: Call me, you jerk!

(Chris slowly picks up the phone.)

KELLY: Uhhh!

BOTH: I can't do this all night.

(He dials her number. Kelly takes her phone off the hook.)

BOTH: This is crazy.

END OF PLAY

Scruples
by Jon Jory

CHARACTERS

LOIS
JANE
MARTI
MRS. DOBBS
MR. SKILES

TIME AND PLACE

The present. A waiting room.

Scruples

Four woman sit in a waiting room. Silence.

They smile nervously at each other. They look away.

Pause.

LOIS: *(Throws a fit in a minor way.)* Aaaaaarrrrgggh!
   (They look at her, startled.)
LOIS: Just thought I'd admit the tension. Anybody want licorice?
JANE: No, thanks.
MARTI: *(Indecisive.)* Ummmm.
LOIS: *(Handing it over.)* Take it.
MARTI: *(Regards it as if it were from outer space.)* Ummmm.
LOIS: You'll have to pull some off yourself; I don't like to touch it. Don't you
   hate to think about how they keep this stuff soft? Think about ingesting
   chemicals that keep things limp indefinitely. Brrrr.
   (Marti hands it back to her wihout eating any.)
LOIS: Listen, what are we doing here?
MARTI: Doing? *(Pause.)* Here?
JANE: In the larger sense, or the smaller sense?
LOIS: In the smaller sense.
JANE: We're auditioning for a Nightsilk commercial.
MARTI: Yeah!
LOIS: *(Regards Marti a moment and then speaks to Jane.)* Well, you've identified
   my problem; what's Nightsilk?
JANE: *(Deadpan, unsmiling, quoting.)* Pantythose, with the elegant sheen of the
   autumn moon on glass-smooth water. Pantyhose so luxurious, so limpid,
   so delicately sensual you will experience across the centuries the serene
   confidence of the Chinese empresses.
   (A pause.)
MARTI: *(Sincerely.)* That was *so* good.
   (A pause.)

LOIS: Jesus!

MARTI: *(Startled.)* What?

LOIS: It's worse than I thought.

JANE: *(Infinitesimally defensive.)* What's worse?

LOIS: Having principles. Having principles is worse.

JANE: You dropped your licorice.

LOIS: See, I dropped my licorice. Great. I dropped my licorice. Wonderful.
    (To Jane.) Would you mind telling me if you're an idealist?

JANE: No, I'm not an idealist.

LOIS: I wanted to eat this licorice.
    (Pause.)

MARTI: I'm an idealist.

LOIS: You're an idealist?

MARTI: Ummmmm.

LOIS: In what sense?

MARTI: In what sense?

LOIS: *(Carefully.)* In what sense are you an idealist?

MARTI: *(Pause.)* Sort of in the sense of hoping for the best.

LOIS: In art?

MARTI: In art?

LOIS: In art, in art.

MARTI: Oh, art.
    (A pause.)

LOIS: *(Tense.)* Do you hope for the best in art?

JANE: Excuse me. When I go up for a commercial, I have to face the fact I am
    one of several hundred women competing for the attention of a casting
    agent with the I.Q. of a chimpanzee and the hostility of a king cobra. In
    that situation it's really a lot better to be calm and centered if you know
    what I mean, and I find that silence is a real help.

LOIS: Really?

JANE: Yes.

LOIS: Wow. *(A pause.)* I find it's such a dehumanizing process that making
    contact with the other women gives me a perspective that allows me to go
    on living. *(Pause.)* So I like to talk.

MARTI: See, I feel you both have better legs.
    (A pause.)

LOIS: Goddammit!

MARTI: What?

LOIS: I don't think we should talk about it.

(A pause.)

JANE: *(Against her better judgment.)* What?

LOIS: I really shouldn't start. *(A pause—to Jane.)* Do you really want to know?

(A pause.)

JANE: Moderately.

(A pause.)

LOIS: All right. *(A pause—when she starts, she goes very fast.)* First of all, I'm an actress. An actress. I am personally committed to holding a mirror up to nature. To show not only what *is* but what *can be*. To say *yes* to life. To illuminate the soul, penetrate literature, and apply the electric shock of truth to a society which is practically moribund and so confused it celebrates form over content and acquisition instead of perception. So, auditioning for a commercial is betrayal on the deepest level of the very vocation I've made central to my existence, but let's not worry about *that!*

JANE: Okay.

LOIS: Let's look at it on a societal basis. Let's take it in terms of images internalized by millions of viewers which provide the raw material for their attitude *toward* and misconceptions *of* women.

JANE: Maybe I'll have a piece of licorice.

LOIS: *(Tearing a strip off and handing it to her while she talks.)* Women are smooth, women are silky, women are meant to be touched. The most important part of women is below the waist, and all, all of this can be enhanced or possessed for less than three dollars a pair. So that both as an artist and a woman I am actively involved in demanding what, up to this point, I have proudly defined as my ideals, my talent, myself, and my body. Is that clear?

JANE: I think I took it in.

MARTI: But you really do have good legs, though.

JANE: I have a very big phone bill. All the people I ever liked now live in Seattle. I am way behind on my rent on a recently remodeled two-level linen closet on the Upper West Side which is about to go condo. I support my boyfriend who has trained for ten years for a classical theater that does not exist, and, currently, the only food in my place is a case of Golden Grahams Crunchy Wheat and Marshmallow breakfast cereal which I won in a telephone promotion. It is perfectly all right with me if they show pictures of legs on television, because it is the truth that I *have* legs, and thus, showing them *is* holding the mirror up to nature.

LOIS: *(Gently.)* You have a slave mentality.

MARTI: Do you have to say lines?

JANE: Lines?

MARTI: I've been a hand and foot model for six years. My dream is to say lines.
> *(Pause.)*

JANE: I think it's legs and a voice-over.

MARTI: Oh.
> *(Pause.)*

JANE: *(Needled.)* For thousands of years people earned their bread by having A—strong arms, B—a strong back, C—strong legs. Just because men view legs as hors d'oeuvres is no reason I have to hide the fact I'm healthy. Plus, lest we forget, truth and beauty. I quote Keats, or somebody, "Beauty is truth, truth Beauty. That is all you know on earth, and all you need to know," or something. I am here defending Beauty, the ideal. To say someone has beautiful legs, you must first idealize the leg, then you judge the leg against the ideal, and the one that comes closest gets the commercial. To the irate feminist I say beauty transcends oppression. The answer to your question is, they keep licorice soft with a chemical called anticoasnibromizine, which is a carcinogen that will eventually melt your intestines and kill you.
> *(Pause.)*

MARTI: I think silence is the greatest sin. I feel so much, but I can't say it. It would be a great step forward for me to speak in front of people on television.
> *(Pause.)*

LOIS: Is Nightsilk pantyhose a good product?

JANE: I don't know.

LOIS: Is it ever right to compromise your ideals for money?

JANE: Yes.

LOIS: I think it's pretty clear that my legs are better than yours, so if I stay here I will get the commercial and you won't.

JANE: In that case, it is wrong to compromise your ideals for money.

LOIS: I'm very close to getting a good role in a Spanish movie about transcending gender in politics that means a great deal to me, but they want to see film on me, any kind of film, so I came here thinking it would be all right to compromise my principles so that I could act on them later.

JANE: You're a very confused person, Lois.

MARTI: My dad raced stock cars, and he used to say that once you got over 130 miles an hour the most dangerous thing to your health was thinking.

(A pause—an efficient woman in a suit enters.)

MRS. DOBBS: *(Pleasant, straightforward, and without artifice.)* Good morning.

LOIS: Good morning.

JANE: Good morning.

(They all look at Marti. She waves.)

MRS. DOBBS: I am glad to see you, Lois, Jane, and Marti. I am Letitia Dobbs.

JANE: Hello, Mrs. Dobbs.

LOIS: Hello, Letitia.

MARTI: *(A pause.)* Hi.

MRS. DOBBS: I handle East Coast casting for Nightsilk pantyhose. The three of you, selected from hundreds of young women, are our final callbacks not for simply *a* commerical, but for a series of commercials, filmed over a two-year period, which the winner will find very, very, very, very, very, very lucrative. Nightsilk, realizing that its products could be categorized as trivial and cognizant that unpopular animal research is crucial to developing world-class pantyhose is donating two cents a pair to African famine relief, which on our annual sales of over a billion dollars will provide over two million dollars of food supplies, so you will be not only body parts but spokespersons and benefactors. Thus, while only your legs will be filmed, we will be wanting you to do a good deal of speaking and traveling on our behalf. Please remember also that legs are not simply sculptural, not simply matter. There are millions of technically attractive legs, but they can be more, much more. Legs can be infused with a sense of self and spirit which animates them on camera and communicates to the viewer with damaged self-esteem new goals and new hope. A beautiful soul makes beautiful legs, and Nightsilk, by enchancing the leg, enhances the soul.

(Jane applauds.)

MRS. DOBBS: Thank you. We are, mincing no words, looking for an uncommon woman for an uncommon job in uncommon times. The callback will begin with a forty-minute in-depth interview exploring your world view and your attitudes toward both our project and our product. Then, of course, in a monitored environment we will be asking you to take off your clothes. Please relax and center yourself for this exciting and challenging process. My assistant, Mr. Skiles will be around shortly with fruit frappes and nibbles. Nightsilk pantyhose apologizes that we are running... *(Checks her watch.)* forty minutes behind schedule; we know your time is valuable. I can tell by speaking with you that you are lovely and intelligent young women with caring and remarkable parents. Are there any questions?

(Pause.)

MARTI: Is there a ladies' room?

MRS. DOBBS: *(Pleasant as always.)* No, I'm afraid not. *(To all of them.)* Good luck. *(She exits.)*

(A pause.)

LOIS: *(In complete moral conflict.)* Dammit!! *(She gets up, starts to leave, stops, returns, and sits down.)*

(Tears run down Marti's face.)

JANE: *(To Marti.)* It's okay. You'll do fine.

(A good-looking young man in a suit enters with a brightly colored plastic tray with coffee, cups, sugar, and cream. He stops.)

MR. SKILES: Hey, babes. I'm Ricky Skiles, Mrs. Dobbs' lackey and designated fantasy sex object. Any of you gorgeous gams looking for a hit of caffeine?

END OF PLAY

The Processional
by Robert D. Kemnitz and Jennifer McMaster

209

CHARACTERS

PASTOR

DILLON

FAY

JAROD

JACKIE

The Processional

A small (black box) church. There are two podiums on either side of the stage.
For the altar, two or three padded steps for kneeling.

At rise, the Pastor and Dillon stand by the altar.

PASTOR: Okay, I know we're all a little tired. But… Once more with feeling.
   (Jarod, the Best Man, escorts Jackie, Maid of Honor, towards the altar.)
PASTOR: Good, good. It's not a funeral, we can put a little pizazz into it.
   (Jarod and Jackie part in front of the Pastor and go to their respective sides.)
PASTOR: And of course tomorrow we will be in step together. Now the Father
   of the Bride takes the Bride-to-Be by the arm to lead the procession.
   (Dillon tries to conceal a yawn.)
PASTOR: *(To Dillon.)* I'm sorry, are we boring you?
   (Fay enters, trying to step to unheard music. She carries with her the bouquet
   of wilted bows and ribbons from last weekend's shower.)
PASTOR: Lovely, lovely—where's the Father of the Bride?
DILLON: He left.
PASTOR: Oh?
DILLON: About thirty minutes ago. He left after the fifth reprise of "O Promise
   Me."
FAY: He said we could meet him and Mother at the restaurant.
PASTOR: Well, apparently he's not as concerned with his daughter's wedding
   as I am. I guess he'll just have to wing it. Generally, I don't approve of
   improvisational weddings. I certainly hope your father doesn't spoil the
   whole ceremony because he had better things to do the night of the
   rehearsal. A wedding day is not a day for surprises. *(To Fay.)* You
   wouldn't want that. On your wedding day.
FAY: Actually, we are looking forward to some surprises.
   (Fay giggles. Dillon beams.)
JACKIE: Fay!
PASTOR: Oh, expecting the big screen TV, are we?
FAY: Something like that.

JAROD: Do we know how much longer…?

PASTOR: I see everyone's got big plans for the evening—I'm sorry to hold you up. But as I explained in my one, brief meeting with Dillon and Fay, I like things to be done right, and I like things to be done my way, and my way is the right way. Of course, we didn't have much time to go over the details, since we only met once, briefly, last week—Tuesday was it?—after I hadn't seen Fay since her confirmation when she was fourteen years old and Dillon, upon whom I had never laid eyes prior to our one, brief meeting. For all I know he's a Catholic.

DILLON: Lutheran.

PASTOR: Whatever. Let's get on with it, shall we. *(Everyone relaxes.)* My critique of the opening pageant is charitable at best. The entrances set the whole tone for the ceremony, and right now I'm greatly concerned—the rhythm is off and the gait is, well, downright downtrodden.

(Quiet grumbles.)

PASTOR: But in the interest of time, we won't go back. I will say a few remarks, dearly beloved, please be seated, that sort of thing, and now, the first scripture reading. I believe the Best Man will be doing the honors.

JAROD: Yes…sir.

PASTOR: Well then?

JAROD: Well—I've been practicing, I think it'll be fine. I don't think we need to hold up things for me.

PASTOR: Oh, you don't, do you? I for one would like to hear it this time round. Those Bible passages can be tricky for plebeians. *(Jarod hesitates.)* Today, son!

(Jarod sprints to the podium. He extracts a crumpled piece of paper from his pocket.)

JAROD: The first reading today is from I, Corinthians— *(He pronounces it "aye.")*

PASTOR: That's First Corinthians.

JAROD: First Corinthians, yes, right, Chapter 7, Verse 1: *(Boldly, and gaining boldness.)* "It is well for a man not to touch a woman. But because of the temptation to immorality, each man should have his own wife and each woman her own husband. The husband should give to his wife her conjugal rights, and likewise the wife to her husband. For the wife does not rule over her own body, but the husband does; likewise the husband does not rule over his own body, but the wife does. Do not refuse one another except perhaps by agreement for a season, that you may devote yourselves to prayer; but then come together again, lest Satan tempt you through lack of self-control. To the unmarried and the widows I say that it is well for them to remain single as I do. But if they cannot exercise self-control, they should marry. For it is better to marry than to be aflame with passion."

FAY and DILLON: Amen.

PASTOR: *(Long pause.)* That's…the passage you chose for your first scripture reading?

FAY: Yes. Isn't it romantic?

DILLON: Well done, Jarod.

PASTOR: Bombastic, to say the least. Did you, by any chance, listen to the words?

DILLON: Of course.

FAY: I know it by heart.

PASTOR: And this is the first scripture you chose to begin your new life as man and wife?

DILLON: *Husband* and wife.

PASTOR: You're prepared for your family and friends to hear these words as a testament to your life together?

FAY: Not just hear it—we've had it printed on the reception napkins. "For it is better to marry…"

DILLON: It is right out of the Bible.

PASTOR: Ah, yes. "Aye" Corinthians, as we've just discovered. What I mean is, it's very…"Old Testament"—do you know? Today, in modern times, we are allowed to interpret the Word of the Lord—

DILLON: No room for interpretation there.

FAY: It says everything we want to say, just how we would say it.

JAROD: *(From podium.)* Can I come down now?

PASTOR: Yes, perhaps you should. Before we invoke the seven plagues.

(Jarod moves back to his position. The Pastor takes a moment.)

PASTOR: Well, I'll have to come up with something to follow that. Maybe I can address it in my sermon.

DILLON: I hate to rush you, but we do have quite a few people waiting for us at the dinner.

PASTOR: Of course, wouldn't want your guests to hog all the stuffed mushrooms, now would we. The church can wait, the rumaki cannot!

DILLON: It's not that I don't appreciate—

PASTOR: No, no, you're quite right. I think that we should move on to the second reading, and yes, I'd love to hear it. I think that's you, Matron of Honor.

JACKIE: Maid of Honor.

PASTOR: I was under the understanding that you were the Matron of Honor.

JACKIE: I was. Until last week. Now I'm the Maid of Honor.

PASTOR: Oh.

JACKIE: It happened pretty quick. Actually, it had been going on for years. First I found out—

PASTOR: *(Changing the subject.)* Which brings up the Maid of Honor with the second scripture reading.

(Jackie moves up to the other pulpit, a deer caught in the headlights.)

JACKIE: *(Meekly.)* The second reading is from Ezekiel, Chapter 16, Verse 30.

(She gently clears her throat. Bellowing.) "Wherefore, O harlot, hear the Word of the Lord! Because your shame was laid bare and your nakedness uncovered in your harlotries with your lovers… Therefore, behold, I will gather all your lovers, with whom you took pleasure, all those you loved and all those you loathed. And I will judge you as women who break wedlock and shed blood are judged, and bring upon you the blood of wrath and jealousy. And I will give you into the hand of your lovers, and they shall throw down your vaulted chamber and break down your lofty places; they shall strip you of your clothes and take your fair jewels, and leave you naked and bare. They shall bring up a host against you, and they shall stone you and cut you to pieces with their swords—"

PASTOR: Stop! Stop! You're melting the pulpit!

JACKIE: Did I do something wrong?

PASTOR: Are you packing snakes?

DILLON: She's just a little tired.

PASTOR: Now, I like to think I know Ezekial, he's an inspiration to us all—but this? Why in God's name did you choose this?

FAY: Because it expresses our feelings about sin and immorality and jealousy and shame and sex out of wedlock.

DILLON: It couldn't be any clearer.

PASTOR: No, it sure couldn't. The blood and wrath of jealousy I'm all for, but your nakedness uncovered in your harlotries…? Wait. You two haven't done the nasty.

DILLON: Your use of the term nasty speaks volumes.

PASTOR: Actually it speaks Genesis to Revelation. Had we had more meetings, maybe we could have covered this. I, of course, just assumed you two had been familiar with one another.

FAY: We're very familiar with one another.

DILLON: She clips her toenails in the bathroom sink.

FAY: He eats M&Ms for breakfast.

PASTOR: I meant familiar in the Biblical sense. I've had a feeling all along about this wedding—something wrong. I knew it, but I couldn't quite put my finger on it. This nagging doubt...

FAY: That's why we've been stuck here for two and a half hours? You've held us hostage all this time because something didn't sit right with you?

PASTOR: Frankly. Yes.

DILLON: You have no right to do that. It's your job to marry us!

PASTOR: This is not McDonald's. I don't have a sign over my sacristy reading "two billion served." And you will not get fries with this.

JAROD: Can we not talk about food right now? I'm starving.

PASTOR: I'm just worried that the two of you haven't really made the commitment, that you're not taking this wedding seriously.

DILLON: I don't see how we could take it more seriously!

FAY: Doesn't our abstinence prove just how serious we are?

PASTOR: It proves that you're taking your Bible, or worse, your Bible School teachings, at face value, that you're not even considering the institution of marriage as a practical, everyday, same as it ever was, mundane situation. That it means more than sharing your lives and your mortgages and your bad days and your tremendously awful days and your really horrifically lousy days and your toenails and your M&Ms together—it means sharing your bed together! Do either of you two know what that means? No, of course you can't, because you haven't had sex!

FAY: But...we have had sex.

PASTOR: You have?

DILLON: Yes, of course.

PASTOR: But you said—

FAY: Well, not with each other.

PASTOR: Beg your pardon?

FAY: Dillon and I have had scads of sex, but we're saving ourselves now for each other.

PASTOR: This doesn't make any sense.

DILLON: It makes perfect sense. Both Fay and I have led reasonably fruitful lives—

FAY: Sex, sex, sex...

DILLON: —But when we met each other, we both knew we had found the one, so—

FAY: So, we decided to abstain, to make our wedding day that much more special.

JACKIE: That's beautiful.

PASTOR: That's weird.

JAROD: Sounds weird to me too, but I'm not the one getting married.

PASTOR: Well, I suppose I'm not the one getting married either.

JAROD: And I can't think of two people who belong together more.

JACKIE: Me neither.

FAY: *(Looking at Dillon.)* Me neither.

(Pause.)

PASTOR: Okay. You're obviously in love. You want to spend the rest of your lives together. You both have some sort of strange affinity for overwrought Biblical passages. Fine. But in this day and age, why do you want to get *married?*

(Dillon and Fay look at each other for a moment, then...)

DILLON and FAY: The presents.

PASTOR: The presents?

JAROD and JACKIE: Why else would anyone get married?

PASTOR: I see. Yes, I see... And frightfully, I understand. This wedding has my complete and utter blessing, and the four of you have a dinner to get to. Let's run it down one more time, just for luck.

(Groans, and the Pastor holds his hands up to squelch their objections. As the Pastor narrates, the others act out the scenario.)

PASTOR: Okay, family enters, Mother over here, other mother over here, bridesmaids-slash-groomsmen, very nice— *(Pointing to Jackie and Jarod.)* You two, in step, good, now Father-of-the-Bride leads in the Bride, everyone stands, she's crying, his tux is too tight, Groom and Bride center themselves around me, I greet, I pray, everyone be seated. *(Pointing to Jarod, then Jackie.)* Old Testament over here conjures up the holy spirit, followed by Mrs., I mean, Miss Fire and Brimstone, who brings the house down. I chat lightly with the convened to explain just how much matrimony means in the eyes of the church, everyone's enthralled, this couple is an example to us all, et cetera, do you take so-and-so to be your lawful whatever to love, honor, and obey—

FAY and DILLON: Cherish!

PASTOR: Cherish, lovely, does anyone object, let's hope not and I now pronounce you *husband* and wife. Snappy guitar music from the bohemian in the fold-out chair next to the video tripod. The wedding party exits, stepping lively, and there you have it.

JAROD: What about the kiss?

PASTOR: Right. The kiss. You may now kiss the Bride. Go ahead, give it a good trial run.

(Dillon and Fay stare at each other.)

(They move closer, but are blocked by Dillon's nose.)

(They counter and are blocked by Fay's nose.)

(Finally, they tentatively kiss as if for the first time.)

PASTOR: Mazel Tov.

END OF PLAY

Mixed Emotions
by Bob Krakower

CHARACTERS

ED: He loves Lex. Just visiting…maybe.

MICHAEL: He loves Lex. And he lives here.

MOIRA: Lex's roommate. Having an affair with Jack.

JACK: In love with Moira, but he's married. Ed's closest friend.

LEX (short for Alexa): Spent last night with Ed. Moving in with Michael.

TIME AND PLACE

Day. Outside. In front of the office of the Mission Rock Café.

Mixed Emotions

Lex—pacing in front of a bench.

Michael enters. Carrying duffel bag, etc.

MICHAEL: *(As he enters, to Jack offstage.)* I'm just going to the office to get something. Hey, Lex.

LEX: Hey, Michael.

MICHAEL: Shit, I don't have my keys. Jack?
(Ed enters.)

LEX: Hi.

ED: Hi. You're here.

MICHAEL: Jack…?

LEX: I have, ya know, the thing—

MICHAEL: …you got your office keys?

ED: The *thing*. The meeting. Right, well. Good. Well, um, can I talk to you?

LEX: About what?
(Jack enters, with bags, etc.)

MICHAEL: You got your keys to the—just ah, put those down for a minute and then we'll move them to the van. Hey, Lex. *(He kisses her on the cheek.)*

LEX: Hi.

JACK: I don't have 'em on me. They're back in the car. *(To Ed.)* Great!!! You're here already. Have a good time? Take one of these, Michael.

LEX: Have a good time doing what?

ED: I was hoping I'd see you here.

LEX: Oh. *(Pause.)* I wanted to see you, too.

MICHAEL: *(Hugs them both.)* And I wanted to see the both of you.

JACK: Let's keep moving these in the van, Michael, the keys are back in the car.

MICHAEL: Yeah, but…

JACK: How are you this morning, Lex?

LEX: I'd say very, *very* good, Jack. Thank you.

JACK: This is good.

MICHAEL: *(To Ed.)* You and Lex have a good dinner last night?

JACK: Michael, can we just…

ED: Huh? Oh, yes. Thank you.

MICHAEL: Michaelangelo's, man, best Italian in town. Worth coming back for, huh?

ED: There's a lot worth coming back for.

JACK: Let's just take these and then come back, Michael, just keep moving and then—

MICHAEL: Ya know, Eddie, there's something I wanna tell ya.

JACK: Michael, can you tell him on the way to the airport—

ED: What's up?

JACK: Michael, please.

MICHAEL: Ya know, Ed, before you came to town, Lex and I, we weren't getting along very well and—

JACK: Michael, I'll tell you what…why don't you go back in the car and get the office keys and I'll transfer these to the van—

LEX: What he's saying is we'll be sorry to see you go.

ED: I was thinking just this morning that I really didn't *wanna* go.

(*Moira enters.*)

MOIRA: Ready to go?

MICHAEL: Hey, Moira.

MOIRA: Hi.

LEX: Hey, Moira.

MOIRA: Lex. I thought you said—

LEX: I lied.

JACK: You look terrific, Moira.

MICHAEL: You know Eddie, now that we're all here, I just wanted to tell ya because I don't think anybody really has, how great it's been to have you here.

ED: It's been great to be here.

MICHAEL: Lex and I were talking yesterday—

LEX: Michael.

MICHAEL: You said we oughta thank him.

LEX: I didn't mean now.

ED: Thank me?

LEX: Nothing, really.

MICHAEL: Nothing? You said if it wasn't for Eddie, we…

JACK: …and I'm sure that Eddie here feels good about it because as we all know Michael, if he can bring a little happiness to one person, each and every day of the their life, here on earth, then he knows, that his time is well spent. Now, can we get this kind man on his plane on time? Come, let's go back to the car…

MICHAEL: Look all I'm trying to say is…

LEX: Michael—

MOIRA: Um, Ed, I um, have something for you. A little, well…going away present.

ED: For me?

MICHAEL: You do?

JACK: For *him?*

MOIRA: A little something.

JACK: Why do you have a gift for him?

MICHAEL: You okay?

LEX: Why wouldn't I be?

ED: *(Pause.)* Oh. Hahaha. Thanks. I um, really needed one just like it. Thank you.

JACK: What is that?

MOIRA: An earring that I knew he was looking for.

JACK: Jewelry?

ED: I was. It is. You must be psychic or something.

LEX: Or something.

MICHAEL: Okay! Let's get the rest of the bags out of the car and—

ED: How much time have I got?

MOIRA: We got ten minutes.

MICHAEL: And why didn't we just take, ya know, *drive* the bags right up to the van?

JACK: Because my *wife* needs to keep the car to take my kids, okay—And this is the third time I'm explaining this to you—to *school*—Fuck it, can we just go back to the car and get the rest of the bags?

ED and MOIRA: Relax, Jack.

JACK: Oh that's just great. *(He exits.)*

MICHAEL: What's the matter with him? I was just kidding. Shit, I gotta get the keys for the office. *(He follows Jack.)*

ED: Moira, I think Jack thinks that you and I—

MOIRA: Let him.

ED: Don't you two have a meeting or something?

MOIRA: No, we cancelled it and we're *all* taking you to the airport.

ED: You're kidding.

MOIRA: No, I'm not. Won't that be fun? *(Pause.)* I think I'll join Jack at the car. Have a little chat with him and his *wife. (As she exits.)* What a happy-go-lucky morning this has turned out to be.

ED: So—

LEX: So—

ED: You said you had the meeting.

LEX: Everybody seems a little frazzled today.

ED: So I see.

LEX: How about they take your plane ticket and we both stay here.

ED: You read my mind.

LEX: This doesn't happen to me very often. You?

ED: Never. *(Pause.)* I was, what would you think if—I was thinking about… staying.

LEX: Staying here?

ED: Not leaving.

LEX: With me?

ED: The thing is…I've decided—yes, with you—I've decided to stay.

LEX: Oh my God.

ED: I could get a job here, ya know?

LEX: I know.

ED: And we could be together.

LEX: Ed—

ED: And Lex, there's no one in the world I'd rather be with. I mean the things you said. Last night? Are you glad you said them?

LEX: Absolutely. And I meant them.

ED: Well, I'm glad you're glad.

LEX: Well, I'm glad that you're glad that I'm glad.

ED: Well, I'm glad that you're glad that I'm glad that you're glad that I'm glad—

(Lex's laughing, they move toward each other as Michael enters.)

MICHAEL: So what else did you guys do last night?

LEX: Why don't you go up and get the…

MICHAEL: Oh yes… On my way. *(To Ed.)* You're gonna love this. *(He exits.)*

ED: What did I do that he likes me so much?

LEX: What did I do that he likes *me* so much?

ED: What do you mean?

JACK: *(Enters.)* My wife says you left some stuff at the house. A shirt, and address book, something else I can't remember.

ED: *(To Lex.)* Yeah, I have a habit of doing that.

LEX: Where's Moira?

JACK: Talking to my wife.

LEX: Gee, I wonder what they're talking about, Jack? They have so much of you in common.

(Moira enters.)

JACK: So, Ed? When are you coming back?

ED: I was just trying to figure that out.

JACK: Well warn us next time, okay? Every time you stay with me for longer than a week, my whole life turns inside out.

MOIRA: You can stay with us.

JACK: And then you two can *share* him.

ED: *(Sits next to Jack.)* Come on Jack! Moira—

MICHAEL: *(Enters.)* Never have so many owed so much toooooo… Never have so many loved one person so much, no that's not it. Never have so many—

ED: Nobody owes me—

MICHAEL: *(Sits next to Ed.)* Eddie, Eddie, Eddie, Eddie. Who else am I gonna find that can drink ten cups of coffee in one sitting in Clown Alley at four o'clock in the morning?

ED: *(To Lex.)* What's a matter, you don't drink coffee?

LEX: No, I'm not a *guy*.

MICHAEL: I figure if a guy like you can like a guy like me, then I must be okay.

JACK: Personally, I can't *wait* for him to get on the fucking airplane.

MICHAEL: What's a matter? Jealous?

JACK: No. You?

ED: *(Pause.)* Um—

LEX: Why don't we get the bags to the van.

JACK: Why don't I get the van and bring it around to here.

MICHAEL: Oh. I gotta get the keys back to your wife.

(They exit in separate directions.)

ED: Uh, Moira, the earring. I don't think Jack, I mean he—

MOIRA: It's good for him.

LEX: Where did you find it?

MOIRA: Where did I find it? Right where I last saw the two of you, before you had the courtesy to move into her bedroom, rolling around on the *carpet*, that's where.

ED: Moira, I know you're enjoying this, but he's like a brother and I don't want him thinking I slept with you last night.

MOIRA: Okay, okay. Too bad though, I was enjoying this immensely. His behavior is always much better when you're around. He drinks too much, he smokes too much, and he's way too married the rest of the time. Why don't you hang around?

ED: Well, we were just talking about that.

MOIRA: *(To Lex.)* And what had we decided?

LEX: Nothing. Nothing's been decided.

(Pause.)

MOIRA: Well folks, it seems somebody better decide something, for the clock she is a'tickin'.

LEX: It's been decided. It just hasn't been discussed.

MOIRA: Well. *(Pause.)* At this point I think I'll stay in town and let you boys ride out to the airport alone together. It appeals to my sense of irony.

ED: Moira—

MOIRA: I'll go head Jack off at the van. *(She exits.)*

ED: I don't like missing people.

LEX: You really want to stay here?

ED: Yes, I really do. Do you want me to?

MICHAEL: *(Enters.)* Jack back? Where's Moira?

LEX: Doing what clandestine lovers do.

MICHAEL: Well, we'll do this without them, then. Ya know Eddie, without you our little budding bistro by the bay would be most certainly…bye-bye! Nice alliteration, huh? So, on behalf of…all the rappin' rockers at the Mission Rock Café, we want to thank you for taking us from red to black and we want to make you an honorary "rocker on a mission." And with this jacket… *(Gives jacket with name on it.)*

ED: I—gee Michael. I—

LEX: Don't feel bad. Go ahead.

MICHAEL: Wear it in good health my man. I love you. *(Gives him a hug.)* Okay. Here we go. Grab a bag, Lex.

LEX: I'm not coming.

MICHAEL: Why not?

LEX: I've got stuff to do.

MICHAEL: It won't take that long.

LEX: I'll say goodbye here.

MICHAEL: *(Pause.)* Why do you need to do that?

LEX: I'll see you over at your place in an hour.

MICHAEL: You can talk to him on the way.

LEX: I just wanna talk to him alone for a minute.

MICHAEL: *(Pause.)* Alone.

LEX: Yes. Alone.

MICHAEL: Okay. Then. Fine. Great. I'll see you at home.

    (He exits as Jack and Moira enter.)

JACK: Jacket looks good on you.

ED: *(To Lex. Quoting Michael.)* I'll see you at *home?*

JACK: I'm sorry Ed, I thought you and Moira, ya know, instead of you and Lex, and I—

ED: It's okay. *Home? Lex?*

JACK: Love'll do that to ya. It's wacky. Huh, Moira?

    (Pause.)

MOIRA: I hope we'll see you soon, Eddie. I'll miss you. *(She hugs him.)* Um, let's go, Jack.

ED: Thanks, Moira.

    (Jack and Moira exit.)

LEX: Well.

    (Pause.)

ED: Something you wanna tell me?

LEX: I—you and I—you're not gonna be here, okay? You don't *live* here. You understand? He loves me and he lives here and—

ED: But I'm gonna stay!!

LEX: It's a fantasy, Ed. And stranger than that, if it wasn't for you—

ED: And this is why he wanted to thank me? Why he really wanted to thank me?

LEX: Yes it is. *You don't live here!* He does. Okay? You're not gonna give up a career so you can come live with me, based on a weekend—yes, a great weekend, but *just a weekend* nonetheless—of unconditional love. That's too much pressure for me, way too much pressure. And I can't live like that. And neither can you. It's totally, totally, *totally* unrealistic, Ed.

ED: *(Pause.)* Unrealistic.

MICHAEL: *(Offstage.)* Eddie, Eddie, Eddie—You coming or going?

ED: *(Long pause.)* I guess, um, I gotta...I'd better get going.

LEX: Yeah.

ED: I'll see you again.

LEX: Or you won't.

MICHAEL: Let's go!!!

LEX: Take care.

ED: You, too.

LEX: I do love you, ya know.

ED: Yeah. I love you, too.

> *(He exits. His bag is left onstage. She stares and crosses to it. She is left alone. Lights fade to black.)*

END OF PLAY

Tattoo
by Jane Martin

CHARACTERS

LINK
JENNY
JONES
VLADIMIR
WILLIAM

Tattoo

Three women in their twenties sit on chairs facing a door upstage. Link (short for Linchovna) is dressed in black slacks, has short blond hair, several earrings and all ten fingers adorned with rings. Jenny is dressed in a suit as a young advertising account executive might for a date. Jones is more in the girly-girl vein with curly hair and Laura Ashley style. She is a graduate student who works also as a waitress.

JENNY: What time is it?

JONES: *(Very Southern.)* 7:45.

JENNY: Where is this guy?

LINK: *(A Russian accent.)* He will come. He is sister's ex-husband. Very reliable person. He will come.

JONES: But...like if they both... I mean what do we do if, you know, they both...

LINK: Very reliable.

JONES: I am sweating like a shot-putter.

JENNY: Calm down. Breathe. *(Knock.)* See.

JONES: But what if it's...

LINK: Is Vladimir. Very Russian knock. Okay? I get.

JONES: But if it's William, do we...

LINK: Only Russian is knocking so deliberate as this. You sit, I do. *(She goes to the door.)* Ah. *(Russian.)* Ooh mᶦᵉyáh b ᶦʰll pree-páh-dok syáird-tsuh. Tih uh-púz-dah-vá-yesh. *(You gave me a heart attack. You are late.)*

VLADIMIR: *(Russian.)* Ahv-tóe-booss pree-shóal púhz-dnuh. Yah lóohch-shuh dyéluhl shtaw smúg. *(Bus was late. I did the best I could.)* *(He enters. He is big, very big, and bearded and tattooed. He has a bag with him much like an old-fashioned doctor bag.)* (K)huh-ruh-sháw, éh-tut chᶦᵈl-uh-vᶦᵈk gdyeh aown. *(Okay, this guy he is where?)*

JONES: My God, he's speaking Russian.

LINK: He *is* Russian. All Russians are coming to your country, get ready. *(Russian.)* Aown nᶦee yesh-cháw nᶦee pree-yéh-(k)hull. Ee-dée zhdoo féh-toy kʷóm-nah-tuh. *(He hasn't arrived. Go in that room and wait.)*

VLADIMIR: *(Russian.)* (K) huh-ruh-sháw now ooh mien-yáh svee-dáh-nyuh ch'ée-ez chahss. Éh-tuh dvair? *(Okay, but in one hour I have an appointment. That door?)*

(Vladimir heads toward the other room.)

LINK: *(Russian.)* Da. *(Yes.)*

JENNY: What did you tell him?

LINK: Be ready. We will tell him when. Call him in.

JONES: Is this really a good idea? Is this really, really, really a good idea?

JENNY: We need closure. He needs closure. There is going to be closure.

(A knock on the door.)

JONES: *(Whispering.)* Oh my God. Oh my God it's him. I have a good idea. You guys do this. You'll be better at this than me. I'll just…oh my God, can I do this?

LINK: Sit down. Not to vacillate. We do this. *(They arrange themselves on the chairs.)* Okay. Very calm. Very good. This is no more than result of his actions. We are a living logic for him. Breathing. Breathing. Good. Okay. We begin. *(Another knock.)* I am liking this.

(She opens the door. The man outside, William, immediately grabs her and pulls her into a passionate kiss. After it has gone on for a while, he has the sense of being watched. He removes his lips from Link and sees the seated women.)

WILLIAM: Oh shit.

JENNY: Hello, William.

JONES: Hi.

LINK: *(Still in his arms.)* Hello, William.

WILLIAM: *(Trying to recover.)* All right, all right, this is really…an intrusion. This is really second-rate is what it is. I cannot believe…have I ever gone through your purses, have I ever gone through…

JENNY: You were going to say "our drawers?"

WILLIAM: No, no, I wasn't, Jenny, I wasn't going to say "your drawers." I was pointing out that there are issues of privacy, that there are questions of trust… *(Realizes he is still embracing Link.)* Oh. Excuse me. *(He releases her.)* I was so…

JENNY: Fucked up.

WILLIAM: No, not fucked up, Jenny, taken aback. Yes. Completely taken aback that you…

JENNY: Knew each other.

WILLIAM: No, I didn't say…you are putting, unfairly, words in my mouth. Look Jenny, if you are looking for the negative, you will find the negative. If you insist something is shoddy, it will look shoddy to you.

JONES: My daddy will come down here and eat your lunch!

WILLIAM: Jones, will you for once in your life wait to start crying until there is something to cry about?

JONES: You slept with me at 6 AM this morning!

WILLIAM: Well, yes I did, Jones. I did that. Well, actually, it was around 6:15.

JENNY: So that was the early meeting?

WILLIAM: Well no, I mean yes, there was an early meeting…

JONES: You said you had to see me. You said you were wracked with desire.

LINK: Wracked with desire?

JENNY: You said that to me at lunch.

WILLIAM: Okay, hold it…

JENNY: It's why I went into the trees with you in the park.

LINK: Wracked with desire, yes, it's very charming.

WILLIAM: Excuse me…

LINK: In the trees his methodology is what?

JENNY: Kissed my neck.

JONES: That's it! That's what he does! He goes for your goddamn neck like an attack dog! And here I was thinking that was because he was wracked with desire!

LINK: Then hand goes up leg. He is then unbuttons the blouse…

JONES: Then he starts saying "please," he says "please" over and over and over! Please, please, please!

LINK: Is like puppy.

WILLIAM: All right, goddammit, I concede the point!

JENNY: He concedes the point.

WILLIAM: If the point is that I am having more than one relationship, you can get off that point because nobody is arguing with you!

JENNY: Oh good.

WILLIAM: We can calm down!

JENNY: Fine.

JONES: You made love to me at 6 AM this morning! You called me your little tuna melt!

JENNY: Tuna melt?

LINK: What is tuna melt?

JENNY: You took me behind the trees at noon.

LINK: And tonight you will teach me *Kama Sutra*.

WILLIAM: This isn't about sex. This is about something way more profound than sex.

JENNY: Oh good, because I thought it *was* about sex.

WILLIAM: Well, it isn't, Jenny it's about…

JENNY: Screwing like a rabbit.

WILLIAM: No.

JENNY: Completely indiscriminate sex.

LINK: Altogether impersonal.

JENNY: Wildly dysfunctional.

JONES: He called me his tuna melt.

JENNY: Okay, Jones, that adds a dollop of romance.

WILLIAM: You may not recognize this but it's about *passion*. It is a frank admission that complex personalities have complex needs, and that…

JENNY: Point of order.

WILLIAM: Each of those needs finds passionate fulfillment…

JENNY: Point of order.

WILLIAM: What?

JENNY: You are the complex personality in question?

WILLIAM: Yes, I am.

JENNY: Just trying to keep up.

WILLIAM: Now each one of you is very different.

JENNY: We are very different.

WILLIAM: And in each case a different part of me responds. I don't give the same thing, I don't get the same thing. The me that is with each of you could not respond to the others. That self is faithful and would never betray you. You wouldn't want that part of me you don't have, and were I not as complex as I am there wouldn't have been enough of each part of me for you to relate to, to care about, in fact, to love.

(There is a long, stunned pause.)

JONES: What the *hell* is he talking about?

LINK: He has many souls.

JENNY: He da three-souled man.

WILLIAM: Go ahead, Jenny, make fun of what you don't understand. You are a wonderful person, a very talented advertising account executive, but you have a demeaningly reductive view of life. That is one of the reasons your spirit has sought me out. You want to be carried into deeper water.

JENNY: Well I will admit that it's getting pretty deep.

WILLIAM: Now I'm not saying there aren't issues here. Matters of the heart, intimacies that I want to discuss with you alone, Jenny, and you too Jones, of course I meant you, too.

JONES: Okay now, I want to get down and talk some Georgia talk here…you know, get right on down in the red dirt here…and what I got on my mind is "am I *is* or am I *ain't* your tuna melt?"

WILLIAM: I am what you need me to be, Jones. *(Link locks the door.)* What are you doing, Link?

LINK: I am making here old-fashioned totalitarian state.

JENNY: *(Moving one chair away from the others.)* Sit down, William.

WILLIAM: I see no reason to sit down.

JENNY: Bill, do you remember when we very recently began seriously to make our wedding plans?

WILLIAM: Yes, I do.

JENNY: Do you remember saying you wanted a really big wedding?

WILLIAM: Yes I do.

JENNY: And I said, "Honey, I just don't know that many people," and you said, "Sweetie, I could list two hundred family, friends, and business associates right now." And I bet you ten dollars and, by golly, you sat right down and did it!

LINK: He has good organizational memory, to do *this* he had to have such a memory.

JENNY: *(Taking a paper out of her briefcase.)* Now, Bill, this is the account of your activities today that I plan to fax to that list if you don't sit down. *(He glances over the letter and sits down.)* I know it's a little heavy on sexual specifics, but you have such a remarkably individual style I thought it made good reading.

JONES: I am never dressing up like that again at 6 AM!

WILLIAM: What precisely is it that you want?

LINK: Ah.

JENNY: Ah.

JONES: Ah.

JENNY: What precisely? Well, we want you to meet someone.

LINK: *(Russian)* Vlah-dée-meer, vuh-(k)huh-dée! Puh-ráh rahbᵃoʷ-táhts. *(Vladimir, come in! It is time to go to work.)* *(Vladimir enters.)* Vladimir, I am wanting you to meet interesting person William. William, this is interesting person Vladimir.
(Vladimir clicks his heels and bows slightly.)

WILLIAM: If you are planning to kill me or harm me, I would like it to be clearly understood that I am a lawyer, my friends are lawyers, my mother is a lawyer, my brother Don is a *ferocious* lawyer, and you will pay. P-A-Y. Pay.

LINK: I like this, William, this is very dramatic, but in this time we don't kill you. This is very funny idea though. You make good Russian joke. Wait, one moment, I tell Vladimir.

(In Russian, Link communicates William's fear. Vladimir laughs and slaps William on the back.)

JENNY: Okay, so it's "the lady and the tiger." Behind two doors, the choice is yours. Here's the deal. I will fax the aforementioned document to the aforementioned list, or Vladimir will tattoo on your butt our version of what you did today.

(Jenny hands William another piece of paper.)

WILLIAM: What?!

JONES: Signed.

JENNY: And dated.

WILLIAM: You are kidding.

JENNY: Take a good look at Vladimir. Does he look like he's kidding?

(Vladimir opens his bag, takes out a small towel, and begins laying out the tools of his trade.)

LINK: In Russia, this man is thoracic surgeon, but in America he is tattoo artist. Such is fate of Russian people. *(Russian.)* N'ee pláhts, moy droohg. *(Do not weep, my friend.)*

(He wipes his eyes.)

WILLIAM: *(Still holding the paper.)* I am supposed to go through life with this tattooed on my butt?

JENNY: William, like many pharmaceuticals, you need a warning label.

JONES: But they can take a tattoo off.

LINK: Not with Russian inks.

WILLIAM: I cannot believe this is happening to me!

JENNY: So you choose the fax?

WILLIAM: You know perfectly well that would ruin my career.

JENNY: Well, see now, we just seem to be on the horns of a dilemma.

JONES: Your career or your rear.

LINK: The lady…

JONES: Or your skinny white butt.

WILLIAM: How the hell did the three of you find out about each other?

LINK: Vladimir is also private detective.

WILLIAM: *(To Link.)* And what made you think you needed a private detective?

LINK: Because, my darling, I am Russian.

JENNY: So what'll it be, Billy?

WILLIAM: Can I have just a goddamn minute here?

JONES: I'm gonna wash your mouth out with soap.

LINK: Man must come to terms with tragic fate. Is good. Okay, while you think, Vladimir will sing you song of suffering and transfiguration from Ukraine. *(Vladimir does; it has no words but great feeling.)* And I will read you *Kama Sutra*.

WILLIAM: Oh God.

LINK: You say tonight our souls, our bodies will become one through *Kama Sutra*. This I don't want to miss.

(Link begins reading the first few sentences of the Kama Sutra, *"Man, the period of whose life is one hundred years, should practise Dharma, Artha and Kama at different times and in such a manner that they may harmonize together and not clash in any way. He should acquire learning in his childhood, in his youth and middle age he should attend to Artha and Kama, and in his old age he should perform Dharma, and thus seek to gain Moksha, i.e., release from further transmigration." Vladimir sings more softly and prepares, the women watch. William fumes and puts his head in his hands. Lights out.)*

END OF PLAY

Just Be Frank
by Caroline Williams

CHARACTERS

DIANE

CHARLENE

JAN

SECRETARY

MR. ROSS

TIME AND PLACE

The present. A busy office.

Just Be Frank

Lights up—Morning in a busy office.

Spotlights focus on two co-workers sitting at adjacent desks. Behind them, other employees are periodically seen passing through, miming office business or huddled around the water cooler. At stage left is a large reception desk and free-standing closed door. Later, just beyond the door will be "the boss's office."
In the spotlight: Charlene, an attractive, overbearing young professional, is wearing a garish, hot pink suit and talking animatedly with her dull-looking colleague, Diane. In dress and posture, Diane is the mouse-like antithesis to Charlene's in-your-face confidence. It is clear who dominates both their work relationship and the conversation in progress.

CHARLENE: *(Striking a pose, modeling her new ensemble.)* It looks expensive, doesn't it? I won't say how much...but let me just tell you...if you even knew—you would *die. (Beat.) Five hundred dollars.* The saleslady said it looked incredible on me. You don't think it's too loud, do you? She said I'd definitely stop traffic...

DIANE: You *are* hard to miss. I mean, it is—*pink.*

CHARLENE: It's not *pink*, Diane, it's *salmon.* I want to look professional when I approach the boss. I really think this suit says, "I'm a woman. I'm not afraid to wear a salmon suit. I can be a valuable asset to this company." *(Beat.)* That promotion has my name written all over it.
(Charlene wears a determined smile.)

DIANE: You mean the Gaines Beefy-Treat account? I'm up for that promotion...I mean, I was thinking of applying. I thought since my proposal saved the Ferber Cheese-Stick account last year...

CHARLENE: Oh, that was you. *Well.* You should know that Ferber Cheese was child's play compared to Beefy-Treats. *(Smiling "helpfully.")* You wouldn't want to be in over your head.

DIANE: *(Dejected.)* I guess you *are* more assertive than I am...and confident. *(A beat, she looks at Charlene.)* And you stand out...

CHARLENE: *(Condescendingly.)* Listen. Since you and I are friends—I'll be frank. *This* is the cutthroat world of business. *You* simply don't have any killer instinct and rarely do you ever have anything exciting to say. Not that those are *bad* qualities—you just lack *verve*.

DIANE: *Verve?*

CHARLENE: Don't worry—you still fulfill a very important role here. Where would people like *me* be without people like *you?* You're punctual and efficient and—meek.

DIANE: *(On the verge of tears.)* Mm-meek?

CHARLENE: *(Big, fake smile.)* In fact, you're *lucky we're such good friends* that we can be honest with each other because, for the most part, Diane, there is no place for honesty in business, and not everyone will be as helpful as I am. Come to think of it, when I become president of this company, my first decree will be to have all of my people be *completely* honest—*all* of the time. *(She thinks.)* It will *revolutionize* the world of business. *(Beat.)* Sometimes my brilliance takes even me by surprise. *(Charlene is transfixed by her vision. Speechless, Diane stares at her in disbelief. Emerging from her reverie, admiring herself, Charlene continues.)* Anyway, my suit *is* sensational, isn't it? *(Charlene turns toward the water cooler and is out of earshot by the time Diane, her face contorting, manages to stammer under her breath.)*

DIANE: What do I know—I'm MEEK!

CHARLENE: *(Smiling over her shoulder, oblivious to Diane's mounting rage.)* No need to thank me—

DIANE: *(Calling after her, sarcastic/bitter.)* Oh yeah, THANKS!!
(Diane turns angrily back to her computer and furiously begins to type. Meanwhile, spotlights follow an obnoxiously cheerful Charlene to the water cooler where fellow employee, Jan, is standing alone, looking paranoid. Dressed in typical middle-management attire [unflattering earth-tone blazer/skirt combo, nude pantyhose, and incongruous stark white tennis shoes], Jan holds a paper Dixie cup and speaks in a flat, nasal monotone. Her face is an expressionless mask of resigned irritation and nausea.)

CHARLENE: Good morning, Jan. How was your weekend?

JAN: Absolute crap.

CHARLENE: Excuse me—?

JAN: I got stood up, my minivan blew a tire, and I have a yeast infection. Do you mind? I'm trying to look inconspicuous here and you're standing next to me like a flashing pink beacon.

CHARLENE: *(Confused.)* Actually, this suit is not pink, *Jan*, it's *salmon*. What's gotten into you anyway? I'm counting on you to nominate me for the new account. You're the only one the old windbag ever listens to...

JAN: Actually, *Charlene*, I'd feel better about *myself* if you'd continue to earn substantially LESS than I do.

CHARLENE: *(Still confused.)* Are you trying to say you're *not* going to give me the recommendation?

JAN: Listen, I'll be blunt. I don't like you. I've never liked you. The way you are *constantly* waving at me from your desk—I have to pretend like I'm writing or looking for something just to avoid acknowledging you—but *you don't get it*...you wave, I ignore you and you keep flappin' away like...some kind of—large, flightless bird.

CHARLENE: Well! *Excuse me*, JAN!

JAN: *(Continuing—she could care less about Charlene's objections.)* ...and, God help me if I ever sit next to you at a lunch meeting again...watching you eat could drive a person insane—it's like watching one of those pointy-faced rodents—incessantly pecking and pecking and...

CHARLENE: *(Seething.)* Of all the rude...

JAN: *(Continuing.)* ...and *speaking* of chewing—your last presentation was so mind-numbingly boring I actually had to *work* to keep from gnawing off my own arm.

CHARLENE: I have heard just about ENOUGH thank-you-very-much!
(Charlene turns to leave.)

JAN: Oh, in that case—before you go, the next time I sleep with the boss in order to advance my own career, I'll be sure and let slip that you called him a windbag...Good luck!
(Jan goes abruptly back to her desk.)

CHARLENE: *(Calling lamely, after her.)* If that's the way you feel, then FINE— I'll meet with him *myself!*
(Charlene stomps off to a large reception desk in front of a free-standing closed door inscribed with the word President *in gold lettering. She addresses a perky, somewhat effeminate male Secretary who wears a constant, obsequious smile. Everything he says is delivered with a cheerful voice and genuinely eager, helpful attitude.)*

SECRETARY: *(Smiling warmly throughout.)* Hello, Ms. Parker. How can I kiss your ass today?

CHARLENE: ...excuse me?

SECRETARY: Would you like some coffee? This is regular but if you'd like decaf I'll just leave and come back with the same pot—you'll never know the difference.

CHARLENE: *(Confused.)* Uh—no. I just want to make an appointment with Mr. Ross ASAP.

SECRETARY: *(Checks appointment book, then looks up, still smiling.)* I'm sorry but I don't think he can squeeze your big pink ass in today. *(Cheerfully.)* Is there anything else I can help you with? *(Charlene's face reddens with anger. She is about to speak when the phone rings.)* Just a moment… *(He holds up a finger to Charlene who waits, fuming.)* Burton and Ross, may I help you? …today? …with Mr. Ross? …how about 2:15? …all right then, buh-bye. *(Back to Charlene.)* As I was saying, are you sure there isn't anything else? I could go fetch some Post-its? Your dry-cleaning, perhaps? *(Charlene looks at him blankly, speechless.)* After all, what am I here to do if not *your* mindless, tedious busywork. Whatever you and all your *over-educated* colleagues with reserved parking and big pink suits think you're just too good for.

CHARLENE: *(Enraged.)* FOR-YOUR-INFORMATION the suit is SALMON and I don't know what your *problem* is but I thought you said Mr. Ross was busy all day— *(Points to phone accusingly.)* What was that?!

SECRETARY: *(Explaining calmly, as if to a small child.)* No, I didn't say he was *busy*—I said I couldn't squeeze you in. He's actually free until *(Glances down.)* 2:15. But, due to my inferiority complex and because this appointment book makes me drunk with power, I've decided to act out my passive-aggressive rage against you.

CHARLENE: *Excuse me* but I will *not* tolerate a secretary with that kind of attitu—

SECRETARY: *(Interrupting.)* That's *administrative maintenance engineer* and I would care what you were saying if you had any power at all in this company. Since you don't, I'll just smile and nod while I look for somebody important to suck up to…Oh! There's an executive! If that will be all Ms. Parker…

(Secretary grabs the coffee pot and rushes off.)

CHARLENE: *(Disgusted, to no one in particular.)* What is wrong with you people? *(Charlene walks past the desk to the boss's door and knocks, opening it gingerly, flooding his office with light. Inside sits Mr. Ross, flanked by stacks of files, behind an imposing oak desk. He wears a dark three-piece suit, red power tie, and is slightly overweight with short hair and kind features. His tone and demeanor suggest an unbearded, corporate Santa Claus.)*

CHARLENE: Mr. Ross?

MR. ROSS: *(Looking up from his paperwork.)* Yes? Come in.

CHARLENE: Hi, I was wondering if I could talk to you for a few minutes about a possible promotion on the new dog-treats account? Last month you had mentioned how I was really up to speed and I was thinking, what with my…

MR. ROSS: *(Cutting her off, leaning back in his swivel-chair.)* Hmmm—yes, the Beefy-Treats. You know, this is quite fascinating. I don't doubt that you do, in fact, work here, and I may, indeed, have commented on your work… I just can't for the life of me seem to remember who in the hell you are. What department did you say you work in?

CHARLENE: Um…marketing and development.

MR. ROSS: Right, right—marketing. You must perform one of those benign tasks that, apparently, I see fit to dole out some measley, pissant salary for… *(Cheerfully.)* in which case I suppose I should hear you out. You were saying…?

CHARLENE: Uh…well, I had actually come in here about a promotion but maybe now's not exactly the right time…

MR. ROSS: *(Interrupting her with a sudden realization.)* Wait a minute! I do remember you—your desk is just across the way there…

(He gestures past the door.)

CHARLENE: *(Excited.)* Yes! That's me! Did you recall how I typed up those reports last term?

MR. ROSS: *(Cheerful and professional.)* Heavens no! I do recall, however, that I quite enjoy looking down your blouse on my way in here each morning…and, considering that my taxes alone are probably twice what you make in an entire year—I suppose it wouldn't hurt to hand over an account I'll probably take credit for anyway. Congratulations Miss…

CHARLENE: Parker…Charlene Parker.

MR. ROSS: Of course. Congratulations Miss Proctor, the promotion is yours. *(Earnestly.)* Good luck and nice ass.

(Mr. Ross gives Charlene a friendly thumbs up and promptly refocuses on his paperwork, effectively sending her on her way. Charlene is speechless. She walks slowly back to her desk, more than slightly disturbed.)

DIANE: *(Bitterly.)* So, how'd it go?

CHARLENE: *(Suddenly crazed.)* GREAT, DI-ANE! As a matter of fact— WONDERFUL. *(Grotesquely enunciating each word.)* Did I not explain to you that a salmon suit like this would command RESPECT? *(Diane, startled, looks at Charlene like she is insane. After a moment, they turn to their respective computers and get to work.)*

END OF PLAY

Plays
for
Six Actors

Pyramid Effect
by Marcia Dixcy

CHARACTERS

(All college-age.)

BUD: Large, congenial, some Texas accent.

STEVE: Was an Indiana high school basketball champ.

ROBBIE: Overcompensates for his inadequacies.

MEGAN: Practical, open-minded, slightly acerbic.

ELAINE: Mellow—has benefitted from yoga.

LULIE: Scampish, very agile. Enjoys herself.

Pyramid Effect

The play starts in blackout.

ROBBIE: No, not there. Jeez, are you crazy?! Move your knee…No, ow!… Not in the middle of my back.

LULIE: Sorry, hon. I thought that was your shoulder there. *(Giggles.)* Wait. Wait. *Wait!* I gotta rest a minute.

ROBBIE: No, there's no way. Get on top or I'm gonna lose it.

ELAINE: You're just wasting energy, Robbie. Take deep breaths. Breeeeeathe in. Breeeeeathe out. Breeeeathe. Breeeeeathe in, Ak! Lulie, watch your nails. No, no, nooooooooooo.

(Lights come up slowly on a human pyramid. Three males at the base. L to R: Bud, Steve, and Robbie. Two females on the middle layer: Megan, Elaine. Lulie has just reached the top.)

LULIE: That's it. Zingo! We're here; we're set. Do you believe it?!

(Leans down to hug the necks of Megan and Elaine. Megan and Elaine speak on top of one another.)

MEGAN: Your knee is squashing my lumbar vertebrae!

ELAINE: No please! You're twisting my neck wrong.

ROBBIE: Stabilize!

STEVE: *(Head turned to Robbie.)* Yo Robbie, our air traffic controller.

(Megan, Elaine, and Robbie speak on top of each other.)

MEGAN: All right, that's better, that's better. Keep your knee right there where I've packed my sweats with Kotex.

ELAINE: *(To Robbie and Steve.)* Don't you two start, I can't hold up over a lot of negativity!

ROBBIE: *(To Steve.)* I think somebody better exert some control or we won't stay up four minutes—let alone four hours.

(Lulie has been back on her haunches straddling Megan and Elaine. She's taken out some suntan lotion from a shoulder bag and is smoothing it over her arms.)

LULIE: Great view guys! That is a *great* view!

BUD: *(The largest, most stalwart of the group.)* Did you say four hours?

MEGAN: Yeh, Bud. Where've you been? What do you think we're doing?

BUD: Fred told me two. Two to break the record.

LULIE: Boy! Fred better have this straight, 'cause way down there two hours means a lot more than it does up here. *(She peers way down.)*

ROBBIE: Two hours for the University record. Four hours, three minutes twenty-nine seconds for *the* record, the Guinness Record. The record that wins us Target's $2,500 Challenge.

STEVE: Is that before or after taxes?

MEGAN: And is it split how? Evenly because of the danger and anxiety on the top versus the weight on the bottom. Or is it...

BUD: *(Calling down.)* Fred, you bimbo! Can you hear me down there?

LULIE: Bud?

MEGAN: This is no time to be unkind to those below you, Bud.

BUD: *(Still calming down.)* You pain in the patootee. Got me here on a wicked hangover.

ELAINE: Calm down, Bud. We all have needs here. Take it one hour at a time. Brea...

ROBBIE: Elaine, dear, even Bud may have better things to do with his mind than concentrate on his breathing. Breathing is something even the lowest forms of life can do without benefit of intelligent thought.

(Bud starts a small hiccup.)

STEVE: *(To Bud.)* C'mon, guy. You can use two hundred bucks. Think ahead.

LULIE: And, Bud, think of my career and the coverage that only four hours can bring.

(Bud hiccups again, slightly stronger.)

STEVE: Hey, four hours is no sweat, Lulie.

MEGAN: *(To Lulie.)* And you've got yourself in a position that cries out for tele-photo lenses.

LULIE: God, I hope so.

BUD: I don't know...HICCUP.

ROBBIE: *(To Lulie.)* So it was Fred's concern for your modeling career that convinced him to place you up there, Lulie?

ELAINE: *(Sincerely.)* That was nice.

MEGAN: *(To Bud.)* What's going on. Are you spazzing out or what's happening?

LULIE: *(Peers down from above.)* Bud?

(Bud hiccups again. Megan, Elaine, and Lulie move up and down slightly.)

STEVE: Cut it out, Megan. Stop bouncing my butt.

MEGAN: I'm not; it's Bud.

ROBBIE: *(To Steve.)* Bud is bouncing your butt?

BUD: *(Hiccuping loudly.)* I've got the hiccups. I've got the dang blasted hiccups!

MEGAN: Great! You just made me bite my tongue.

ELAINE: He just got too upset. Hiccups are simply a stress reaction.

MEGAN: Gross, my tongue is bleeding, oh gross.

ROBBIE: Stress reaction! What you're hearing are the dying bellows of two six-packs of Moosehead.

(Loud hiccup and commotion.)

ROBBIE: Down, Bullwinkle, steady, boy.

STEVE: Chill out, Robbie. You're giving me an earache.

MEGAN: I'm serious guys. This is like a hemorrhage. In a minute I'm gonna be choking.

ELAINE: You need to apply pressure to stop the bleeding. Do you have a Kleenex or something?

LULIE: *(Pulls scarf from around head.)* Here, take my bandana. *(Leans over to let Megan grab it in her mouth.)*

ROBBIE: Yes, Elaine, why don't you make a tourniquet?

(Loud hiccup. Megan screams muffled by scarf.)

LULIE: I think we oughta do something hiccupwise.

STEVE: Don't worry, Lulie.

ELAINE: Well, it's muscle relaxation, really. His esophagus is going into traumatic spasms.

STEVE: Ya know, I think I did read about that somewhere…some guy who had hiccups for eight years! They tried…

ROBBIE: Oh sure. Is this helping to relax you over there Bud?

(Loud hiccup.)

ELAINE: *(Just barely hanging on.)* Perhaps if he tried holding his breath…

(Megan makes muffled sounds of agreement.)

ROBBIE: I thought you just said *taking* a breath was supposed to be so relaxing.

ELAINE: Well…

LULIE: Cut it out, Robbie. Holding your breath is a valid cure for hiccups. Anyone knows that.

(Loud hiccup. More muffled sounds from Megan.)

STEVE: Yeh. This guy with the hiccups for eight years? They held him under water in one of those backyard swimming pools? Something like five minutes. The hiccups just kept rising to the surface.

(Loud hiccup prompting Megan to spit out scarf in an outburst.)

MEGAN: Shut up and let him hold his breath before I get really nauseous!

LULIE: OK, Bud, get ready, big breath: one, two, three…

(Bud heaves a massive breath, almost toppling all above…several beats of silence.)

ELAINE: Lulie, could you move that knee back about two inches?

MEGAN: There's no way we're going to keep this up four hours, no way. How long have we been up here already?

ROBBIE: I don't know. Steve, turn your wrist around so I can see your watch.

LULIE: *(Showing her jazzy Swatch to Megan.)* Here, I've got it.

MEGAN: How am I supposed to read that? They're no numbers. They're no hands are there? Are they those little lightening bolts?

LULIE: *(Cupping her hand over her watch face.)* Yeh, they glow in the dark… it's…ah…

ROBBIE: *(Finally reading Steve's watch.)* Two fourteen.

LULIE: I say twenty after.

MEGAN: So how much longer?

ROBBIE: Three hours, fifty-four minutes.

(Large subterranean hiccup.)

MEGAN: *(Swaying.)* Not of this there won't be.

ELAINE: Just keep holding on, Bud. Just hold right through the hiccup.

STEVE: You know what finally stopped 'em? His wife fired a gun point blank, right at his face. I mean it was empty, but it scared him so bad it finally stopped 'em.

(Bud glares over at Steve, face beet red.)

LULIE: Hey, Bud, how's it going?

(Bud begins quivering.)

STEVE: But after that, they got divorced. It was just…

MEGAN: Are we going to follow this man to his grave?

(Bud now vibrating the whole group, starts to let air out like a trumpet.)

ELAINE: I think you better release now, Bud. Just let the air out slowly.

MEGAN: Yeh, we're liable to go out like the Hindenburg.

ROBBIE: *(Looking down to folks below.)* OK, OK, hang on down there. We're experiencing technical difficulties.

(Bud lets all his air out with a large lurch … silence for a few beats.)

STEVE: You feeling better now guy?

LULIE: Bud?

ELAINE: Give him space.

ROBBIE: Oh fine.

(Small hiccup from Bud.)

ROBBIE: Was that you again, Bud?

MEGAN: I think I just felt my two hundred dollars heave its dying breath.

LULIE: What about water? What about the thing of drinking water upside-down?

MEGAN: That ought to be a cinch.

LULIE: *(Smacking top of head with joy.)* I've got my thermos! *(Reaching into bag.)*

ROBBIE: Did you consider there might be a minimum baggage allotment on this venture, Lulie?

LULIE: Here, Bud. Here's some V-8.

ELAINE: *(Perking up.)* Oh, can I have a sip?

BUD: Give me a break. *(Large hiccup.)*

MEGAN: *(Taking control.)* No! Now you take this and try to drink it upside down.

> *(Megan takes cup from Lulie and bends down to reach Bud's mouth.)*

BUD: I can't drink V-8 juice right side up.

> *(Lulie pours another Dixie cup for Elaine.)*

MEGAN: Well, this is important, so you got to try. Lulie, move from my shoulder a sec so I can get this cup under his mouth backwards. *(Contortions trying to execute this maneuver.)*

STEVE: OK, Buddy. This glass of V-8 is your ticket to fame and fortune.

BUD: Mmmm, hurrah, gurgh, cough, cough...

STEVE: Steady.

MEGAN: Don't spill it, Bud.

BUD: Hnah, phah! It went up my nose!

ELAINE: You ought to watch out. He could actually become asphyxiated that way.

ROBBIE: Fine, as long as it cures his hiccups.

> *(Spastic painful hiccup from Bud.)*

STEVE: Bummer.

MEGAN: Now I'm starting to feel really discouraged.

LULIE: C'mon Megan!

ELAINE: I've heard about breathing into a paper bag. That way the carbon dioxide accumulates and the body thinks it's kind of an emergency situation, so the whole digestive system just shuts down.

ROBBIE: And do the hiccups stop or are you sharing a form of dietetic breathing?

> *(Another large hiccup.)*

ROBBIE: Lulie, we're now waiting for the bag.

LULIE: *(Looking furiously through her stuff.)* Darn! I had my Oreos in a kind of a... I don't know, they must be back on the counter...but...I thought it was a balloon.

MEGAN: What?

LULIE: A balloon. You blow up a balloon for hiccups.

MEGAN: Do you have a balloon?

LULIE: Course not. Why would I bring a balloon with me?

BUD: I *(Large hiccup.)* don't want a balloon.

ROBBIE: But you do want two hundred dollars. And it's not just your two hundred dollars you're hiccuping away; it's two thousand, three hundred belonging to your friends. Friends who need it.

ELAINE: Putting pressure on him will only make them worse.

STEVE: Ah, I might have it. *(Tries to reach for his left shirt pocket but can't maintain balance.)*

MEGAN: Watch it, Steve.

LULIE: Whoa!

STEVE: OK, listen, one of you has to reach inside my left shirt pocket.

MEGAN: Yeh…and what?

STEVE: Just do it.

MEGAN: All right, all right. Lulie, can you move over to Elaine for a minute? *(Lulie does so—much unsteady hanging on. hiccup from Bud.)*

ELAINE: Lulie your knee, no your knee has got to go…uh…OK. *(Megan gets to Steve's shirt pocket and pulls out…)*

MEGAN: A condom? You have got to be kidding me. *(Lulie laughs.)*

ELAINE: Oh please!

ROBBIE: Ready for a little safe sex up here, Steve?

STEVE: *(Blushing badly.)* No, I mean it was just there.

MEGAN: Just there? You just carry these in your shirt pocket?

STEVE: Yeh, as a matter of fact…

JULIE: So what's Bud supposed to blow it up? *(Giggles.)*

BUD: Go to h… *(Large hiccup.)*

MEGAN: *(After recovering from that one, she rips the packet open with her teeth and passes it up to Lulie. Urgently.)* Here Lulie, pull it out.

LULIE: *(Really giggling.)* Hope this is as bad for hiccups as it is for sex.

ELAINE: Is that the kind made out of sheep bladders?

STEVE: Uh…

ROBBIE: Uh oh, you're not a vegetarian are you, Bud?

BUD: Robbie, you many not live to spend that two hundred dollars. *(Hiccup.)*

MEGAN: Here it is; here it is; here it is. Take it Bud.

STEVE: Bud, ya got nothing to lose, right?

BUD: *(Grabs condom with a fury. Begins to huff and puff into it.)* Dang! Puff…puff…puff…puuuuuufff…puff. *(Hiccup.)*

LULIE: Bud?

BUD: Puff…puff, pufff. *(Hiccup.)*

LULIE: Bud, please try 'cause… *(Growing slightly more hysterical.)* It's not just the publicity. I mean I do have to make a move if I'm ever going to catch the public eye.

BUD: Puff…puff… *(Hiccup.)*

MEGAN: Lulie, do you think you're…

LULIE: No let me say this. Bud! OK now listen this is important. I can't just fall down from here, Bud. I can't just throw this all away 'cause… I'm pregnant! *(Bud and Steve react simultaneously.)*

BUD: *(Let's the balloon fly away.)* What!!!?

STEVE: What??!

(Beat of silence.)

ROBBIE: This row is beginning to feel very crowded.

MEGAN: Lulie, what in the world are you trying to pull?

ELAINE: Steve, you're shaking, I don't think I can…

BUD: *(To Steve.)* What d'you mean what?

STEVE: What d'you mean what do I mean what? What do *you* mean what?

MEGAN: I'm beginning to have serious regrets.

BUD and STEVE: Lulie!

LULIE: Yes?

(Bud and Steve speak simultaneously.)

BUD: Are you saying that I…

STEVE: When did you start…

(Bud and Steve stare each other down.)

LULIE: Notice anything?

ROBBIE: Could you be a bit more specific, dear?

LULIE: Notice any hiccups lately?

(Brief silence. All heads turn to Bud who looks out, concentrating.)

ROBBIE: It's fairly quiet, Bud.

ELAINE: *(Kindly.)* Lulie, when is your baby due?

(Heads turn toward Lulie.)

LULIE: What baby?

STEVE and BUD: What d'you mean what baby?

LULIE: I was just trying Steve's story. You know that guy who got shot in the face?

MEGAN: Lulie!

LULIE: Well it scared him didn't it?

(*General surprise and dismay.*)

STEVE: I don't even want this two hundred dollars anymore.

BUD: You don't want the two hundred dollars? After what I've been through you don't want the two hundred dollars?

STEVE: I don't want to hear what you've been through. We've been busting our chops to help you, Buddy.

MEGAN: (*Getting bounced.*) I've got to hand it to you, Lulie. At least with the hiccups it was only one of them.

LULIE: You guys! Cut it out. We've got some time to spend here together.

ROBBIE: We've got three hours and twenty-seven minutes to spend here together.

MEGAN: Lulie's right guys. Two hundred dollars is still two hundred dollars.

STEVE: I'm not saying a word.

BUD: That two hundred dollars better be in my hands by tomorrow. Fred! (*Calling down.*) Thanks again, pal.

(*Lights begin a very slow fade.*)

LULIE: This'll be an achievement, something we'll never forget.

ELAINE: (*Dreaming.*) You know, I've heard that Minoan Acrobats could hold a lift for up to twelve hours...some of them even performed on the backs of bulls.

MEGAN: So what else is new?

ROBBIE: I wonder if the Minoans were as well equipped for medical emergencies.

LULIE: Do you see that van? Is that Channel 7? It is; it's the Action Cam!

ROBBIE: Be sure to give them your best side, dear, whichever that may be.

(*Lulie gives a squeal of anticipation.*)

MEGAN: I'm beginning to think we might make this.

(*Lights are almost out.*)

STEVE: A-CHOOO!

LULIE: Steve?

STEVE: AAAAACHOOO!

(*Blackout.*)

MEGAN: Ooooh noooo...

END OF PLAY

Jerry Springer Is God
by Matt Pelfrey

CHARACTERS

VIV: Female.
LAURA: Female.
DANA: Female.
RC: Male.
JIM: Male.
TEX: Male.
All are in their twenties.

TIME
The end of the twentieth century.

PLACE
An apartment.

Jerry Springer Is God

A funky living room.

Five unmatched chairs are in the center of the room. Sitting in these chairs are Viv, Laura, Dana, RC, and Jim. Tex stands off to the side watching them.

VIV: She's been sleeping with my man!

LAURA: I have not!

VIV: Oh yes you have!

LAURA: I don't know what this bitch is trippin' about!

VIV: Bullshit! I see how you check him out! You call my place when you know *damn well* I'm at work!

LAURA: Oh, stop your lying! And don't *even* pretend that's your real hair!

VIV: Excuse me?

LAURA: Did I stutter? You're bald, ass-ugly, and there is no way in hell I would go sniffing around some piece of trailer-park tube steak like him!
(*Viv gets up and rushes at Laura. Laura meets her halfway and they start to struggle with each other. Their fight is rather pathetic. After a minute of this they both start to laugh and turn to Tex.*)

VIV: This is so stupid.

LAURA: It really is.

TEX: No, come on! You're doing great!

RC: Nice try, but this is not gonna work.

TEX: You guys, don't do this to me…

JIM: We've humoured you long enough. Slap that video in. Move these chairs back.

TEX: Come on! Hold up…

JIM: Who wants some more grog?

VIV: Right here. Grab me an Anchor Steam.

LAURA: (*Raising her hand.*) Rolling Rock.

RC: See, Tex, we can't go on that show for one basic reason; we aren't freaks. We aren't mutants. We are normal. We're real. We have all our teeth. We aren't humping our brothers and sisters and living in trailers.

LAURA: He's right, Tex. Everyone they parade on that show is a human cock-roach.

VIV: ...Trailer park monstrosities.

DANA: One guy was so inbred, I could swear I saw *gills* on him.

JIM: Iggy the Porpoise Boy.

TEX: So you do admit watching?

JIM: Of course. Human cockfighting is quality television.

RC: I think they should expand the premise of the show...make it life or death...like gladiator combat, search through all these small towns for human oddities and make them fight each other. Like they do with pitbulls. Not only would it clean out the gene pool, but it gives us another spectator sport.

DANA: What a little Nazi you are.

JIM: That would be *humongous* entertainment. I would *pay* to see that.

DANA: Coming from a guy who's paid to see an armless stripper, that is not saying much.

JIM: First off, that was in Mexico. Second, I've always supported the rights of the handicapped, and third, she was a skilled dancer. It was an intensely erotic experience that I shall cherish into ripe old age. I swear, how many times are you going to bring that up?

RC: Why would we want to go on national television and humiliate ourselves while a studio full of sociopaths chant "Jerry! Jerry! Jerry!"

TEX: It's about the quest for interesting, human experience. It's about taking off all your clothes and doing a big cannon ball dive into the cultural Zeitgeist.

VIV: More like diving into the cultural sewage of late twentieth century television.

TEX: We cannot pass this up. I've got it all set. I've got one of the producers hooked, and I'm ready to reel the bastard in. He just wants to meet with the rest of you, conduct a preshow interview...we are *in there*.

VIV: You mean this guy is already interested in us?

TEX: After the shit I slung at him, bet your ass he is.

LAURA: I'm confused...what in the hell would we go on the show and say?

TEX: That's what I was hoping we could hash out tonight. That's what our lit-tle improv was about...

JIM: So your concept is we lie? That's your plan?

TEX: I prefer to think of it as role-playing, but basically, yeah. We'll lie our asses off.

LAURA: This is so insane.

JIM: Really Tex, no offense, I want you to feel like you can come to us with anything. I think as friends it's important to be a sanctuary where you can be comfortable sharing any idea, thought, or feeling...but this is one of the most utterly fucking stupid ideas I have ever wasted my time listening to, and if you ever try to foist another idea this pathetic on us again, I'll stand on a chair and pee on you.

TEX: You guys have no vision. Like it or not, Springer is a trademark of our times. And think about it…wouldn't it be cool to be able to say we were part of it? The boomers had their marches and protests…

VIV: Did you know four out of five claim they were at Woodstock—

DANA: A mathematical impossibility.

TEX: Right, but listen: Springer is not long for this world. Powerful forces are already surrounding him…pressuring him to clean up his act, to sanitize his wacky hijinks. But mark my words: the Springer show is going to go down in TV history as a legend. Twenty years from now, some Oliver Stone wannabe is going to make a three-hour biopic of this cat's life… and we'll be able to say we were on the show. It's gonna be a *classic*. Think of it like being on *American Bandstand*, except with bitch-slapping, hair-pulling, and an occasional thrown shoe.

RC: I have to disagree with Jimbo. I think Tex is making a provocative and compelling case.

LAURA: The hell he is. They're already touchy about those fake fight accusations. We can't pull this off even if we all agreed to your little scheme.

TEX: You don't think you're smart enough to fool the producers of *The Jerry Springer Show?* Is that what you're saying? *(Beat.)* We could totally pull this off. It'll be epic!!

JIM: So what would our yarn be?

TEX: Okay, well, this is just what I've kinda thrown together…feel free to mix and match, but okay, here it is: Viv will go on and say she wants to confront her boyfriend with a dark secret, okay? I'll come in and she'll tell me she's having an affair with Jim. Jim will come in, I'll charge Jim, and we'll choreograph a little fight. Then Jim will say he's got a secret of his own. And he'll say he's been sleeping with Dana, who will say she was supposed to be Viv's maid of honor at her upcoming wedding. Then RC, you come in and rush Jim, saying you're Dana's boyfriend.

JIM: That's a crappy scenario.

TEX: Well, come up with something else…it's not written in *stone*.

DANA: I'm not doing it.

JIM: Me neither.

LAURA: Good. That's settled. Let's watch a video. What is it we rented?

VIV: *Bring me the Head of Alfredo Garcia*. Peckinpah.

TEX: You guys suck. I can't believe you won't rise to the occasion.

RC: I dunno…it almost sounds fun, except I think you'd need to work on the scenario a little more.

TEX: Let's hear your critique.

RC: Well, you've kinda got a credibility problem…

TEX: Where?

RC: The Jim-Dana thing.

TEX: Yeah, so?

RC: It's just not…credible.

TEX: Why not?

RC: C'mon… I mean…"come on." *(Looks around.)* Someone help me out here.

JIM: No. What exactly do you mean?

RC: *(Thinks a moment, trying to be as diplomatic as he can.)* I just think if the plan is to go on national television and perform what is basically a hoax, we should have a plot that lends itself to the suspension of disbelief a *tad* more.

JIM: What's not believable about me and Dana having an affair?

RC: Isn't it obvious?

JIM: No, it's not. Educate me.

DANA: Let's not and say we did. Throw in the video.

JIM: I want to know what he fucking means.

RC: *(He looks at Jim for a beat or two before speaking.)* Who's gonna believe you could get somewhere with Dana? I mean, I'm sorry, but the issue had to be brought up.

DANA: Ray, why do you always have to do shit like this?

RC: Like what? If we're gonna go on this show we have to—

DANA: *(Frustrated, angry.)* We're not going on the goddam show! Let's just drop this and have a nice little time watching this movie!

TEX: Ray, what are you trying to do here, man—

RC: You can't go on the tube with *science fiction,* okay? We have to be able to suspend disbelief or—

JIM: You don't think I could…

LAURA: Time out! Time fucking out!

JIM: Wait—

LAURA: No! We are forgetting this crap right now! I'm not going to have you guys in here talking about who could score with who, like we're just… just appliances or something and not even in the room!! Fuck that!

JIM: *(Ignoring Laura.)* Hold on! I don't have a shot with Dana? Is that your statement?

RC: *(Mockingly pretends to think it over.)* Um…yep.

JIM: And why is that?

TEX: We're getting off track here. None of this is serious, okay? Jim...
Jimbo...you're a studley, sexual predator...any woman would gratefully
accept your manhood in a heartbeat. Okay? Are egos healed now? Can we
move on?

JIM: Tex?

TEX: Yo?

JIM: Shut up and sit down. *(To RC.)* Why couldn't I get anywhere with someone like Dana?

DANA: Ladies, are we gonna let this toxic testosterone kill the evening? Viv?
You've been quiet over there...

VIV: I'd kinda like to know RC's answer.

DANA: This is *so* stupid.

RC: You wanna know?

TEX: No, she doesn't, let's—

RC: There are leagues in everything. Take baseball. You've got pee-wee league.
Little league. High school. The professional minors and of course, major
league baseball. You follow so far?

TEX: Just get to the point so we can move past this, please...

DANA: I'm outta here!

(Dana exits down a hallway.)

TEX: You guys are really fucking up my plans here. I could get some tasty
exposure being on that show and—

JIM: *(To RC.)* I said, go on.

RC: Think of Dana, then look in the mirror. She's the majors, so to speak, and
you, this pains me to say, are still running around in the pee-wee league.

JIM: *(To the others.)* Can you guys believe this?

LAURA: Ray, you are being so goddam stupid it's not even funny.

RC: I'm just giving it to you straight.

TEX: I hate to break the news to you, RC, but I've seen Alec Baldwin on the
movie screen, I've seen him on television, and you sir, are no Alec Baldwin.

RC: What the fuck are you talking about?

JIM: I guess you don't talk to Dana much.

RC: What's that supposed to mean?

JIM: I mean, there's not a lot of sharing between the two of you. Maybe you
should spend some time talking. You might learn something.

RC: Like what? What should I be learning about my girlfriend? Educate me.

TEX: Alright, fuck this. Fuck Jerry Springer. You guys are—

VIV: What's up with Dana?

JIM: Viv, shut up.

TEX: Hey, hey, hey—

VIV: I'm on your side here—

JIM: I don't need help with—

RC: Wait, wait, wait…what is this?

TEX: I'm getting some brews.

(Dana enters wearing her jacket. She heads for the front door.)

RC: Whoa, where are you going—?

DANA: Home.

RC: Come here…

DANA: Fuck off.

RC: What the hell is this? Get over here!

JIM: Easy…

RC: Fuck you. *(Shoves Jim.)* Say what you have to say! You got advice for me punk? *(Shoves him again.)* Say it!

JIM: *(Shoves RC away.)* Forget it…

RC: *(Moves close to Jim.)* Say it! *(Shoves Jim.)* Spill your guts! *(Shoves Jim.)* Tell me! What is behind that shit-eating grin you're always wearing?

DANA: Stop it, Ray!

(RC tries to shove Jim again. Jim grabs RC's arm, looks him in the eyes.)

JIM: You want me to spill my guts? That what you want, Mr. Major League?

RC: Yeah, that's what I want…

JIM: Then take one guess who's been groovin' on my stick…

TEX: Aw, crap…

RC: *(To Dana.)* You slept with him?

JIM: Fucking is really a more appropriate word there, Ray. Looks like I just took a step up to the majors—

(RC dives on Jim. They go sprawling into the couch, fighting each other.)

LAURA: *(Looking over at Dana, her voice quivering with rage.)* The two of you…?

DANA: I can explain—

LAURA: YOU FUCKING BITCH!!

(Laura takes off her shoe and throws it at Dana, missing.)

(Laura charges Dana, they start fighting.)

(Tex and Viv try to pull the different combatants apart but are themselves pulled into the insane tangle of punches, bites, kicking, and hair pulling.)

(As the chaos continues, the sound of The Jerry Springer Show rises, a TV audience chants "Jerry! Jerry! Jerry!" over and over as lights fade.)

END OF PLAY

The League of
Semi-Super Heroes
by Val Smith and
Michael Bigelow Dixon

CHARACTERS

The League—dreamers all, but real, very real.
>   EL GRANDE DE SAYER DE NAY
>   MASTER OF THE OBVIOUS
>   PUSHY BOB
>   WABBIT WOMAN
>   THE HUMAN PUDDLE
>   CAROL, The League Receptionist.

TIME
Oh, who cares.

PLACE
The League of Semi-Super Heroes' sparsely furnished office. A spartan desk with chair. The desk is noticeably devoid of papers or implements of any kind. The only object is a gold glittery phone with wings—and an answering machine. Maybe there's something else to sit on in the office, but it's not a normal piece of furniture. Some good rousing "Super Hero" preshow theme music is in order.

The League of Semi-Super Heroes

At rise, the gold telephone is highlighted. It rings. The answering machine picks up. Carol enters but makes no effort to pick up the phone. Instead she busies herself with putting away her coat, her purse, and shopping bags, putting on lipstick, and picking up and looking through the mail, all under the following.

CAROL'S VOICE: Hello. You have reached the number of The League of Semi-Super Heroes. If this is an emergency, please stay on the line and an operator will pick up shortly. *(Pause.)* If this is a message for only The Human Puddle, please press 1 now. *(Pause. The Human Puddle flies in the door, listening intently. When the messages goes on to the next Semi-Super Hero, The Human Puddle bursts into tears, just as Wabbit Woman hops into the room with her snorkel. Smocking, she smirks in anticipation.)* If this is a message for Wabbit Woman, please press 2 now.

WABBIT WOMAN: *(Pause.)* Oh wats!

CAROL'S VOICE: If this is a message for Master of the Obvious, please press 3 now.

(Master of the Obvious has entered the room, all smiles.)

MASTER OF THE OBVIOUS: Hey!! We got a call?

(Pause. El Grande De Sayer De Nay enters frowning as usual.)

CAROL'S VOICE: If this is a message for El Grande De Sayer De Nay, *(Pause.)* …

EL GRANDE DE SAYER: *(A look of hope and cynicism and simultaneously with tape.)* …don't bother to press anything.

CAROL'S VOICE: …don't bother to press anything. If this is a message for Pushy Bob, press 4—

PUSHY BOB: Yow! Watch out!

(Pushy Bob blasts through the doorway, scattering everybody.)

CAROL'S VOICE: —and get out of the way. If this is a message for the entire League, please leave it at the tone—

(The League leans in eagerly to listen. The sound of the tone. There is the sound of snorts and giggles and then a hang-up.)

EL GRANDE DE SAYER: Told ya.

HUMAN PUDDLE: It could have been something. It might have been something.

EL GRANDE DE SAYER: They only call 'cause they think we're a joke.

(Human Puddle bursts into tears.)

MASTER OF THE OBVIOUS: You've upset the Puddle.

EL GRANDE: So what else is new?

WABBIT WOMAN: *(Through snorkel she sings "Rain Drops are Falling on My Head.")*

PUSHY BOB: So! Carol, whaddaya doin'? What are you working on there?

CAROL: *(Working on her crossword puzzle.)* Oh, I don't know, Pushy Bob. What does it look like to you?

MASTER OF THE OBVIOUS: Say, isn't that a crossword puzzle you've got there?

CAROL: I'm surrounded. I give up.

PUSHY BOB: *(Looking over Carol's shoulder.)* Oh, way-way-way-way-wait! Forty-four down, a five-letter word for "screw-up!" Hold on, hold on. No, hold on now, hold on! Ahhhhh—

CAROL: *(Grabbing crossword puzzle back from Pushy Bob.)* Look! Instead of working MY crossword puzzle, why don't we deal with your bills? For instance. Here. The bank statement. Oh, my. Surprise, surprise. You've overdrawn on all your accounts.

MASTER OF THE OBVIOUS: Ooh bummer.

CAROL: Exactly. Ooh bummer. And what is this? Why, it's an eviction notice from the landlord. Oh dear. What should you do? Any semi-super money to take care of this? Any semi-super ideas? Any ideas at all? *(An embarrassed silence among the Semi-Super Heroes.)* No? Well then, there's a little matter of my salary. You are familiar with the word "salary"? Money in exchange for work provided?

MASTER OF THE OBVIOUS: Ah c'mon, Carol. We know what salary means.

PUSHY BOB: Hey, we'll write you a check!

CAROL: I'll start clearing out my desk.

MASTER OF THE OBVIOUS: Our bank account is overdrawn.

(Carol begins emptying out her desk, collecting her personal belongings in a box. Pushy Bob hovers around her, checking out her stuff.)

WABBIT WOMAN: Hizth izth ridiculuzzz! *(Without snorkel.)* They can't take away our *office*, for cwying out wowed. How will we do ouh bidness?

EL GRANDE DE SAYER: Look around, Wabbit Woman. Don't you see? *(They all look around.)* Oh, c'mon! All of you? Any of you? Don't you see?

(Puzzled, they all look round again.)

WABBIT WOMAN: Well. We're wookin'—

EL GRANDE DE SAYER: I'm speaking metaphorically!

MASTER OF THE OBVIOUS: No fair! You can't expect *me* to figure that out.

WABBIT WOMAN: He's Master of the Obvious.

EL GRANDE DE SAYER: Don't you see, it isn't working! We *have* no business! In a year, nobody has called for our services. It can't work! It will never work! Never, never, never!

(The Human Puddle sobs loudly.)

MASTER OF THE OBVIOUS: Geez. There goes the Puddle.

EL GRANDE DE SAYER: Oh what else is new!

PUSHY BOB: Look out everybody! The glass is half empty again.

EL GRANDE DE SAYER: This time it's completely empty. We're being evicted. Carol is thinking of leaving.

CAROL: Correction. Carol *is* leaving. *(To Pushy Bob.)* Will you *please* get out of the way.

PUSHY BOB: Okay! Have a big gigantic ding-dong cow!

EL GRANDE DE SAYER: I mean, who are we kidding? "Semi-Super Heroes!" Our talents make no sense!

CAROL: Finally. Thank you, God.

HUMAN PUDDLE: Ordinary people with *unusual* skills helping other people in need.

MASTER OF THE OBVIOUS: That was the whole idea.

EL GRANDE DE SAYER: Sounds good, Human Puddle. Only one problem. Who *needs* stupid skills?

WABBIT WOMAN: My skiffs ant stoofid! *(Removes snorkel from mouth.)* Can you smock, snorkel AND smirk? I can!

EL GRANDE DE SAYER: Who cares?

MASTER OF THE OBVIOUS: It may not be obvious to everyone but even if it is—doesn't it follow, El Grande de Sayer de Nay, that you also have a stupid skill?

ALL: Hmmmmmmmmmmmmmmm?!

EL GRANDE DE SAYER: NO!

ALL: Oh.

CAROL: Guys, there's one more piece of…

PUSHY BOB: Look! Right now, somebody out there might *need* a pushy guy! And if I can help by bulldozing my way in somewhere, hey—I'm there!

HUMAN PUDDLE: Or just someone who likes to—who can't help—crying—

(The Human Puddle sobs uncontrollably.)

CAROL: Guys, you're not listening.

WABBIT WOMAN: We're wisionaries!

EL GRANDE DE SAYER: We're the League of Personality Disorders!

MASTER OF THE OBVIOUS: Some people choose not to see it that way. While others obviously do.

PUSHY BOB: I've always thought we could use more aggressive advertising. Loud and In Your Face.

WABBIT WOMAN: Yah! *Willwe* Wowed!

PUSHY BOB: Yeah! Wilwe willwe Wowed!

CAROL: Guys. If I could have your attention…

PUSHY BOB: Ah! "Gaffe"! Five letters meaning screw-up—could work.

CAROL: Thank you, Pushy Bob! I wanted to spare everyone's feelings, but there is one more piece of information I need to share with you. The Grant? *(The group looks puzzled.)* Remember The Grant? *(The group looks puzzled.)* The last glint of rescue in an otherwise dark sea of despair?
(Human Puddle weeps, a high-pitched sob.)

PUSHY BOB: *(A flash.)* Oh! Yeah! The Grant! *(He knocks Carol's box off the desk accidentally.)* Helping people with our unusual skills.

CAROL: Well. You didn't get The Grant.

WABBIT WOMAN: Oooooooooooooo.

HUMAN PUDDLE: Oh God! How much rejection do they think we can take?!

MASTER OF THE OBVIOUS: Maybe the word "semi-" gave them pause.

EL GRANDE DE SAYER: That's it! I, El Grande de Sayer de Nay, propose we disband!

WABBIT WOMAN: Ooooooooooooooooooooooooooooooo.

EL GRANDE DE SAYER: You heard me! Quit! We follow Carol on out of here.

CAROL: I walk alone!

MASTER OF THE OBVIOUS: You mean—give up the office.

WABBIT WOMAN: Look. We have to have faith. Faith that somehow our talents, howevah stwange, howevah cweative, howevah—meager—amount to something. I'm not giving up smocking for nobody. I'll continue to smock—and smirk—and, yes! snorkel *(Puts snorkel in mouth.)* wheorbel I foltb libit.

MASTER OF THE OBVIOUS: Smock on, Wabbit Woman!

HUMAN PUDDLE: We just wanted to help people.

PUSHY BOB: Well, what the hell do people want! I mean, excuse me for illuminating the human condition, but we do so have something to offer! Can't they see that?!

MASTER OF THE OBVIOUS: Push on, Pushy Bob!

EL GRANDE DE SAYER: No! This is the end. We have to accept that. We have to be big enough to say yes to no!

(A moment while they all ponder this statement.)

MASTER OF THE OBVIOUS: We didn't get our grant.

PUSHY BOB: And who's to blame? *(Pause.)* Carol. We'll miss you. You're fired.

CAROL: Thank you, Pushy Bob. Look guys. I'm sorry. But there is such a thing as appreciating the reality of a situation.

> *(Pause.)*

EL GRANDE DE SAYER: Exactly, Carol. Reality! When we walk out that door, we must know who we are and always will be—unwanted, useless, distracting, irritating, unloved, and unlovable strange-ohs. When we walk out that door, we're gonna know we face a world that has no use for us and our hopeless, pathetic little lives!

> *(El Grande has rested his case. Stunned silence. After a moment, The Human Puddle sobs loudly. A pause.)*

CAROL: Well. Let me put it this way. I've enjoyed my time here, but I never really understood how smocking and snorkeling and crying and being pushy and telling people what they already know—or being negative on a continual basis—I mean, how are those qualities supposed to help other people? Huh?

> *(Pause.)*

WABBIT WOMAN: OK. It's a wittle weird. But is that any weason to weject us?!

CAROL: Yes. Yes, it is. *(Pause during which the lights flicker and then go out.)* Well, there it is. Reality. Third and final notice from the electric company. Tell ya what. I'll take the answering machine in lieu of a check. *(Carol disconnects the answering machine and tucks it under her arm.)* Good luck to all of you. And I really mean that.

> *(Carol exits.)*

THE LEAGUE: *(Sadly.)* Bye, Carol. Bye…

MASTER OF THE OBVIOUS: She's gone.

EL GRANDE DE SAYER: We don't need her.

PUSHY BOB: She left her crossword puzzle.

WABBIT WOMAN: *(Sings another chorus of "Raindrops" sadly through snorkel.)*

> *(Long pause. The phone rings. They all look at it. It rings again.)*

MASTER OF THE OBVIOUS: Phone's ringing.

> *(Phone rings.)*

HUMAN PUDDLE: Aren't we going to answer it?

EL GRANDE DE SAYER: No.

PUSHY BOB: Just another 'noxious nincompoop lookin' for a cheap laugh. Prob'ly.

(Phone rings.)

HUMAN PUDDLE: But what if…

EL GRANDE DE SAYER: What!!

(Evocative heroic music plays quietly under the following, slowly building as it progresses.)

HUMAN PUDDLE: Well, what if it's a guy in Sault Ste. Marie who's in big trouble 'cause he can't accept what's happening in his life.

MASTER OF THE OBVIOUS: He needs help hearing some hard—but obvious—truths.

(Phone rings.)

HUMAN PUDDLE: Or, like, what if it's some shy kid in Cheyenne who never gets picked when they're choosing up teams and never gets called on in class, who's always last in line and who always walks home alone.

PUSHY BOB: Maybe all she needs is an assertive role model, a little jolt of brass, somebody to tell her not to be afraid to just barge in and make it happen.

(Phone rings.)

HUMAN PUDDLE: What if it's a guy in St. Louis who can't say no to a boss who keeps making him stay late to work and that's ruining his home life.

EL GRANDE DE SAYER: He needs help, he needs someone who can help him see the importance of saying no! Emphatically. And often.

(Phone rings.)

HUMAN PUDDLE: Or maybe it's—uhhh—maybe it's—uhhhhh—

(Human Puddle turns to the rest of the League in his desperation—)

PUSHY, GRANDE, MASTER, and PUDDLE: Or maybe it's—uhhhhh—

WABBIT WOMAN: A synchwonized swim team!—who want a cewtain fashion nostalgia to their swimsuits!—And who despwately need to—learn to—you know—smirk for the judges!

(Phone rings.)

HUMAN PUDDLE: Or maybe, just maybe it's a bunch of people right here in this city. A group of dreamers who've lost their way. And maybe what they need most of all, maybe all they need in fact, is just a darn good—

(Dissolving in tears.)

(The phone keeps ringing. The League of Semi-Super Heroes, some with a look of hope, some anxious and teary, watch the phone, which continues to ring as the Human Puddle looks heavenward and Wabbit Woman hops toward the phone ever so slowly as lights go to Black and music swells to terrific climax.)

END OF PLAY

The Intervention
by Anne Washburn

CHARACTERS

KATY

LU

BRET

WILL

DOUG

NINA

All are somewhere in their mid- to late twenties.

TIME

The present.

SETTING

The living room: a dumpy couch, a dumpy chair, a coffee table.

NOTE

The play takes place in five scenes and is punctuated by swift blackouts, which indicate the passage of a small chunk of time. Blackouts should be accomplished by an interesting blur of music and sound.

The Intervention

I

Katy, Lu, Bret, and Will.

KATY: She needs help. *That's* not the issue. But to lure her here, and confront her, and suddenly put it all out there: is this really the best way to deal with it?

LU: But what about that thing, you read about or hear places, that thing where someone says "that was the turning point for me; if that wouldn't have happened, very painful though it was, I would never have turned it all around." They say: I was very angry, at the time, *very* angry, but now I am very grateful.

KATY: Yes but that's what you say in retrospect. After it all works out. But what if it doesn't work out. *That's* the thing. Then you say: that was the turning point. That was the precise moment when my life turned into a horror movie.

LU: How can the Truth turn your life into a horror movie?

KATY: I thought it was *precisely* the Truth that turned your life into a horror movie.

BRET: It's like in a war, okay? And you're in the trenches with the smoke rushing at you from the burning tank stalled sixty feet ahead of you on the battlefield, or they're knocking on the door late at night and you're lunging for the back window—or if you're just waking up in a cold sweat, fallen halfway out of bed, and you're pretty certain you dreamed the knock—but you're not *sure:* this is how you become someone. That's what I'm saying. This is how you form a character, or, an identity. You can't *become anyone* without a catalytic event. A national *or* personal catastrophe. Massive crisis. Lauren should count her lucky stars.

(*Pause.*)

LU: To begin with: they don't even *do* war like that anymore. Now it's all with computers.

KATY: Where is everyone?

WILL: What do we *say?* When she comes in?

BRET: We all shout: Surprise!
(Blackout.)

II

Doug and Nina burst in and stand for a moment, frozen with tension.

DOUG: Okay, we're not late.

NINA: We are late. Where's Lauren?

KATY: She's late.

NINA: I was like: "*Fuck*. We cannot be late." Do you think Lauren knows?

KATY: I think she's just late.

NINA: I can tell you, right off the bat, that this is way too casual a… *(Searches for the word.)* tableau. If she comes in and sees this, and *then* everyone scrambles around and straightens up and looks concerned, she's not going to take this seriously.

DOUG: *(Lightly sarcastic.)* What do you want us to do—all line up facing the door?

LU: I think that would make her laugh.

WILL: That would scare *me* shitless.

BRET: I think the crucial thing is that no one blows this because these moments are so delicate. They hang by threads. We've all got to be preternaturally alert, really thinking, really focused, and just completely compassionate, just—everyone open your heart. All the way.
(Pause.)

NINA: Okay. Everyone do that. And while you're doing that— *(She gestures.)* Katy—I swear this'll work—on the sofa, with your hands folded on your lap, and Lu, if you are literally standing behind her *(Indicating Katy.)* and Doug, over there *(She indicates the chair to the side.)* so we can get some surround on this. Bret, on the sofa. Will, on the sofa.

WILL: Hands in my lap?

NINA: No, on a guy that looks silly. Try crossing your arms. *(He scrunches them against his body.)* Try crossing them in a relaxed manner. No. Try to look firm. But casual. But firm. Okay, we'll get back to you.

BRET: Nina, she's coming in that door at any moment. It's not going to matter what we *look* like if our mental attitude is completely unfocused.

KATY: I don't know that confrontation is the best way. Maybe we should try to change her from within.

DOUG: Should I look authoritative or should I move back into the shadows and look menacing?

LU: I feel like we should be saying "cheese."

NINA: Okay everyone just shut up. Let me look at you. *(She steps back. Looks at them. Starts to back towards the door.)* Okay now I'm Lauren, coming into the room:

(She exits. Knocks.)

(Pause.)

(Knocks again. Will nudges Katy.)

KATY: Oh! Come in.

(Nina enters. Looks at everyone for a moment.)

NINA: I don't feel at all moved, or, motivated by you guys. Bret's right. We have to focus. The mental attitude here sucks.

(Blackout.)

III

Bret is sitting in the center of the couch staring intently at a cheapie tourist-quality voodoo doll. Everyone else is gathered around him on the couch.

BRET: This isn't the kind that comes with instructions. Some of them have the places all marked out where you put the pins in. Where do we put the pins in?

KATY: Do we need special pins?

NINA: Does anyone *have* pins?

(Pause.)

DOUG: We could just pinch it.

NINA: But where. Heart? Brain?

DOUG: Um, is it supposed to work…are we supposed to be working on it like a machine, or, symbolically?

WILL: You can't just stick pins into it. You have to have a ceremony. I saw a ceremony at the voodoo museum in New Orleans, but halfway into it the two guides got into a tussle for hegemony of the exhibit and the fake chicken was crushed and we all snuck out the back way. So I didn't see all of it. Not that they show you the real ceremony anyway. They keep parts back. The important parts.

LU: Okay, no. This isn't about any ceremony or system. This is about the power of raw belief.

DOUG: Well, I respect that but in fact, practically, there's no way I'm believing without some kind of rigmarole. There is no express elevator out of Western Consciousness for me; if you're going to take me away you've got to take me by the stairs.

(*A pause.*)

KATY: Oh fine. (*She stands up.*) I've got some pins somewhere…

BRET: (*Looking up.*) Someone turn down the lights.

(*Instant blackout.*)

IV

In the dark.

WILL: If we were Bodysnatchers, all we'd have to do would be to wait for her to fall asleep—*which is inevitable*—and then we'd just position a Pod by her sleeping body. And then we could sit back and relax.

(*Pause.*)

NINA: *What?*

WILL: Don't you ever do that? When I'm watching horror movies, and I'm getting really stressed out, I just think: well, why am I identifying with the humans? Why don't I just identify with the powerful alien entities? And I do. And then the movie is really enjoyable. Unless the humans win in the end. But then I just think to myself: *Earthling propaganda.*

(*Pause.*)

NINA: *What?*

BRET: Will, shut up. I'm trying to concentrate.

WILL: Right. Okay.

V

The lights are low. Everyone is sitting on the floor around the coffee table. Bret is in the middle and he holds the doll upright. He pivots it, slightly, so that it appears to look at each member of the circle. They are (on the whole) hushed and expectant.

BRET: Say hello to Lauren, everyone.

LU: (*Solemnly.*) Hello, Lauren.

NINA: (*Crisply.*) Hello, Lauren.

WILL: Hello, Lauren.

(*Katy reaches out to touch the doll's hand with her fingertip.*)

KATY: Hello, Lauren.

(*Pause. The doll "waits."*)

DOUG: (*Terse.*) Hi.

(*Pause. A few glances are exchanged.*)

DOUG: Well? Is she going to do anything? Or are we supposed to do something.

BRET: She's suspicious.

NINA: Katy, do you want to start this off?

KATY: Um…

BRET: We're going to have to restrain her.

KATY: Physically?

BRET: She's figured out what's up and she's turning to go.

KATY: Okay, well—

(Bret presses the doll flat into the table.)

BRET: Okay, you can talk now.

DOUG: Is this necessary?

BRET: If you walked into this room would *you* stay?

(Pause. They stare at the doll.)

KATY: *(Intent.)* Lauren. I know this is all a shock. I know that this seems like we're ganging up on you and it seems like a betrayal but believe me, this wasn't easy.

LU: No.

(Katy takes up a pin and sticks the doll with it, thoughtfully.)

KATY: It would have been far easier to let you go on with your life and let you go. We wouldn't do this if we didn't love you, and this isn't about what's *wrong* with you. This is about all of the ways in which you aren't *you* anymore.

LU: This is about reaching into you and pulling you out of yourself. Before you really become a different person. Bret, can I?

(She carefully transfers the doll from Bret's grasp and holds it to her chest, clutching it tightly as though it might spring away.)

LU: *(Carefully inserting a pin.)* Sweetie, I know it's been rough. But you're wrong to believe that you've lived your life in this extra intense way and it's much more deep, and that now you've moved beyond, like, the bounds of your perception and that we can't understand you and we have no idea what you're going through and that we have no *insight* on your life. You're wrong to think that we can't help you. Because we can. And you have to let us. You have to.

DOUG: *(Impulsively.)* Lu, give me Lauren.

(Lu passes the doll to Bret who passes it to Doug.)

BRET: Hold on tight, 'cause she's pissed.

DOUG: I agree with Katy. To me it's as if there's some *thing* inside of you that's gone wrong, a foreign object lodged inside you. And I'd like to just…shake it out of you; cut you open and pull it out and sew you up again and you'd be fine. And I know now why they used to—to get demons out of people—why they used to do horrible things to them; I'd like to punish you—not for anything you've done to me, I mean, we aren't close, but I watch the way you treat yourself and I think: she shouldn't be allowed to get away with that. And I've never said this to another human being, but I think you should bow down and pray. And I'm an agnostic.

(He pauses. Then sticks a pin into the doll. Will reaches out.)

DOUG: Wait just a sec. I'm not sure I'm done yet.

WILL: I just remembered something and I know exactly what I want to say. And if I don't say it right now I'll forget it.

DOUG: Okay.

(They transfer the doll. When it is in his grasp, Will turns away and huddles over it, whispering inaudibly into its ear. He sticks it with lots of pins, very insistently and methodically.)

NINA: Will, what are you doing?

WILL: This is private.

DOUG: I thought what *I* said was pretty private. But I said it in pubic.

LU: Will, this is supposed to be—

NINA: There's a group dynamic we're trying to maintain here.

WILL: Almost done.

LU: *(With a facial expression.)* Well. Whatcha gonna do.

(He turns around and flings the doll violently onto the center of the table.)

DOUG: *Jesus*, Will.

(Katy and Bret dive for the doll at the same time. Bret grabs it first and holds it upright on the table, as at the beginning of the scene.)

KATY: Is she okay?

NINA: Will, that's completely uncool.

BRET: *(Neutral.)* She's mad.

WILL: Good.

BRET: No, I mean she's really mad.

WILL: Good. She's mad. I'm mad.

(Bret starts to move the doll toward Will, doll step by doll step.)

BRET: She's coming toward you, Will.

WILL: Forget it, Bret.

BRET: She's coming closer. And closer. And closer.

(There is a knock on the outside door. Nina and Katy shriek, Doug yelps. Everyone turns to face the door, frozen.)

WILL: Oh my God! Don't let her in!

(Blackout.)

END OF PLAY

Labor Day
by Sheri Wilner

CHARACTERS

ONE: Male or female, age twenty-one to twenty-eight.
TWO: Male or female, age twenty-one to twenty-eight.
THREE: Male or female, age twenty-one to twenty-eight.
FOUR: Male or female, agetwenty-one to twenty-eight.
FIVE: Male or female, age twenty-one to twenty-eight.
SIX: Female age twenty-nine.

TIME AND PLACE

The night before Labor Day, 11:50 PM. A party.

Labor Day

Labor Day Eve, 11:50 PM. A nondescript room, save for some white decorations and furnishings. Six friends, all dressed completely in white, sit in a circle. Characters One, Two, Three, Four, and Five range in ages from twenty-one to twenty-eight. Character Six is twenty-nine.

They are playing a party game and strike their chests with their hands before speaking.

Author's Note: Although individual directors and casts are encouraged to create their own way to play the fictional game, a particularly effective method was discovered for the Actors Theatre of Louisville production. After each player called out a word and hit his or her chest, the other players, one at a time in counterclockwise order, would hit their chests, as well. The next word was not called out until a complete round of chest-hitting had been completed. The method created a ritualistic rhythm and set a good speed for the game.

ONE: *(Hits chest.)* Sale.
TWO: *(Hits chest.)* Noise.
THREE: *(Hits chest.)* Pages.
FOUR: *(Hits chest.)* House.
FIVE: *(Hits chest.)* Collar.
SIX: On rice.
ALL: One word!
SIX: Close enough.
ONE: It is not. No way.
THREE: And you didn't tap your chest.
SIX: *(Hits chest.)* On rice.
FOUR: It's not one word and you didn't tap your chest.
SIX: *(Hits chest repeatedly to get a reverb effect.)* O-o-o-o-n-n-n r-i-i-i-i-c-c-c-e.
FIVE: You're out.
SIX: It's just a game.
FIVE: Right. And you lost it. Sit over there.

SIX: It's my white party and I'll sit where I want to. Sit where I want to. Sit where I want to.

(*They watch her in silence as she chooses a location for herself. It is off to the side and near a white table covered with an array of white foods.*)

ONE: Actually, it's my white party.

SIX: Obviously. If it were my WHITE party, I wouldn't serve WHITE wine.

FIVE: (*Hits chest.*) Wine.

SIX: White wine is white in name only.

ONE: (*Hits chest.*) Head.

TWO: (*Hits chest.*) Out.

THREE: (*Hits chest.*) Face.

SIX: Anyone want more Wonder Bread balls? Popcorn? Milk?

ALL: No.

(*They continue with their game, ignoring her while she speaks.*)

FOUR: (*Hits chest.*) Russian.

SIX: (*Shrugs.*) More for me.
(*Six pours herself a glass of milk. She raises her glass.*)
Here's snow in your eye.
(*She drinks.*)

FIVE: (*Hits chest.*) Wash.

ONE: (*Hits chest.*) Wedding.

TWO: (*Hits chest.*) Meat.

THREE: (*Hits chest.*) Fish.

FOUR: (*Hits chest.*) Cap.

SIX: What will you miss the most?

FIVE: (*Hits chest.*) Christmas.

Me, I'll miss the danger. The terror felt at every fork-ful, at the possibility that a dozen dots of marinara will spray onto your chest. Or that a fist-size clump of chocolate ice cream will lean off its cone and fall right into your lap.

ONE: (*Hits chest.*) Lines.

TWO: (*Hits chest.*) Chocolate.

THREE: (*Hits chest.*) Guilt.

FOUR: (*Hits chest.*) Man.

SIX: No, you can never feel
    safe wearing white. That's what
    I'll miss, believe it or not.
    Somehow, it makes you more
    sensitive. More awake. More
    aware of every wave pattern in
    the atmosphere. Is that a rain
    cloud? A sticky-fingered child?
    Do I look like a nurse?
    My period was last week, right?
    In white, all your senses are
    heightened. You hear new
    sounds, smell more smells.
    You develop a whole new set
    of senses.

FIVE: *(Hits chest.)* Wall.

ONE: *(Hits chest.)* Bread.

TWO: *(Hits chest.)* Castle.

FOUR: *(Hits chest.)* Slavery.

FIVE: *(Hits chest.)* House.

ALL: Said it!

FIVE: No sir.

ONE: Yes sir.

FIVE: No way!

TWO: Yes way.

THREE: Oh please, of course someone said White House.

FIVE: Who did?

FOUR: I did.

FIVE: I didn't hear you.

ONE: I heard her (or him).

FIVE: Well I didn't.

FOUR: I definitely said White House.

FIVE: When?

SIX: *(Hits chest.)* Sale. *(Hits chest.)* Noise. *(Hits chest.)* Pages. *(Hits chest.)*
    House. Fourth item called. Then *(Hits chest.)* collar, then the fatal *(Hits*
    chest.) on rice.

FOUR: *(To Five.)* Have a seat.

FIVE: I thought she said mouse.

ONE: *(Hits chest.)* Mouse.

TWO: *(Hits chest.)* Album.

THREE: *(Hits chest.)* Lie.

(Five walks over to the food area. Six offers Five a glass.)

SIX: Milk?

FIVE: No thanks. *(Five pours a glass of white wine.)*

SIX: You're better off. It's a stupid game. Limited to one word. How much is neglected because of that punishingly arbitrary rule? *(She hits her chest.)* Sands of time. *(Hits chest.)* Cliffs of Dover. Hills like *(She hits her chest.)* elephants.

FIVE: *(Hits his chest.)* Men can't jump.

SIX: That's actually not one I'll miss.

FIVE: Ha! That's a good one! *(Hits chest.)* Men can't jump. Hey, is there any more vanilla ice cream left?

ONE: In the freezer. *(Hits chest.)* Fang.

FIVE: Excellent! *(Five starts to exit.)*

SIX: Wait!

FIVE: What?

SIX: Tell me what you'll miss. The most. About wearing white.

FIVE: I never wear white. This party every year is the only time I ever do. *(Five exits.)*

FOUR: *(Hits chest.)* Trash.

ONE: *(Hits chest.)* Race.

TWO: *(Hits chest.)* Flag.

THREE: *(Hits chest.)* Tie.

FOUR: *(Hits chest.)* Flight.

ONE: *(Hits chest.)* Knight.

TWO: *(Hits chest.)* Owl.

THREE: *(Hits chest.)* Supremacists.

FOUR: *(Hits chest.)* Lightning.

TWO: *(Hits chest.)* Diamonds.

THREE: *(Hits chest.)* Sox.

FOUR: *(Hits chest.)* Haired.

ONE: *(Hits chest.)* Rabbit.

TWO: Water.

SIX: *(To group.)* Did you hear that? *(Yelling after Five)*. You're not invited next year.

THREE: *(Hits chest.)* Light.

TWO: *(Hits chest.)* Market.

THREE: What the hell's a *(Hits chest.)* market?

TWO: I don't know. There's a black market. That means there must be a *(Hits chest.)* market, right?

ONE: No.

FOUR: Buh-bye.

TWO: Who's got a dictionary?

ONE: I do. But it's red.

THREE: Buh-bye.

TWO: Shit.

(Two sits down next to Six. Six offers Two a bowl.)

SIX: Mashed potatoes?

FOUR: *(Hits chest.)* Hot.

ONE: *(Hits chest.)* Squall.

TWO: Yeah. Thanks. *(Two takes the bowl and a fork and begins eating.)* Any salt?

THREE: *(Hits chest.)* Pride.

FOUR: *(Hits chest.)* Sauce.

SIX: Need you ask? *(Six hands Two a salt shaker.)* What will you miss the most? About wearing white?

ONE: *(Hits chest.)* Mountains.

TWO: *(Thinks for a moment before answering.)* If you don't have a tan, it looks like you do. If you do have a tan, it looks even darker.

THREE: *(Hits chest.)* Plains.

FOUR: *(Hits chest.)* Rat.

SIX: I'll miss the possibilities. There's nothing quite like that giddy post-Memorial Day moment when you open up your closet and think: "Anything. Absolutely anything." There's no reaching for something and then stopping yourself. No fears, no hesitations. You thrust

ONE: *(Hits chest.)* Satin.

THREE: *(Hits chest.)* Pine.

FOUR: *(Hits chest.)* Paper.

SIX: *(Continued.)*
in your hand and can pull anything out. Absolutely anything.

ONE: *(Hits chest.)* Tailed.

TWO: That's not true for me.

THREE: *(Hits chest.)* Rage.

SIX: Why not?

FOUR: *(Hits chest.)* Space.

TWO: I don't wear red in
summer. I could have the
greatest tan, but I put on red
and some moron inevitably
says, "Ouch, bad burn."

ONE: *(Hits chest.)* Hope.

THREE: *(Hits chest.)* Chapel.

THREE: *(Hits chest.)* Gold.

FOUR: *(Hits chest.)* Knuckled.
(Five re-enters.)

FIVE: You guys know what time it is? It's 11:59. *(Everyone but Six screams, stands, and then runs around the room retrieving their white bags and backpacks.)* Man, if I didn't go into the kitchen—!

ONE: Oh my god, where's my bag? Who's seen my bag?

TWO: What color is it?

ONE: Very funny. Where is it? Where the hell is it?

TWO: Everyone, quick, get your stuff. Quick!

SIX: *(A quiet pronouncement.)* This year I won't do it.

THREE: You're standing on my strap, move!

SIX: *(Still quietly.)* This year I won't do it.

THREE: Get your stuff, hurry!

SIX: I won't do it. I won't give it up. The danger. The freedom. The possibilities. I won't give it up.

FOUR: You have to.

SIX: Why? Who says that I do? Who's issuing the order?

FOUR: Forty seconds to Labor Day!

ONE: Thirty seconds. On your mark, get set...GO! *(Suddenly everyone but Six starts to take off their white clothes and quickly replaces them with colored clothes.)* Twenty seconds. Watch the clock.

TWO: *(Struggling.)* Shit. This button won't—!

THREE: Hurry. Hurry!

FOUR: *(To Six.)* Come on.

ONE: Ten seconds.

SIX: STOP! *(Time stops. They all freeze except Six.)* Why does today feel like the saddest day of the year? It always has. From early on. I died a small death every September. Every first day of school. The feeling that some-thing was over. Something glorious and light and free was over. Why do we follow clocks and calendars? Daylight Savings and New Year's? Why the divisions? Why the markers? Do we really have to make it so obvious that time is passing? That our sisters are now mothers, our parents now grandparents? That the last remnants of our childhood have all but slipped through our fingers? *(Beat.)* I am staying in these clothes. I am staying in these clothes and safe from breast cancer and ovarian cancer and all other diseases that ignore the young. My legs will stay smooth with thin, hidden veins. My parents will not turn sixty but stay the age they were when they each took a hand and lifted me over puddles. I will not allow another season to pass. I can't stop that blasted ball dropping on New Year's, but I will stop this.

(Time restarts, they all resume changing clothes.)

ALL: *(Except Six.)* 10, 9, 8

SIX: Stop it.

ALL: *(Except Six.)* 7, 6, 5

SIX: I said stop it.

ALL: *(Except Six.)* 4, 3, 2

SIX: Stop it

ALL: *(Except Six.)* 1! Happy Labor Day!!

(They cheer, yell, hug, and blow noisemakers.)

SIX: EVERYBODY STOP IT!!

(They stop what they are doing and stare blankly at Six. On her hands and knees, she moves about the room, gathering all their white clothes, and in the process, one of the white balloons. She holds the clothes tightly to her chest and buries her face in them. Pause.)

FOUR: It's just pants and shoes. You can still wear white shirts.

ONE: Yeah, and there's always winter whites.

SIX: None of you know. None of you have any idea.

(Hits chest.) I miss the freedom.

(Hits chest.) I miss the freedom.

(Hits chest.) I miss.

(Six releases the white balloon and watches it float up into the air.)

END OF PLAY